Issues in Agricultural Trade Policy

PROCEEDINGS OF THE 2014 OECD GLOBAL FORUM ON AGRICULTURE

OECD
BETTER POLICIES FOR BETTER LIVES

Please cite this publication as:
OECD (2015), *Issues in Agricultural Trade Policy: Proceedings of the 2014 OECD Global Forum on Agriculture*, OECD Publishing, Paris.
http://dx.doi.org/10.1787/9789264233911-en

ISBN 978-92-64-23388-1 (print)
ISBN 978-92-64-23391-1 (PDF)

Photo credits: Cover © Thinkstock/Dominiquedelacroix.

Foreword

This book brings together a collection of papers prepared for the Global Forum on Agriculture which took place at the OECD in December 2014. It reviews current knowledge about agricultural and agricultural trade policy settings and asks how pertinent that knowledge is in the light of profound market and structural changes that have been taking place in the global agro-food sector in recent decades. It aims to inform and assist policy makers and negotiators as they seek to overcome the problems that have made the agricultural pillar of the Doha Agenda trade negotiations particularly difficult. The data and analysis presented cover OECD and major G20 and emerging economies which account for the great bulk of global food production, consumption and trade.

Chapter 1, prepared by Jared Greenville of the OECD Secretariat, provides a short overview and synthesis of the main conclusions which can be drawn from the papers which make up the book. Chapter 2, by Stefan Tangermann, Professor Emeritus at the University of Göttingen, examines the validity of analysis undertaken by OECD since the conclusion of the Uruguay Round, in light of the profound changes that have occurred in agricultural markets and policies in recent years. It asks in particular whether earlier policy recommendations and analyses of reform impacts remain pertinent in a world of higher and more volatile international prices, and where the role and influence of key emerging economies is much greater than in the past. Chapter 3, by Lars Brink, Independent Advisor, examines current policy settings in 20 major agricultural producing and consuming countries against their Uruguay Round commitments and against the 2008 draft modalities drawn up in the context of the Doha negotiations, with a view to gauging the degree of further reform effort that would be required to give effect to the draft modalities in today's policy and market environment. Finally, Chapter 4, by Annelies Deuss of the OECD Secretariat, reviews recent experience in the use of buffer stocks and social safety net stocks, mainly in emerging and developing countries, with a view to determining how effective they have been in meeting their seemingly contradictory aims to raise or stabilise prices for producers while lowering them for consumers.

A summary of the discussion during the Global Forum on which this proceedings volume is based, as well as the presentations made during the Forum, are available from the Forum webpage (http://www.oecd.org/agriculture/global-forum-agriculture-2014.htm).

Table of contents

Tables

Figures

Boxes

Chapter 1

Issues in agricultural trade policy: An overview

by
Jared Greenville[1]

This chapter presents a synthesis of the work presented to the OECD's 2014 Global Forum on Agriculture: Issues in Agricultural Trade Policy, held in Paris on 2 December 2014. It first provides an overview of the main developments in agricultural markets that have occurred since the Doha round of negotiations began in 2001. Second, significant policy developments in OECD and other major agricultural producing countries are briefly discussed. Third, the relevance of the lessons from past OECD reviews of agricultural policies in the context of market and policy changes is explored. The chapter concludes by analysing why agricultural market liberalisation remains an important tool for continued sector growth, rural development and food security.

Agricultural trade and related domestic support policy remains a contentious international issue. The current round of negotiations on world trading rules officially began 14 years ago in 2001.[2] Since that time, agriculture has proven to be a critical element in the effort to reach agreement on a single undertaking outlining new international trading rules. During the period of negotiations, world agricultural markets and domestic agricultural support policies have changed significantly. Agricultural production centres have shifted in relative importance and world price trends have altered. In policy terms, some countries have continued the reform path established by the preceding Agreement on Agriculture (AoA) agreed in 1994, while others have taken a different route. Further, increasing populations, rising incomes and changes in agricultural production have all fundamentally altered world agricultural markets.

1.1. Evolving agricultural markets

Balance of global production growth is shifting to emerging economies

During the 2000s, global agricultural production growth was strong, returning to growth rates seen in the past (Figure 1.1, top panel). Annual compound growth rates for the decade outperformed those seen during the 1990s, returning to past decadal growth rates of around 2.5% per annum. Moreover, of particular note, the 2000s saw the fastest per capita agricultural production growth rates – close to twice those seen in previous decades. This means that during this period, agricultural production growth outstripped population growth at a faster pace than what has occurred over the previous 40 years.

Growth in production was not uniform amongst agricultural producing regions across the globe (Figure 1, bottom panel). Significant differences are observed between developed agricultural producing regions and emerging production centres. The 2000s saw continued strong production growth in South America and Southeast Asia, continuing trends from the 1990s. Similarly, other regions in Asia (excluding western Asia) also experienced strong growth. In per capita terms, both South American and Southeast Asia also saw an acceleration in agricultural production volumes in the 2000s compared with past decadal growth rates. For Africa, while overall production growth was strong, in per capita terms growth was significantly lower than in other developing regions. Production growth in Europe and North America was significantly lower, and fell in per capita terms in North America, indicating the reduced importance of these regions to world agricultural output growth.

Real agricultural prices for many products have increased

Between 2000 and 2014, prices have been volatile and there has been a fundamental shift in longer-term price trends. Of particular note, the sustained period of structurally declining food prices came to an end in the mid-2000s, and was followed by a series of food price spikes from 2007-08 to 2012 (Figure 1.2). Since then prices have stabilised, albeit at higher levels than before 2007.

Food price rises were driven by a confluence of mutually re-enforcing longer-term structural changes, short-term market shocks, and importantly, policy responses (OECD, 2008; Piesse and Thirtle, 2009; Naylor and Falcon 2010; Headey, 2011). On top of underlying structural changes to world agricultural markets from rising levels of food and feed demand, falling stock-to-use ratios and increasing production being channelled to biofuels production, world markets were hit by a number of short-term shocks that placed further upwards pressure on prices. Droughts in key grain producing regions and other weather effects, exchange rate movements, along with hoarding and panic buying by private agents helped spur already rising prices. On top of this, government policy interventions through trade restrictions and import measures, coupled with panic purchases by some governments, helped create the spike in prices that was observed. Government policies surrounding biofuels mandates and subsidies also contributed. Price rises were particularly witnessed for wheat, coarse grains, rice and oilseed crops – all of which experienced strong real price growth between 2005 and 2010.

Over the medium term, real prices for most agricultural products are projected to decline from 2013 levels (OECD-FAO 2014). Prices for cereals are expected to decline in real terms over the period from

2014 to 2020, with falls for rice expected to be the largest. Meat prices, on the other hand, are expected to only see modest real price declines over the projected period. Nevertheless, the projections suggest structurally higher prices than those seen between 1990 and 2006.

Figure 1.1. Net agricultural production

Period compound annual growth rates (per cent)

Decadal growth rates

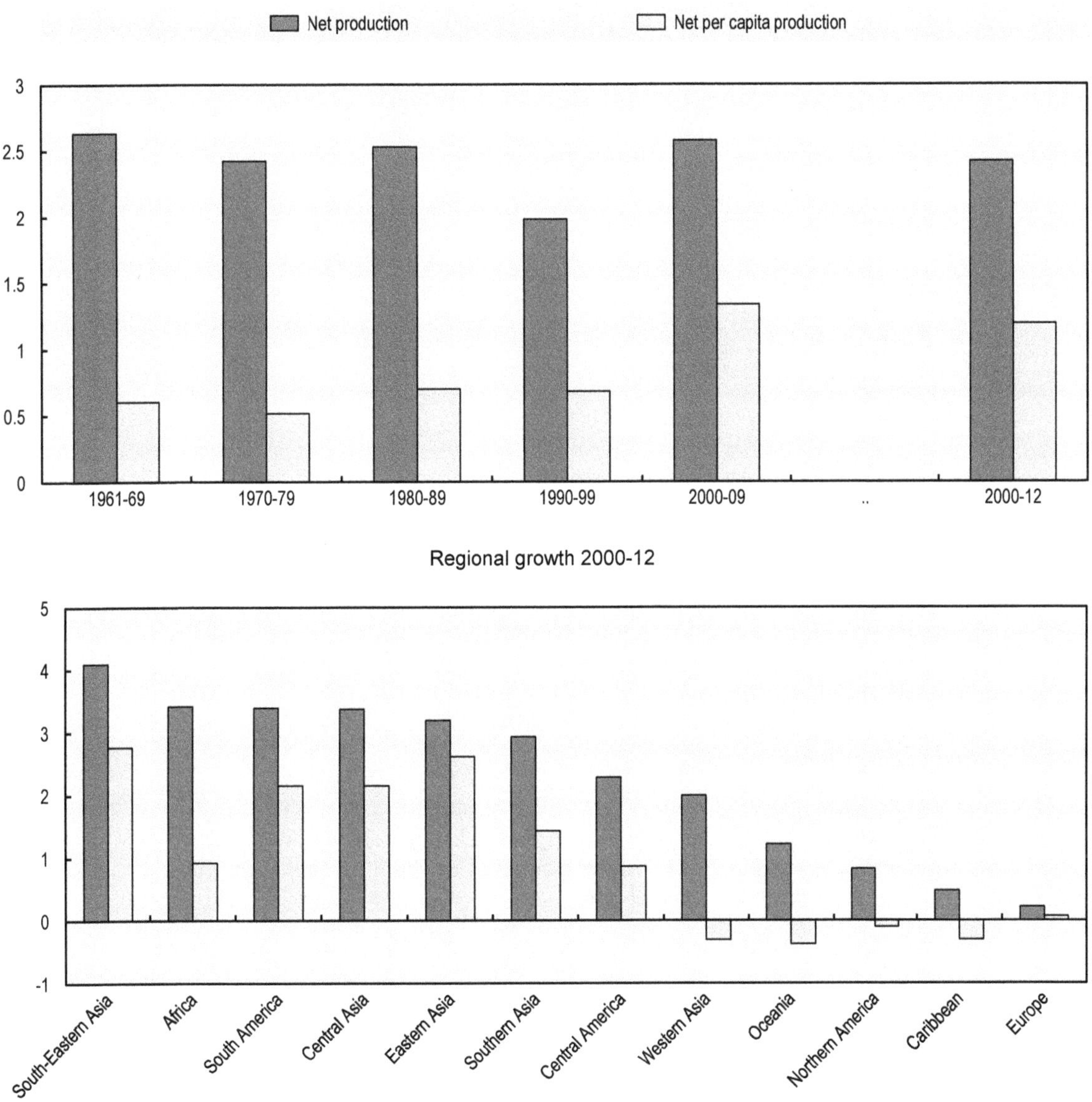

Note: Net production refers to total production less cereal use for livestock feed.

Source: OECD estimates based on FAOSTAT 2014.

Figure 1.2. Real food prices

1957 to 2014

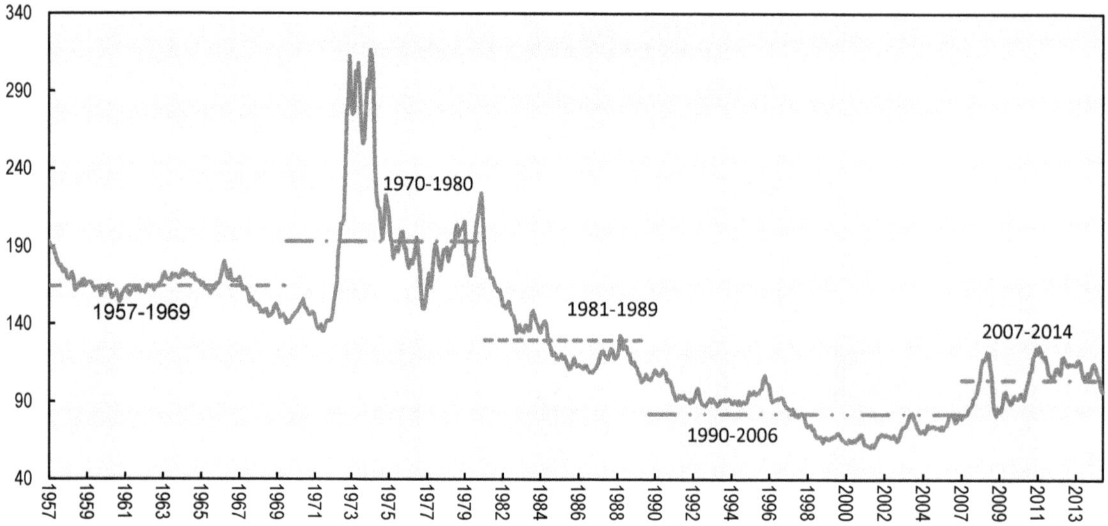

Notes: Nominal food prices were deflated by the US deflator. To convert to real prices, the average annual US GDP deflator was applied to each monthly observation.
The horizontal bars depict average price levels for selected periods.

Source: OECD calculations based on IMF IFS database 2014.

Alongside the structural change in world food price trends, price volatility on international markets also increased for some products. Measured by coefficients of variation, price volatility between 2007 and 2014 increased for rice and wheat compared with the 1990 to 2006 period. However, price volatility for all commodities and food overall was much lower than what was experienced between 1970 and 1980. Despite this, in most recent years (between 2010 and 2014), volatility for many crops (except maize) and food has fallen.

World trading patterns have altered

Over the longer term, the real value of agricultural and food products traded internationally has grown strongly. Since the mid-1990s, growth in agro-food trade has averaged around 5% per annum.[3] Since the start of the new round of WTO negotiations on agricultural trade, growth rates in agro-food trade have been significantly higher than what was seen between 1994 and 2000 (Figure 1.3).

A major development in world agricultural markets since 2000 has been the increased importance of developing countries, in particular the emerging "BRIICS" economies.[4] Between 2000 and 2013, the BRIICS's share of world agricultural exports increased from 9.9% to 17.4%, while their share of world agricultural imports increased from 6.5% to 15.6%. Most of the increase in the BRIICS's share of world agricultural exports represents increased trade with other BRIICS countries. For example, around 24% of Brazil's total agricultural exports are to the People's Republic of China. The *OECD-FAO Outlook* (2014) suggests that these trends will continue over the next ten years. At a regional level, the Americas will strengthen their position as the dominant export region, both in value and volume terms, while Asia and Africa will increase their net imports in order to meet growing demand.

Figure 1.3. Growth in agricultural trade

Compound annual growth rates in real value (USD)

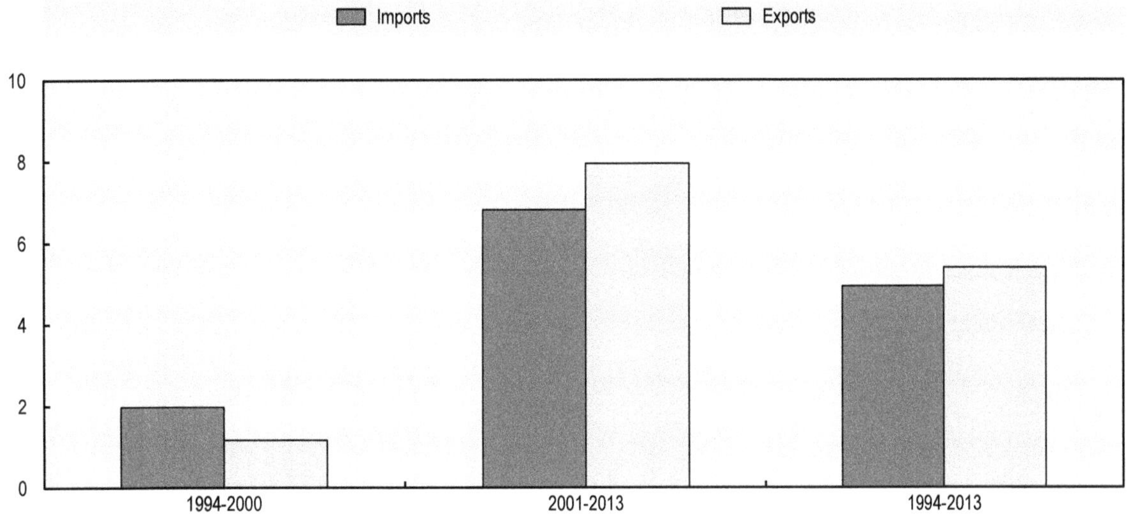

Note: Trade values converted to real terms by applying the US GDP deflator from IFS Online.

Source: OECD calculations based on WITS data.

While multilateral negotiations have stalled, many countries have sought to pursue further trade liberalisation though bilateral and regional trade agreements. In absolute terms, since 2000 there have been an increasing number of new agreements notified to the WTO each year (Figure 1.4). This has significantly increased the "stock" of agreements in place and has resulted in an increasing proportion of world trade now being covered by these agreements – in 2014 only seven WTO countries are not part of a notified and in force goods bilateral or regional trade agreement. For example, in 2008, slightly more than one-third of all world merchandise trade (excluding intra-EU trade) was conducted within RTAs, up from 18% in 1990 (WTO 2011: 64). The share of global trade in agricultural products flowing between countries connected through RTAs also grew from slightly above 20% in 1998 to nearly 40% in 2009 (Bureau and Jean, 2013).

Despite the political sensitivity of the agricultural sector, a number of bilateral and regional trading agreements have made inroads into agricultural protection levels, enabling liberalisation beyond the levels of the WTO Agreement on Agriculture (AoA). The OECD (2014a) found that in terms of market access, the majority of trade agreements have included tariff cuts and other market access concessions that exceed those of individual countries' WTO commitments. Despite this, sensitive areas remain and often reflect those at the multilateral level.

In other respects, bilateral and regional trade agreements also go beyond WTO commitments. About a third of those examined by OECD (2014a) incorporated obligations that went beyond areas covered in the AoA; these are mostly related to provisions for technical assistance and are largely couched as best-endeavour provisions. Within this, a number of agreements include a WTO-plus framework for sanitary and phytosanitary (SPS) measures and for technical barriers to trade, although in some cases these do not constitute enforceable obligations. Finally, over half of bilateral and regional agreements strengthen disciplines for export restrictions and subsidies, although these provisions are not exclusively geared towards agricultural products.

Figure 1.4. Notified bilateral and regional trade agreements

1957 to 2014

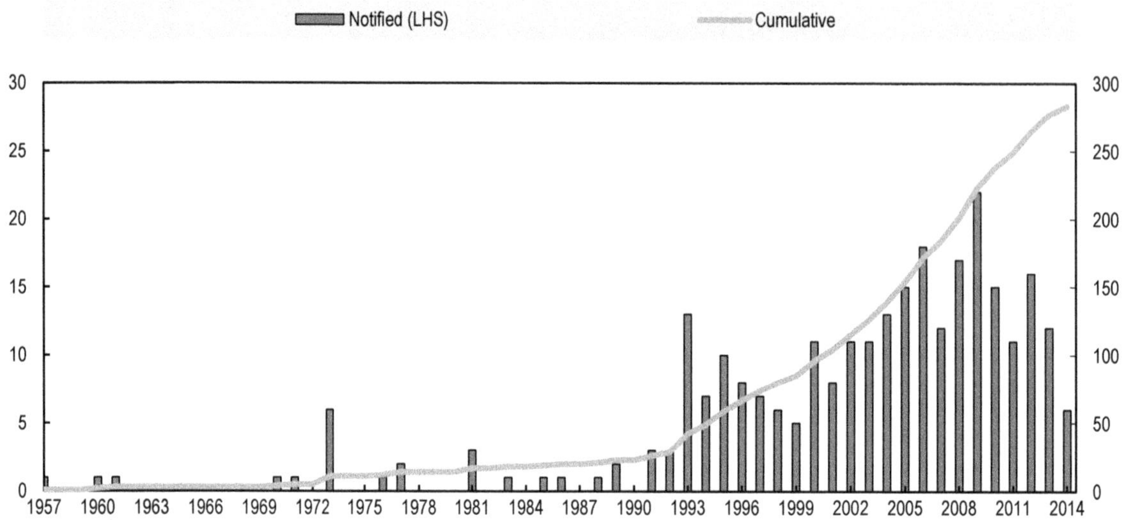

Source: WTO RTA database (2014).

1.2. The landscape of agricultural support policies has evolved

Alongside developments in domestic and international agricultural markets, the extent and nature of government involvement in the sector has also changed since 2000. Increasingly, there appears to be a convergence in the use of producer policies of developed and developing countries – in particular those that directly support individual farmers. Since 1995, income transfers to individual farmers by emerging and developing countries have been increasing, driven in part by rising levels of development and incomes within these countries, and for some, a push towards policies aimed at achieving self-sufficiency in particular agricultural products.

Producer support estimates (PSE) measured by the OECD show the contrasting developments between developed and emerging economies. In 1995, the seven emerging economies for which the OECD collects information on agricultural policies accounted for just under 4% of the total measured PSE (OECD and emerging economies). By 2012, these seven countries accounted for over 45% of the total (Figure 1.5). This rising share is made up of stable nominal expenditures by OECD countries (therefore falling real expenditures) and growing expenditures in emerging countries.

The makeup of the PSE within emerging countries shows a move to greater use of policies that are most distortionary in terms of their impact on trade – those of market price support, output-based payments and input subsidies. In contrast, for most OECD countries, the share of the PSE made up of most distortionary policies has fallen since 2000. Emerging countries' use of such payments exceeds the OECD average, and for some, the share of transfers due to these policies has increased since 2000.

Along with changes in domestic support, on average, market access for agricultural products has increased. Average applied tariffs have continued to fall globally, including amongst OECD and BRIICS countries (Figure 1.6).

However, despite improvements in market access, tariff barriers for several agricultural commodities remain very high. In many cases the maximum duty for any agricultural tariff line is significant above the average tariff level, often as high as several hundred percent and, in the cases of Norway and Switzerland, more than 1 000%. Further, potential tariff levels remain high. Many countries, developed and developing, have bound tariff levels that significantly exceed their applied levels.

Figure 1.5. Trends in PSE: OECD and emerging economies

Nominal PSE spending 1995 to 2012 (USD billions)

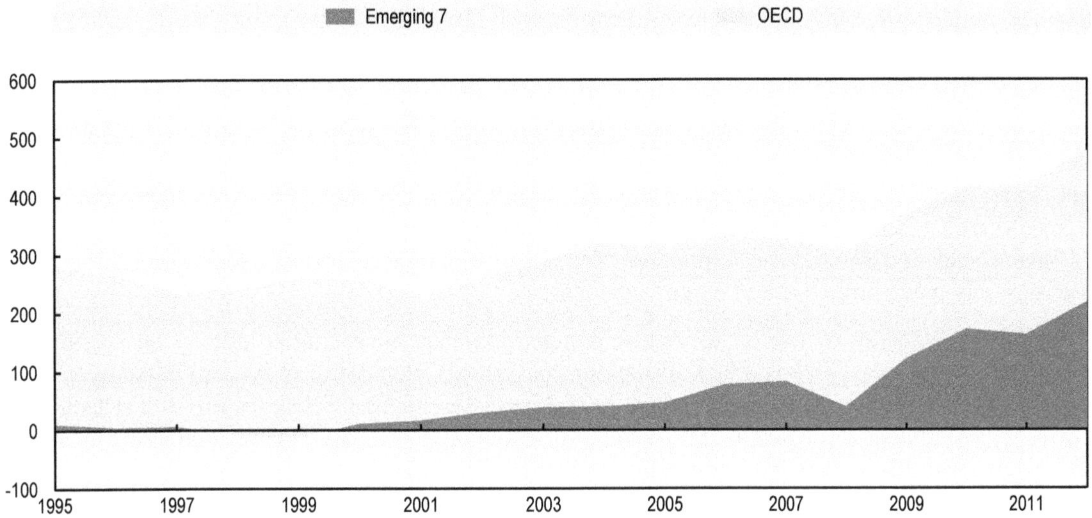

Source: OECD Stat.

Figure 1.6. Applied agricultural tariff rates

Weighted average 2000 to 2013

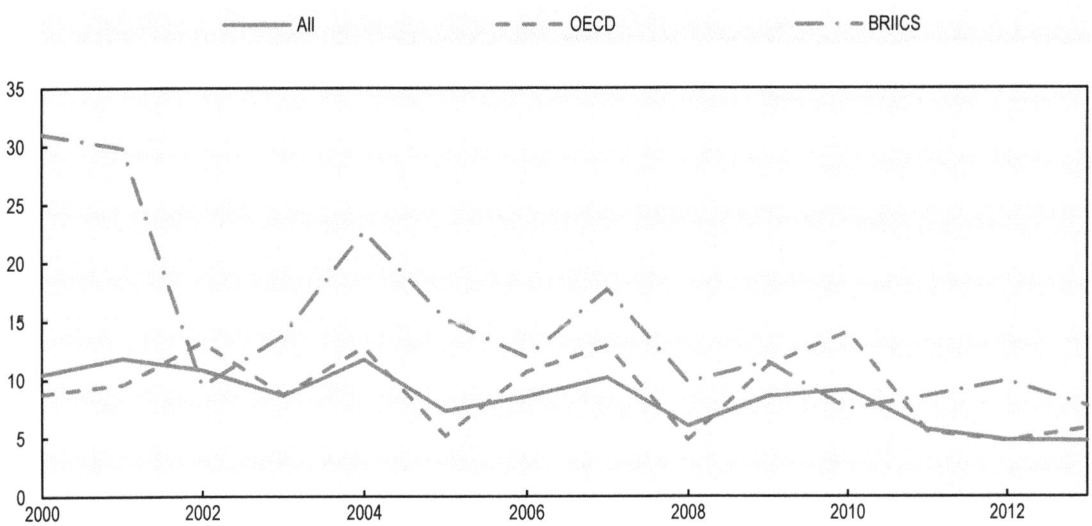

Source: WITS (2014).

Tariffs, however, constitute only one category of the host of "traditional" border measures. Many countries continue to make use of other forms of protections, including tariff-rate-quotas (TRQs). Across all WTO members, 1 094 TRQs for agricultural products were in use in 2011 (WTO, 2013). While the number of TRQs in use has fallen, from 1 430 in 2002, their use has remained nearly unchanged since 2007. Fill rates of these TRQs vary across countries, products and methods of administration. On average (unweighted), the fill rate over the 2002-2011 period was 61%.

Actual use of export subsidies has also declined notably in recent years, in part as a result of high prices on international markets, but in part also due to policy reforms. Of the 18 WTO members (counting all EU member countries as one) that had agreed non-zero export subsidy commitments in the Uruguay Round, 10 countries have not used export subsidies in all years notified since the beginning of the Doha Round in 2001. Of the remaining, three have reported continued use, and one, the United States, has only made limited use of export subsidies.

Changes in other areas related to export competition that have similar effects on world trade, however, are less clear. There is a lack of data on the subsidy element of provisions relating to export financing, food aid and state trading enterprises making assessments of changes difficult. Despite this, the WTO Secretariat has suggested that overall, since the launch of the Doha round, there have been positive developments in the export competition pillar (WTO, 2014).

Emergence of "defensive" trade policy measures

The 2007-08 food price crisis also initiated a number of changes to governments' agricultural trade policy stances. In the short term, a number of governments imposed export restrictions and varied import duties in an attempt to insulate domestic consumers from rapidly rising international prices. For larger exporting countries, these interventions helped moderate the price increases faced by domestic consumers.

However, the use of defensive trade policy measures came at a cost. During the period of rapidly rising food prices, Anderson, Ivanic and Martin (2013) found that such policies exaggerated overall price movements. Similarly, Headey (2011) suggests that trade policy-related decisions were a major driver of the observed price spikes. For rice, wheat, maize and soybeans, trade actions by countries related to export restrictions, buying to increase stockholdings, and removal of import restrictions or import subsidies all contributed to the price spikes.

The effects of these policies were particularly felt by net food importing countries that already had low trade barriers. The exaggerated price movements created by the application of insulation policies in other countries created worse outcomes than would have otherwise occurred. From a global perspective, the various individual country interventions targeted at improving food security lessened it. Anderson, Ivanic and Martin (2013) found that the trade based food price insulation policies implemented in 2007-08 could have actually increased the number of people living in poverty around the world.[5]

In the period since, many countries have maintained a more defensive stance towards international markets. Many have begun to pursue food self-sufficiency policies, often with reference to a desire to improve food security. The policy levers employed have varied, and many employ a raft of measures that range from market price support provided by trade barriers to input subsidies, and for some, the use of public stockholding programmes (Box 1.1). Many have also made use of less distortionary policies with significant investments in agricultural infrastructure and research and development.

Box 1.1. Increasing use of public stockholding policies

The 2007-08 food price hike led to a renewed interest in stockholding policies as a way to deal with price volatility and food shortages. Public stocks have grown significantly since 2007 and many developing countries intend to continue expanding their public stocks in the future.

Public stockholding programmes that influence prices can have significant impacts on the domestic economy and can have spillover effects on neighbouring countries and international markets. There are two types of public stocks that can influence prices, namely buffer stocks and social safety net stocks (dependent on their size and operation). Emergency stocks have no impact on prices since they are only released to respond to humanitarian emergencies and the stocks held are usually not sufficiently large so that acquisition or disposal of stocks has any significant price effects on markets. Buffer stock programmes influence prices directly as they aim to stabilise prices and/or alter the level of producer and consumer prices. Social safety net stock schemes aim to assist the impoverished and chronically food insecure by distributing food at subsidised prices.

The different types of stockholding programmes are not easily distinguishable in practice. Often one agency is in charge of different types of stocks, each potentially with multiple purposes. The purpose of a stock can also change over time. For example, a stock that was acquired to serve as a buffer stock can be released through a regular distribution programme. Finally, there are no uniformly used definitions to differentiate between the different types of stocks. As a result, it is not straightforward to associate certain effects to one particular type of stock.

Past experiences with buffer stocks are not encouraging. In developed countries, they have resulted from unsustainable levels of price support and have led to the accumulation of huge stocks which were dumped or sold at a loss. They also generated negative spillover effects in international markets as they often triggered the creation of trade barriers such as import tariffs, and at the same time export subsidies to guarantee the functioning of the programme. These trade measures protected domestic markets but depressed international prices.

Currently, buffer stocks are mostly held in countries in Africa and Asia. They are often operated by agencies that also manage social safety net stocks. The performance of buffer stocks can be evaluated by analysing whether they were able to achieve their objective(s) of reducing overall volatility, increasing producer prices and/or stabilising consumer prices. The effectiveness of social safety net stocks can be analysed by examining food security indicators. Of importance to both is a consideration of the opportunity costs of these policies and their relative performance compared with policy alternatives.

Research has found that inefficient targeting and conflicting objectives prevent stockholding programmes from achieving their objectives. Inefficient targeting can increase inequality when higher producer prices or subsidised cereals are not received by the intended beneficiaries. Buffer stock programmes that pair producer price support objectives with the objective of providing lower prices to consumers often achieve only one goal at the expense of the other. Schemes that raise prices for producers frequently lead to higher consumer prices, which is in conflict with the food security objective of the scheme.

Even though public stockholding policies are designed as domestic policies, they can create unwanted international spillover effects. When large amounts of grains are acquired to build or replenish public stocks, world supplies can be decreased and hence world market prices potentially increased. Conversely, releasing large amounts of grains from public stocks may depress world market prices. In addition, the import tariffs and export restrictions that are required to ensure the working of buffer stocks can have detrimental effects on the economies of neighbouring countries.

Source: Deuss (2014).

However, despite the shifts by some countries towards increased levels of domestic support and more defensive agricultural trade policies, most comply with current and proposed WTO commitments. Analysis of 19 significant agricultural producing and internationally trading countries suggests that most current policy settings would comply with potential commitments that could be made under the 2008 draft WTO modalities on agricultural trade (Box 1.2).

Box 1.2. Current trade policies and Doha draft modalities

Given the raft of changes in international agricultural markets and in policy settings, it is useful to understand where major agricultural traders sit relative to their potential WTO commitments as set out in the set of negotiated, but not agreed, modalities – the Revised Draft Modalities for Agriculture TN/AG/W/4/Rev.4 (hereafter Rev.4). With assumptions over possible implementation decisions (as the necessary steps to transform the draft modalities into a legally binding agreement have not yet taken place and it is unknown what options countries would pursue with respect to the flexibilities that exist within the modalities) the policy settings of 19 countries (12 developing and 7 developed) were assessed with respect to the Rev.4 modalities as if they were agreed and fully implemented in 2014.

The Rev.4 provisions provide for cuts to support across the three pillars of the GATT Agreement on Agriculture: market access, export competition and domestic support. Regarding market access, many bound tariffs would be reduced and tariff rate quotas introduced or expanded. There are, however, many exclusions. Special and sensitive products and other provisions limit the extent of the possible improvements in market access. In export competition, export subsidies are to be phased out (including those which result from the intervention of state trading enterprises), along with some changes to the conditions placed on export financing support programmes.

In relation to domestic support, the draft changes are more complex. Rev.4 would reduce the Bound Total AMS for most countries that have one. The *de minimis* percentage would be reduced for most countries with a Bound Total AMS, but not for others. Caps on product-specific AMSs would be introduced. Rev.4 would see an expansion in the set of blue box payments, but also place a cap on the total support in this box and product-specific caps on such payments. There would also be the addition of a bound ceiling on what may be termed Current Overall Trade-Distorting Support.

Overall, the examination of current policy settings suggests that few countries would need to change their policy settings to conform to the rules and commitments under Rev.4. There is, however, some variation across the pillars and countries.

Regarding market access, the reductions in bound tariffs would in many cases not affect, or would affect only minimally, countries' applied tariff levels. However, a handful of developed countries could see their average applied tariff reduced by several percentage points, and particular tariff lines for some countries would face larger reductions. Regarding export competition, the elimination of export subsidies would today require only little policy change for most, although there are a few specific sectors in some countries where the elimination would imply considerable policy change. Likewise, implementing Rev.4 rules in the other areas of export competition would generally require little policy change, although there are specific instances where ongoing reforms have not yet brought policy in line with the requirements of Rev.4.

As the modalities surrounding domestic support are more complex, so is the analysis of what might need to be done to meet the potential commitments as laid out in Rev.4. On the AMS and Total AMS front, in general most countries currently meet the Rev.4 limits, with some variation for individual products in a few countries. The reduction in the *de minimis* percentage for some countries would make a difference under current policy settings for very few products and countries. For the future, the values of production of many products will grow in nominal terms and thus increase the associated *de minimis* thresholds and limits, which can result in complicated interactions with other limits that are fixed in nominal terms.

Limits placed on blue box and current overall trade distorting support are also not likely to bind most countries under current policy settings. However, for some a caveat applies. If subsidies provided under the "development box" (Article 6.2) were to be included in current overall trade distorting support, some countries may exceed their cap.

Source: Brink (2014).

1.3 Do changes in agricultural markets require new principles for formulating future agricultural trade and domestic policies?

As noted, there have been some significant changes in trading patterns and the trade policy landscape since the 2000s. Notably, prices have risen, prompting some countries to make use of a range of policy measures that had not been used much in the past, such as export restrictions. Further, many countries have continued to decrease or restructure their support programmes in line with the commitments made under previous WTO agreements.

Exploring the policy landscape also suggests that the motivations behind some countries' market interventions in agriculture have changed. Underlying the increase in producer support is often a policy objective of increasing production to promote food security and to achieve self-sufficiency targets. However, the instruments at play are very similar to those used in the past by OECD countries. For example, concerns over food security are prompting some governments to implement domestic market price support and stability programmes, often with the help of public stockholding programmes. Similarly, programmes targeted at improving rural incomes and production often make use of interventions aimed at lowering the costs of inputs.

Box 1.3. Principles for agricultural policy design from past OECD analysis

Past OECD analysis has explored ways in which governments can develop policies that can deliver the gains from a market-orientated and trade-exposed agricultural sector while also addressing domestic policy objectives. Central to good agricultural policy making is the explicit definition of measurable policy objectives. With clear objectives, governments are better placed to address objectives and intended beneficiaries directly, thereby avoiding distortions to markets and trade. Specific instruments can be designed to address market failures at their source, and remaining income issues should be resolved with measures targeted to farm households that have persistent income problems. OECD analysis has highlighted the role of decoupling support; targeting and tailoring support programmes to the source of market failures and accounting for the multifunctional character of agriculture; and addressing those negatively affected by reforms through accompanying policy measures or compensation.

Decoupling support from production provides a means to achieve objectives while minimising markets distortions. Payments made directly to farm households elicit a significantly lower production response and result in higher farm incomes compared with policies that seek to do this indirectly by inflating producer prices through trade barriers or market price support schemes. These policies can provide a path for governments to follow to move away from market price support and payments based on output and input use.

Any decoupled payment to producers must be both targeted and tailored to the policy objectives of governments. Income support (or poverty alleviation) payments should be targeted at poor households. Similarly, payments for the production of environmental goods and services should only accrue to those who produce them and not to all producers. And while governments may be tempted to combine payments (e.g. income support and environmental payments) to save on transaction costs, it represents a blunt way to achieve any one objective and risks being ineffective. Agriculture has multifunctional characteristics and can provide, in addition to food, feed and fibre, several non-commodity outputs such as rural community well-being or environmental amenities. In the absence of truly joint production, it is best to stimulate provision of non-commodity outputs through directly targeted measures, rather than broad-based forms of production or price support.

Policy reforms following the principles above, while increasing overall returns to society from agriculture, will adversely affect some. To help those made worse off, and to lessen the political costs of reform, targeted transitional measures are warranted.

The OECD has also investigated policies designed to help manage the risks faced by farmers. This work has highlighted the differences between the types of risks faced and the respective role of government in addressing them. Namely, some level of fluctuations in output or price represent normal risks and should be managed by producers. On the other extreme, there are catastrophic risks from extreme, uncertain and infrequent events that create damage beyond the capacity of farmers or the market to cope. Governments should deal with only such catastrophic risks. The last type of risk, termed marketable risk, lies in between (such as hail damage). Such risk can often be dealt with through market instruments such as insurance, and when such instruments are not available governments should be concerned with creating the institutional environment that allows the market to provide such services.

Source: Tangermann (2014).

The countries that are becoming increasingly active in their domestic agricultural markets also have a different agricultural demographic compared with most OECD countries. Their agricultural sectors are often characterised by a large number of mostly poor producers who face a number of challenges, including relatively low levels of productivity and a lack of access to well-functioning markets.

Of issue then is whether or not these differences would suggest that the previously used domestic support policies that were found to be both ineffective and inefficient in OECD countries would be more efficient and more effective in developing countries?

For OECD countries, past analysis has suggested that good agricultural policy making centres on the key principle of addressing objectives and intended beneficiaries directly, thereby avoiding distortions to markets and trade. Specific instruments should be designed in response to market failures, and remaining income issues should be resolved with measures targeted to farm households that have persistent income problems (Box 1.3). These principles are well supported on theoretical and equity grounds, but have also proven sensible in practice. Undistorted markets (including corrections to ensure that unpriced elements are taken into account) allow resources to flow to their most efficient use, maximising the returns achievable from the agricultural sector and the broader economy. Such policies ensure agricultural incomes and production are both at high and sustainable levels. On practical grounds, avoiding negative international spillovers from domestic policies can create a more respectful and stable international trading environment.

The principle of addressing objectives directly through correcting for market failures and addressing barriers is valid whatever the level of prices prevailing on international markets. Creating distortions, on the other hand, is costly to the economy, at low and at high prices. Avoiding distortions as far as possible therefore remains a critical principle in formulating current policy advice. Further, with the emergence of new major agricultural producers, there is renewed importance in avoiding the pitfalls of past policy paths. Where distortionary policies are used by countries with limited fiscal resources and a large number of rural poor households, developing policies that provide for a more effective and efficient response to targeted market failures are perhaps more important. The ineffective nature of many distortionary policies in addressing policy objectives and the efficiency costs imposed potentially carry a higher opportunity cost as they direct government attention and limited resources away from policies that can, in the long run, overcome the challenges faced by their domestic producers.

1.4. Agricultural market liberalisation remains important, including for food security

While a number of countries have continued to liberalise their agricultural markets by decreasing levels of trade-distorting producer support and increasing levels of international competition through reducing barriers to market access, further liberalisation remains important.

Higher international prices for many agricultural products have in part been responsible for the shift in focus of agricultural support policies. They have also helped some governments move away from export subsidies. However, without any international agreement that will lock in existing reforms, and continue the trend to lower levels of protection, there remains a risk that if price trends were to reverse, there could be a shift back towards protectionism.

The risks of no further multilateral agreement on agriculture could be significant. Bouët and Laborde (2009) suggest that without an agreement, a shift towards protectionism by countries increasing tariffs to bound rates would be costly in both trade and welfare terms. These costs could be significantly mitigated through the signing of an agreement.

Agricultural trade and open markets are also an important requirement for countries to achieve key objectives such as improving food security and encouraging rural development to reduce poverty (OECD 2013; Box 1.4). The use of market insulating policies are likely to be counterproductive to these desired objectives in the longer term by increasing domestic prices paid for food by consumers while providing no extra incentive for improved productivity for producers, thereby ultimately having little impact on producer incomes. Further, for large agricultural producers, recent World Bank research suggests that the imposition of export restrictions to lower domestic prices in the face of sustained increases in world prices will be net costly, and particularly so for poor rural households (Jacoby, 2013).

In the longer term, policies that lead to rising incomes of poorer households, such as those targeted at promoting productivity, which can include education and training, innovation, infrastructure policies, and domestic competition-based reform, among others, are of critical importance. It is particularly important that government policies do not unnecessarily hinder the ability of producers to alter the production mix and expand output in the face of sustained price increases. This process is crucial to the flow on income effects from price increases that help deliver much of the improvement in incomes of poor households. Such policy prescriptions are generally accepted by most.

But such policies take time to have effects and poor households within countries may still be threatened by sudden price movements. Governments should rightly act to help alleviate some of the effects of price increases as they can increase poverty levels and lead to social unrest, as seen by the riots in some countries in response to the 2007-08 rapid price increases.

Redistribution policies can help cushion some of the impacts of such price movements and importantly avoid many of the unintended impacts that stem from other less targeted policy interventions. Indeed, such policies are becoming increasingly important in their own right with the distribution of the gains from economic growth in many developing countries becoming less equal over time.

Key features of the future outlook for agricultural markets also suggest that trade and agricultural market liberalisation are likely to play an increasingly important role in maintaining access to food, limiting price pressures and improving food security more generally. Both climate change and population growth, coupled with increased prosperity, will play an increasingly important role in food supply and demand, and therefore influence food security.

Box 1.4. Trade and food security

Food security is a multi-dimensional concept. People will only be food secure when sufficient food is available, they have access to it, and it is well utilised. A fourth requirement is the stability of those three dimensions over time. Trade openness can help a country improve food security across each of these four dimensions.

On availability, trade allows for products to flow from surplus to deficit areas. Longer-term trends in agricultural markets show increasing volumes of trade (export shares of production for most products have increased). Openness to trade also increases the diversity of products on offer to consumers, opening up the potential for a more varied diet.

On accessibility, trade allows for production to occur where it is of lowest cost to do so. This increases productivity and lowers prices compared to what they may otherwise be. International food prices have fallen in real terms over the longer run, making food more affordable to poorer households.

On utilisation, open markets are generally beneficial for economic growth, which if a country's institutional settings are correct, promotes development and reductions in poverty. As countries develop, they also invest more heavily in health systems, sanitation and clean water, education, and other social infrastructure. These investments, coupled with higher incomes, contribute positively to food utilisation.

On stability, open markets generally improve the stability of supply, for the simple reason that the risks associated with own food production exceed those of pooled production on international markets. For the same reason, open markets can provide a means to hedge against the volatility in price movements caused by changes in domestic production. Further, trade openness provides a solid ground for continued economic growth and good domestic policy setting, thereby helping provide a platform for stability in the provision of services that aid in the utilisation of food.

Source: OECD (2014b).

Climate change will alter production patterns and variability on both a domestic and international scale. For individual countries, it is likely that food production will become more variable, with changes also possible in terms of land use and the variety of products produced domestically. Trade openness allows countries to secure supplies from a wider range of producers, who are likely to face different climate risks than those of domestic producers.

Across the world, populations will continue to grow and become richer. This will both increase the demand for food and create shifts in relative food demands with a likely greater demand for proteins and more processed products. Trade openness provides a number of advantages in helping countries better adjust to these developments. It provides for a greater diversity of products to be available and accessible for consumers – helping consumers meet their full range of nutritional needs. It also allows for the benefits from changing patterns of specialisation to be realised and provides access to global and regional agro-food value chains. With income growth, there has been increased demand for more processed products, which means for many commodities, the value chain involved in getting the product from the farm gate to the final consumer is being extended. Participation in value chains is facilitated by low barriers to trade and improved regulatory coherence that allow products at various states of transformation to flow across borders: in other words, imports play an important role in creating a competitive export sector. It is a mistake to believe that imposing barriers on inputs into value chains, for example by restricting the export of raw materials, will help spur competitive value-adding within the domestic economy, thereby allowing producers to "capture" the value created in upstream processing. Such policies only increase the final price paid by consumers, with little influence on producer returns and domestic food security.

In respect of both climate change and population growth, trade openness will allow production to be centred in areas of comparative advantage. This helps place downward pressure on world prices, which is particularly important for accessibility when demand is rising, when a country's domestic production is becoming more variable, and when climate change may lead to permanent (and unknown) shifts in comparative advantage.

With greater participation in global and regional markets, based around comparative advantages, the opportunities for economic growth are maximised. If domestic policy settings are robust, this provides for the best opportunities for income growth amongst the poor, reducing poverty and therefore having the greatest impact on improving food security domestically.

Notes

1. This overview presents a synthesis of the work presented to the OECD's 2014 *Global Forum on Agriculture: Issues in Agricultural Trade Policy*. The work draws heavily on the contributed papers to, and insights provided by participants at, the forum held in Paris on 2 December 2014. Copies of the contributed papers and presentations are available at: http://www.oecd.org/agriculture/global-forum-agriculture-2014.htm.
2. In fact, agricultural negotiations started a year earlier, in 2000, with respect to Article 20 of the Agreement on Agriculture.
3. Estimates represent compound annual growth rates in the real value of reported agricultural product imports and exports respectively, based on Comtrade data for the period between 1994 and 2013.
4. The BRIICS countries are Brazil, Russia, India, Indonesia, China and South Africa.
5. Model results indicate that around eight million additional people would have been had incomes that classified them as living in poverty when the trade based insulation policies were modelled compared to when such policies were not implemented (both cases assuming the observed initial price increases pre policy responses). Despite this, the authors note that the estimate was not significantly different from zero.

References

Anderson, K., M. Ivanic and W. Martin (2014), "Food Price Spikes, Price Isolation, and Poverty", *Policy Research Working Paper*, No. 7011, World Bank Group.

Bouët, A. and D. Larborde (2009), "The Potential Cost of a Failed Doha Round", *IFPRI Discussion Paper*, No. 00886.

Brink, L. (2015), "Current Domestic Policy Settings in the Context of Past and Potential International Agreements", in *Issues in Agricultural Trade Policy*, OECD, Paris.

Bureau, J. and S. Jean (2013), "The Impact of Regional Trade Agreements on Trade in Agricultural Products", *OECD Food, Agriculture and Fisheries Papers*, No. 65, OECD Publishing, Paris.
DOI: http://dx.doi.org/10.1787/5k3xznkz60vk-en.

Deuss, A. (2015), "Review of the Performance and Impacts of Recent Stockholding Policies", in *Issues in Agricultural Trade Policy*, OECD, Paris.

Headey, D. (2011), "Rethinking the Global Food Crisis: The Role of Trade Shocks", *Food Policy*, Vol. 36, pp. 136-46.

Jacoby, H.G. (2013), "Food Prices, Wages, and Welfare in Rural India", *Policy Research Working Paper*, No. 6412, World Bank Group.

Naylor, R.L. and W.P. Falcon (2010), "Food Security in an Era of Economic Volatility", *Population and Development Review*, Vol. 35(4), pp. 693-723.

OECD (2015), "Regional trade agreements and agriculture", *OECD Food, Agriculture and Fisheries Papers*, No. 79, OECD Publishing, Paris.
DOI: http://dx.doi.org/10.1787/5js4kg5xjvvf-en.

OECD (2014b), "Trade Dimensions of Food Security", *OECD Food, Agriculture and Fisheries Papers*, No. 77, OECD Publishing, Paris.
DOI: http://dx.doi.org/10.1787/5js65xn790nv-en.

OECD/FAO (2014c), *OECD-FAO Agricultural Outlook 2014*, OECD Publishing, Paris.
DOI: http://dx.doi.org/10.1787/agr_outlook-2014-en.

OECD (2013), *Global Food Security: Challenges for the Food and Agricultural System*, OECD Publishing, Paris.
DOI: http://dx.doi.org/10.1787/9789264195363-en.

OECD (2008), *Rising Food Prices: Causes and Consequences*, OECD Publishing, Paris, http://www.oecd.org/trade/agricultural-trade/40847088.pdf.

Piesse, J. and C. Thirtle (2009), "Three Bubbles and a Panic: And Explanatory Review of Recent Food Commodity Price Events", *Food Policy*, Vol. 34, pp. 119-29.

Tangermann, S. (2015), "Are Past OECD Analyses of Agricultural Policy Reforms Relevant to Current Policy and Market Settings?", in *Issues in Agricultural Trade Policy*, OECD, Paris.

WTO (2011), *World Trade Report 2011: The WTO and preferential trade agreements: From co-existence to coherence*, Geneva.

WTO (2013), *Tariff Quota Administration Methods and Fill Rates 2002-2011*, Background Paper by the Secretariat? Document TN/AG/S/26/Rev.1, 28 March 2013, Geneva.

WTO (2014), *Annual Export Competition Review: Submission from the Cairns Group to the 74th Meeting of the Committee on Agriculture (COA) in June 2014*, Document G/AG/W/129, 2 June 2014, Geneva.

Chapter 2

Are past OECD analyses of agricultural policy reforms relevant to current policy and market settings?

by
Stefan Tangermann[1]

This chapter looks at how the conditions and policies for global agriculture have changed since the major international agreements of 2008, how work done in OECD up to 2008 may be relevant to current negotiations, and where new analyses may be needed. Section 2 looks at developments in international markets for agricultural products. The evolution of the policy landscape is considered in Section 3, as well as how it relates to commitments under the Agreement on Agriculture and potential future commitments along the lines agreed in 2008 for the Doha Development Agenda (DDA). Section 4 reviews relevant OECD work on market and trade impacts of agricultural policies, while implications for achieving optimal policy performance are briefly summarised in Section 5. Some possible implications for the post-Bali negotiations on agriculture are suggested in Section 6. A few issues that might benefit from future analysis are proposed in Section 7.

2.1 Introduction

Given the importance of trade as an economic activity, and of trade policy as a cornerstone of economic policy making, the OECD has always placed much emphasis on analysing trends in international trade, and on investigating developments in trade policies both at the national level and in the multilateral framework of the GATT/WTO. In that context, agricultural trade has required particular attention. Though the share of food and agricultural products in global trade is small and declining, agricultural trade continues to play an important role for both overall economic development and food security in many developing and emerging economies. Moreover, in multilateral trade negotiations, tensions over agriculture have time and again caused particular difficulties and retarded progress in other sectors.

Over the years, OECD analysis has contributed significantly to identifying the nature of challenges faced in global agricultural trade, to investigating the trade impacts of alternative agricultural policies, and to clarifying options for improving policy performance and reducing impediments to well-functioning international markets. OECD work in this area has, for example, made an important contribution to preparing the intellectual and political ground for successful negotiations on agriculture in the Uruguay Round of the GATT. The Agreement on Agriculture (AoA) concluded in the Uruguay Round was a milestone in multilateral efforts to create operationally effective disciplines governing agricultural trade. It established firm rules and clearly specified quantitative reduction commitments. It also called for another round of negotiations, to deal with the "continuation of the reform process". There was hope that much of the large amount of "water" the Uruguay Round results had left in the new disciplines would then be wrung out of the reduction commitments, and that agriculture could eventually be integrated fully into the WTO regime, without any sectoral exceptions.

It turned out that the agricultural negotiations mandated in the AoA could be integrated into the Doha Round – where agriculture began to cause tensions from the start. It took a major effort to agree on the precise wording of the objectives for agriculture in the Work Programme for the new round. The real difficulties began when the negotiations turned to the details of new modalities for agriculture. At a mini-ministerial in July 2008, the time appeared ripe to reach closure on the modalities for future disciplines and commitments. However, it proved impossible to reach a compromise on a number of elements in agriculture. Though agreement on most other issues was in sight, the mini-ministerial collapsed as a result. The possibility of calling a WTO ministerial in December 2008 was explored, in the hope that it might finalise the modalities. The chairs of the negotiations on agriculture and on non-agricultural market access issued revised texts of draft modalities, reflecting results from the July mini-ministerial and subsequent negotiations. However, gaps between negotiating positions remained so wide that risk of yet another failure appeared too high, and the ministerial was postponed.

In the absence of any significant progress in the Doha negotiations, the draft modalities of December 2008 documented for a long time what had, or had not, been achieved in the Doha negotiations on agriculture. Often referred to as "Rev.4", in reference to WTO document TN/AG/W/4/Rev.4, these modalities are extensive and highly detailed, specify a large number of qualitative provisions and contain all the quantitative parameters needed to define reduction commitments regarding market access, domestic support and export competition. Since 2008, however, negotiations made little, if any, progress. As a result of the Bali Ministerial in 2013, however, a new dynamic emerged and negotiations became more intensive again. One of the questions considered by negotiators in the first half of 2014 was to what extent the conditions in global agriculture and policies affecting it have changed since Rev.4 was drafted.

2.2 Market situation and outlook

Price level

International markets for agricultural commodities are notoriously volatile.[2] Most of that volatility originates on the supply side: output depends on the vagaries of weather and other natural factors, which vary from year to year. Cyclical swings of output, reflecting lagged response of supply to price changes, can inject an additional degree of volatility into agricultural markets. As it happens, such output fluctuations on agricultural markets hit a demand that does not respond much to price variations. Hence prices have to change rather much in order to restore market balance. International trade could, in principle, even out much of that intrinsic volatility, given that weather variations and other supply shocks are typically regional phenomena. However, the balancing potential of trade is diminished as many governments to try to stabilise their domestic markets through various policy interventions. In effect, such policies export instability to international markets and prevent fluctuations on these markets from being absorbed in national markets. In consequence, international markets tend to be more volatile than most domestic markets for agricultural commodities.

In "normal" periods, volatility on agricultural commodity markets is essentially symmetric: prices are sometimes above and sometimes below their trend, and the highs are more or less matched by corresponding lows. Occasionally, however, such "normal" (though pronounced) volatility is interrupted by an extreme price spike, usually accompanied by particularly high volatility. This phenomenon of asymmetric price movements (or "skew") on agricultural (and other) commodity markets is closely related to stock changes. For storable commodities, stock variations can contribute to evening out some part of market volatility. However, once stocks are depleted, they can no longer compensate for a decline in output. In that situation, an output shortfall can drive up prices to very high levels. Uncertainty and nervousness of market participants can then add to volatility. If panic spreads to governments and some of them resort to *ad hoc* policy interventions such as export restrictions, price spikes and volatility are amplified even further.

Most of the time, such episodes of extreme price spikes do not last very long. Output recovers, stocks are replenished and prices return to their usual levels. This was, for example, the nature of the pronounced price spike on international cereals markets in the mid-1970s. After the extreme price spike was over, markets calmed again and continued their secular decline in real terms (Figure 1.1). More recently, in 2007 and subsequent years, the world experienced another extreme price spike on international markets for cereals. This time, however, the subsequent development of markets differed notably from the usual episode of a transitory price spike. After the original extreme price explosion was over, prices did not revert to their pre-spike levels. On the contrary, further peaks followed, prices continued to exhibit much volatility, and even though they declined again from their extremely high levels of 2007/08, prices remained significantly higher than before 2007, even in real terms (Figure 1.1).

While market projections for the coming years differ somewhat between authors and institutions, there is general agreement that the prices of most agricultural commodities are likely to remain at a high level for the foreseeable future. The *OECD-FAO Agricultural Outlook* (2014) projects real prices of cereals to decline again slightly over the whole of the 2014-23 period, but would remain considerably higher than before the 2007-08 price spike at the end of that period (Figure 2.2). Real prices for most other agricultural commodities are also projected to attain levels significantly higher than in the past. Average prices for the ten-year period 2014-24 are projected to be higher than those in the 1992-2006 period by 15% to 35% in real terms for cereals, oilseeds and sugar, by 40% to 60% for poultry meat and dairy products, and by 25% for beef/veal (Figure 2.2). Only pigmeat prices are projected to remain slightly below their 1992-2006 average. Relative to the base period 2000-06, which does not include the above-trend prices of the mid-1990s, the projected increase of real prices in the coming ten-year period is even larger, for some products reaching as much as 80% (Figure 2.2).

Figure 2.1. International market prices of cereals in real terms, 1971-2023

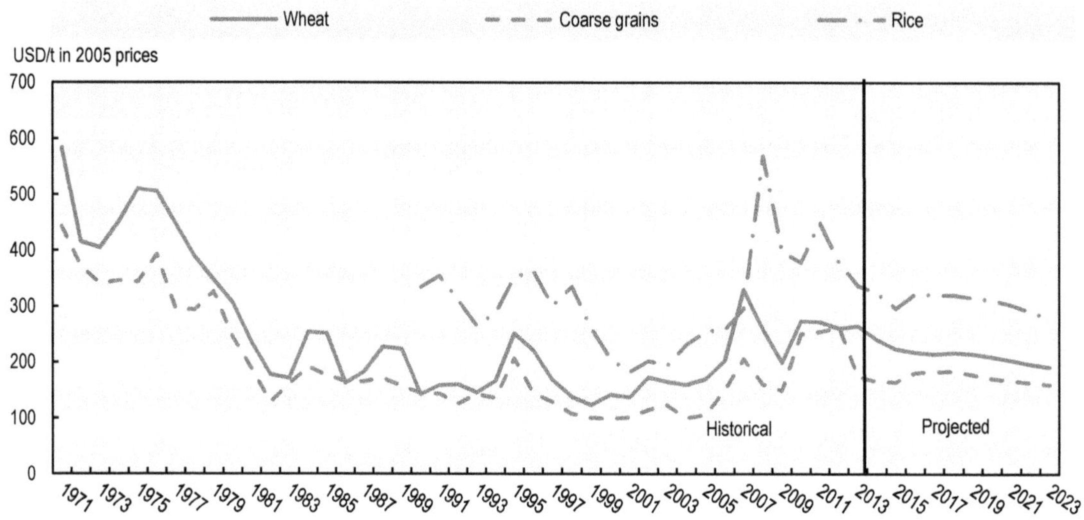

Source: Author's calculations based on database of OECD-FAO (2014).

Figure 2.2. Price projections for selected agricultural commodities for the average of years 2014 to 2023

Percentage change of real prices relative to averages in two alternative base periods

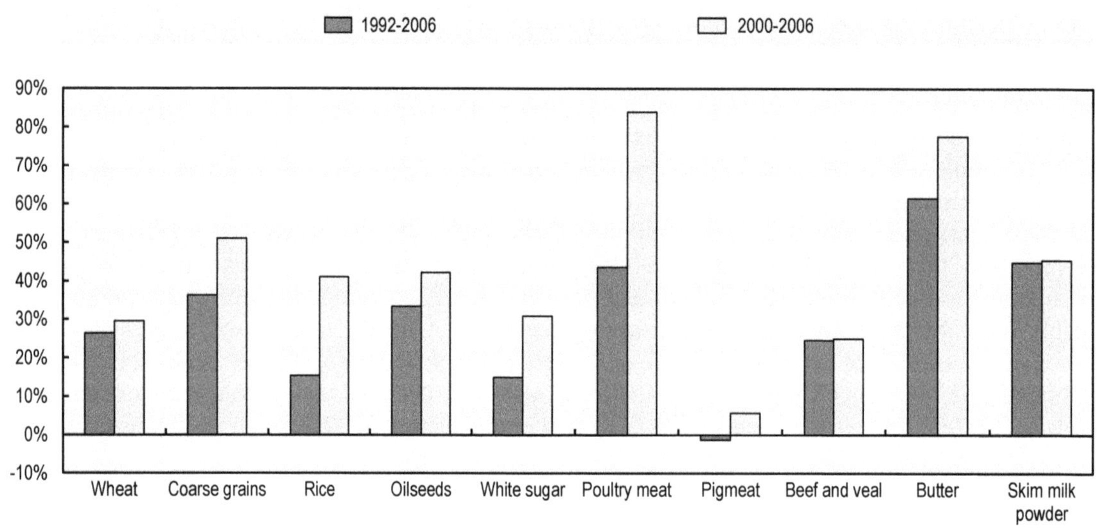

Source: Author's calculations based on database of OECD-FAO (2014).

It thus appears that in 2007 and subsequent years, the world has not only experienced an extreme price spike and hefty volatility, but also a notable step increase in the price level of agricultural commodities.[3] This is a remarkable departure from past trends on world markets. Real prices for agricultural commodities have trended downwards for a long time.[4] Around the year 2000, that downward trend slowed, and then was interrupted by what appears to have been an upward step in the price level on the order of magnitude of approximately one-third.[5] A number of factors may explain that step increase. A major influence is attributed to high and rising energy prices and the resulting cost push in world agriculture, both through direct energy consumption (e.g. tractor fuel) and through their impact on other input prices, in particular fertiliser. The most recent *OECD-FAO Outlook* (2014) projects the average price of crude oil in the 2014-23 period to be above that in the 2000-06 period by about 160%

in real terms, and the average price of fertiliser to be higher by nearly 70%. Another factor on the supply side is what appears to be a slowdown in yield growth and productivity improvement on a global scale. Moreover, resource constraints are increasingly apparent, specifically regarding the availability of water and land. On the demand side, food consumption continues to be stimulated by population growth and rising incomes, in particular in emerging economies. Growing use of agricultural commodities as feedstocks for the production of biofuels also contributes to demand expansion. All of these factors appear to be of lasting nature for the foreseeable future. Thus it seems that the step increase in the level of real agricultural commodity prices that has occurred after 2006 is not short-term phenomenon.

Volatility

The future volatility on world markets of agricultural products is more difficult to project. Fundamentally, the degree of volatility depends on two sets of conditions: the frequency and size of shocks, most of which originate from the supply side; and the ease by which markets can adapt, which reflects factors such as price elasticities of demand and supply, and the availability of stocks.

The occurrence of shocks is essentially impossible to predict, given that shocks are deviations from the expected. However, there are reasons to assume that the frequency and size of shocks in global agricultural output may be higher in the future than in past decades. In particular, climate change is expected to be accompanied by increasingly frequent and violent occurrences of extreme weather events (storms, flooding, drought, etc.), resulting in growing output variability. This may be exacerbated by the fact that agricultural production is increasingly moving into marginal areas, which are particularly susceptible to yield variations. New shocks enter the agricultural system as energy prices become increasingly important in the cost structure of the global farming industry, not least because expanding global agricultural output will depend on growing use of fertiliser. On the demand side, volatility may increase as the consumption of bioenergy, and hence of agricultural feedstocks, will depend more and more on the price-driven profitability of substituting biofuels for fossil energy.

At the same time, the flexibility of markets in adapting to output variations may decline. As incomes rise on a global scale, food demand becomes less and less responsive to price changes. Where consumption of biofuels is driven by government policies through fixed mandates, the price responsiveness of that component of demand for agricultural products is essentially zero. As global demand for agricultural products approaches the frontier of production capacity of world agriculture, markets become progressively tighter and hence less able to adapt to shocks. Stock levels of cereals are projected to recover somewhat from their very low levels in the recent episode of price spikes and volatility, but may tend to remain low as global output struggles to keep pace with the growth in demand. Macroeconomic conditions may also remain somewhat fragile as high government debts and low interest rates continue to reflect the emergency actions pursued in fighting the global financial crisis and then the European currency crisis. All this would suggest that, in addition to a higher level of prices, the future may see larger volatility on agricultural markets.

2.3. Evolution of the policy landscape

While the situation on international markets has changed noticeably in the recent past, agricultural policies have also evolved, partly in response to the changes in market conditions, but also reflecting changes in policy pursuits. This evolution of the policy landscape is best illustrated by changes in estimated producer support. Additional specific insights can be derived from the development of policy settings in domestic support, import measures and instruments affecting exports.

Producer support

In its annual *Agricultural Policy Monitoring and Evaluation* (M&E), the OECD now provides estimates of producer support for a total of 47 countries. Included are the 34 members of the OECD, 6 non-OECD member countries of the European Union and 7 emerging economies.[6] On aggregate, these 47 countries cover almost 80% of value added in world agriculture (OECD, 2014: 24) and thus provide a good impression of the global picture. It should, therefore, be useful to review developments in these countries during the DDA negotiations, comparing the most recent M&E data (2012) with the average of the six-year period 2002-07, the period before the 2008 draft modalities were tabled. Over that time, the Producer Support Estimate (PSE) for the aggregate of these 47 countries grew by nearly 60%, from USD 308 billion in 2002-07 to USD 486 billion in 2012.[7] During the same period, gross farm receipts (inclusive of support) for these 47 countries grew even more rapidly, by nearly 90%. Thus the average of the share of producer support (%PSE) in gross farm receipts of the 47 countries declined from 20.3% in 2002-07 to 16.7% in 2012. The decline began in 2007 and continued in 2008, after which the support rate increased again somewhat, suggesting that much of the decline was a result of the rise of international market prices in 2007-08 (Figure 2.3).

Within this aggregate, the evolution in producer support in different country groups have diverged notably. In the OECD area,[8] the %PSE has declined significantly since the beginning of the century, while the %PSE for the aggregate of the seven emerging economies has increased equally significantly. In both these groups, the change in %PSE was about 15 percentage points since around the year 2000 (Figure 2.3). As a result, the shares of these country groups in aggregate producer support for the 47 countries covered in the M&E have shifted fundamentally. While the group of seven emerging economies made up for no more than 17% of the total in the period 2002-07, its share had grown to 45% by 2012 (Figure 2.4).

Behind these averages for country groups there is a large variation across individual countries. While the %PSE declined by 9 percentage points from 2002-07 to 2012 in the OECD area overall, it decreased by 17 percentage points in Iceland and went up by 2 percentage points in Japan (Figure 2.5). Among the emerging economies, changes in %PSE during that period range from - 4 percentage points in South Africa to 10 percentage points in Indonesia. Given these large differences in the evolution of countries' producer support despite facing similar developments in international market prices, it is clear that changing market conditions can explain only partially the changes in producer support in several countries. Exchange rate movements and changes in policy settings must account for the remainder.

Figure 2.3. Producer Support Estimate as a share of gross farm revenue, 1995-2023

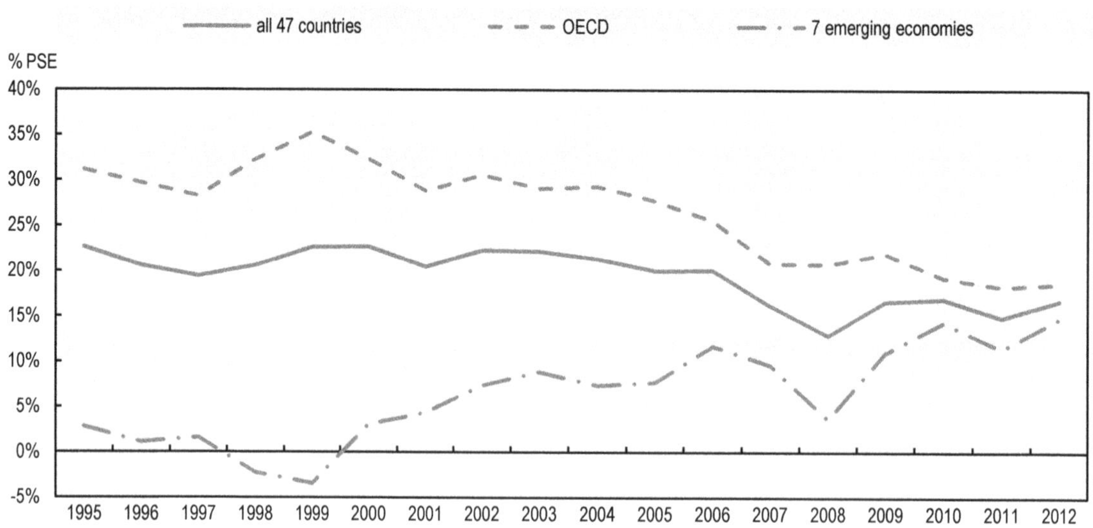

Source: Author's calculations based on PSE database of OECD.

Figure 2.4. Shares of country groups in aggregate producer support of all 47 countries covered in the OECD's M&E

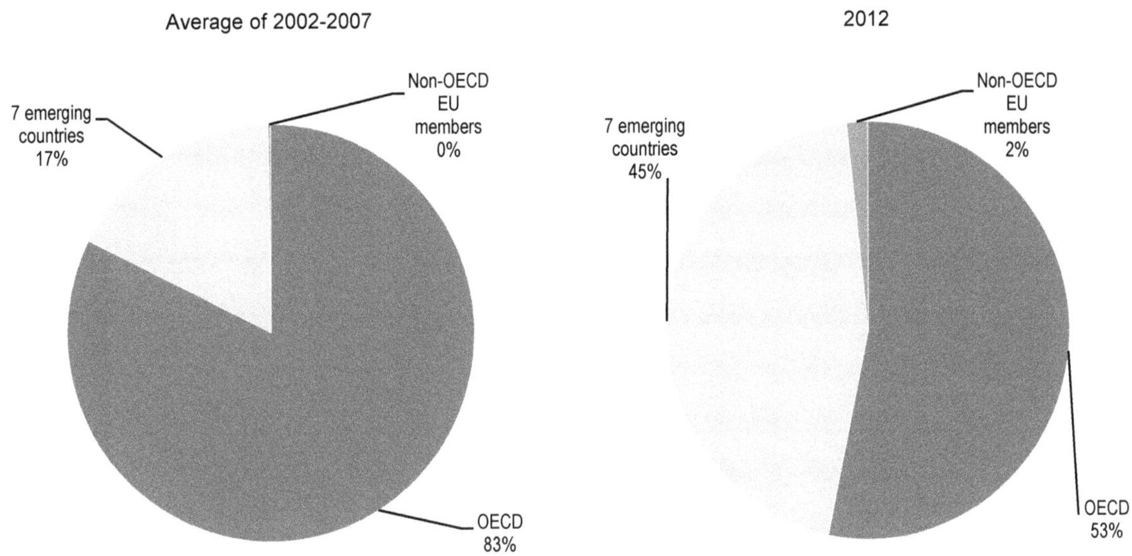

Source: Author's calculations based on PSE database of OECD.

The same conclusion can be drawn from the wide variation in changes to the producer Nominal Protection Coefficient (NPC) during the same period (Figure 2.5). In most countries where the %PSE has declined, the producer NPC has also been reduced and vice versa, indicating that a reduction in support based on commodity output has contributed to the decline in overall producer support.[9] In the OECD area overall, the NPC declined by 0.13, from 1.23 in 2002-07 to 1.10 in 2012. This means that the gap between domestic producer prices (inclusive of payments per unit of output) and international market prices was reduced by 13 percentage points. In the seven emerging countries, the (unweighted) average of NPCs increased from 1.07 to 1.08 during this period.

The change in NPCs is one indication of the evolving composition of producer support. Another indicator, often used by OECD in presenting M&E results, is the share of potentially most distorting support in the PSE, consisting of support based on commodity output and payments based on variable input use without input constraints. This indicator varies across OECD member countries, both in terms of its level and in its change over the period considered here (Figure 2.6). The composition of support has become less distortive in nearly all OECD countries, with the exception of Israel and Canada.[10] For the OECD area overall, the share of most distorting support in overall producer support has declined from 63% in 2002-07 to 52% in 2012. In the emerging countries covered, the (weighted average) share of the most distorting policies in all producer support is not only higher than in the OECD area, it also increased during the same period, from 68% in 2002-07 to 75% in 2012.

The overall picture then is that since the beginning of the Doha Round negotiations, the evolution of producer support has diverged notably between the OECD area and the emerging economies covered in the OECD's M&E. In the OECD area, producer support as a share of gross revenue declined, while it increased for the aggregate of the emerging economies. The result was that the emerging economies' share of producer support in the aggregate of all countries covered has grown significantly. Also, while the composition of support has changed in the direction of less distorting measures in the OECD area, the opposite was true in the emerging economies.

Figure 2.5. Change of %PSE and Producer NPC from 2002-07 to 2012

Percentage points for %PSE, absolute for NPC

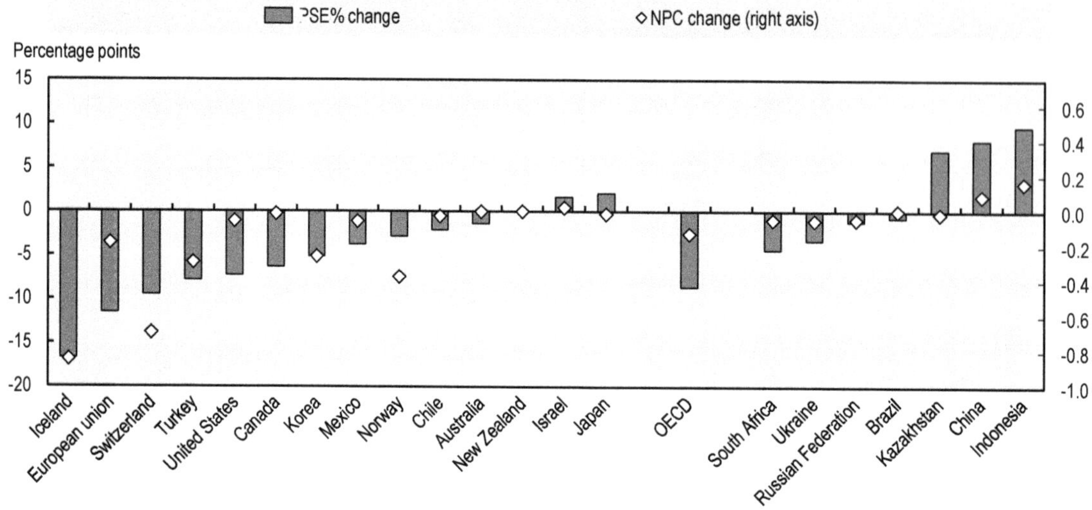

Source: Author's calculations based on PSE database of OECD.

Figure 2.6. Share of potentially most distorting support in all producer support, 2002-07 and 2012

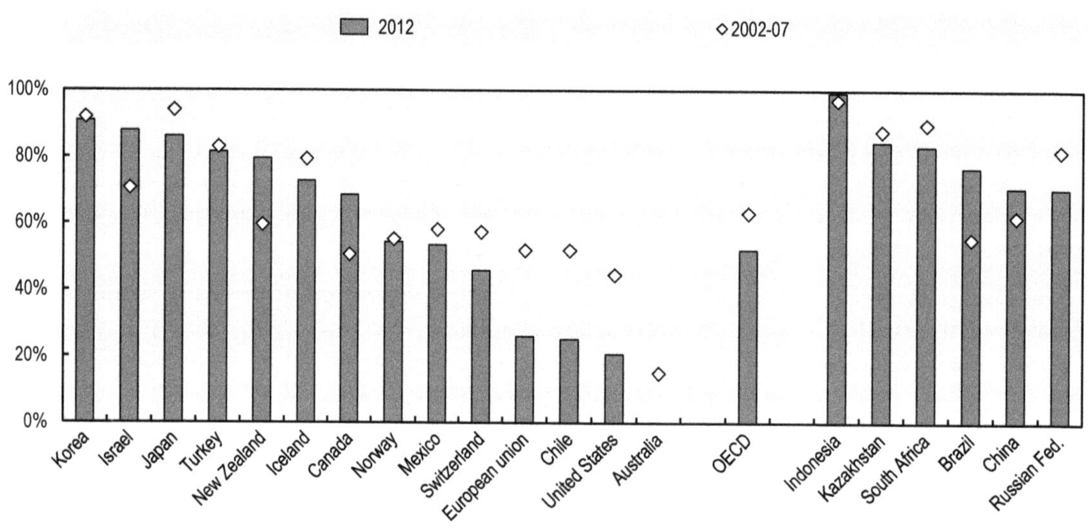

Notes: Potentially most distorting support is defined as support based on commodity output and payments based on variable input use without input constraints.

The Ukraine is not included in this figure as its share of most distorting support in the PSE was negative due to negative support based on commodity output.

Source: Author's calculations based on PSE database of OECD.

Import measures

The level of tariffs in agriculture, averaged across all agricultural tariff lines (unweighted), differs very much across the countries covered here (Figure 2.7).[11] In 2012, averages of MFN applied tariffs ranged from 1.2% in Australia to 53.2% in Norway. Among the emerging countries covered here, India's MFN applied tariff level in agriculture is highest, at 33.5%. It is also notable that in many countries, the tariffs actually applied (MFN) are far below the bound tariffs. This "binding overhang" is largest in Norway and India, where in both cases it amounts to nearly 80 percentage points. Contrary to what is sometimes suggested, large margins of binding overhang do not exist only in emerging and developing countries.

In most countries, tariffs for individual agricultural products vary widely across tariff lines. In many cases, the maximum duty for any agricultural tariff line is very far above the average tariff level, often as high as several hundred percent, and in the cases of Norway and Switzerland even above 1 000% (Figure 2.8). Only Chile has a schedule of uniform tariffs: 6% for all agricultural products. Among the countries covered here, only in China, India and New Zealand is the maximum tariff less than five times as high as the average.

From 2007 to 2012, average applied tariffs in agriculture declined in all OECD countries except Korea (Figure 2.9). Tariff averages also declined in all emerging economies covered here except for a minor increase in Kazakhstan. Some countries tend to adjust tariffs from time to time to compensate for changes in international market prices. China and Indonesia are cases in point (OECD, 2013: 36). There are also cases where governments change import tariffs in an *ad hoc* manner. Examples of this latter practice include Argentina's temporarily increased tariffs on certain products from 20% to 35% from 23 January 2013; the customs union between the Russian Federation, Belarus and Kazakhstan, where some tariffs were increased and others reduced in 2010 and subsequent years; and the application of interim tariffs in China in 2011, resulting in a reduction of tariffs on several products (WTO, 2014b). As tariff bindings have not changed much since the end of the implementation period of the Uruguay Round (except where countries acceded later to the WTO), increases in binding overhangs have accompanied reductions in applied tariffs.

Figure 2.7. Bound and MFN Applied Tariffs for Agricultural Products, 2012

Simple average of all agricultural tariff lines

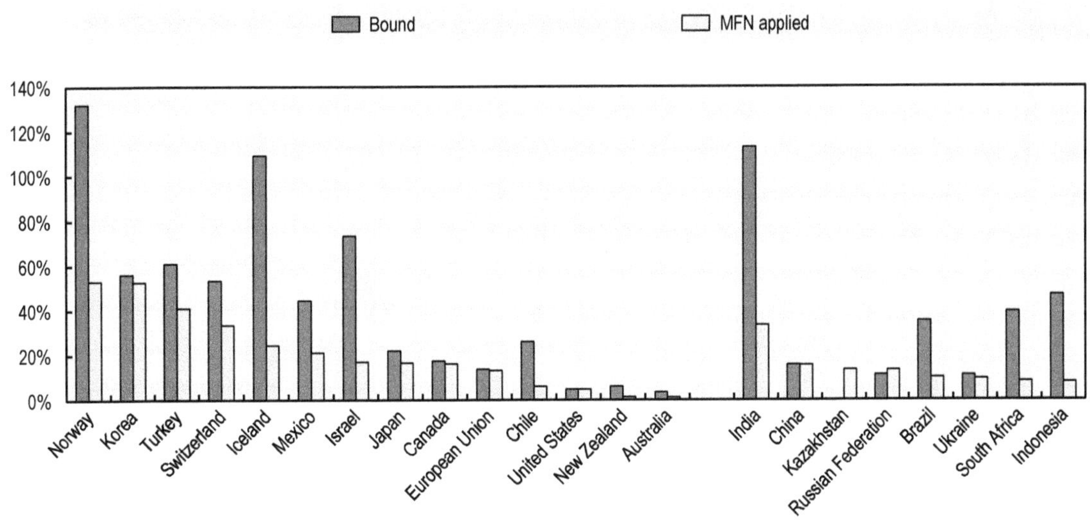

Notes: For some countries, data relate to 2011.
In the WTO database, agricultural products are defined as under the WTO Agreement on Agriculture, and specific tariffs are converted to *ad valorem* equivalents.
Source: WTO (2014a).

Figure 2.8. Maximum duty (MFN Applied) among all tariff lines for agricultural products, 2012

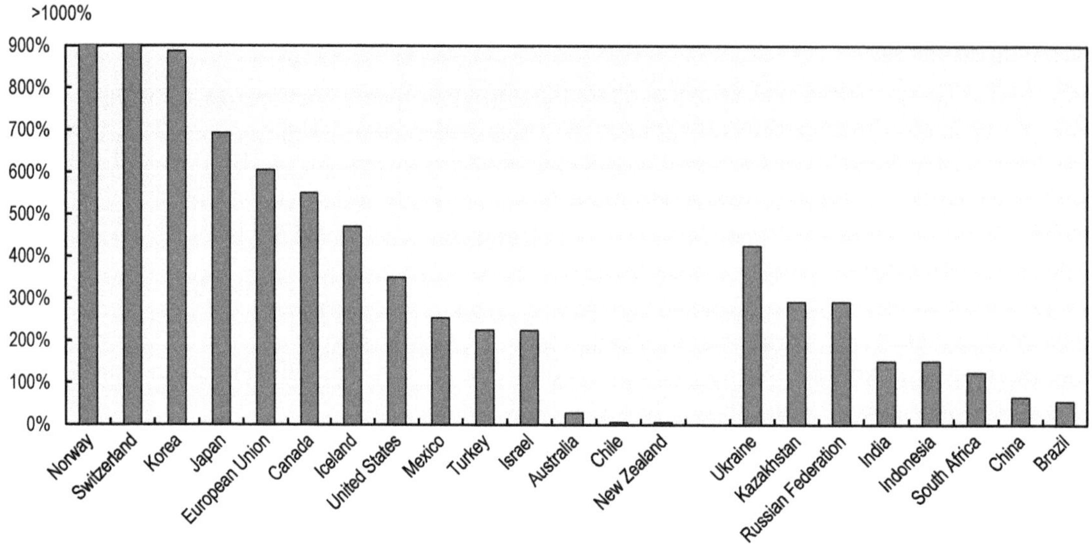

Source: WTO, ITC, UNCTAD (2008), and author's calculations.

Figure 2.9. Change of average tariffs (MFN Applied) for agricultural products from 2007 to 2012

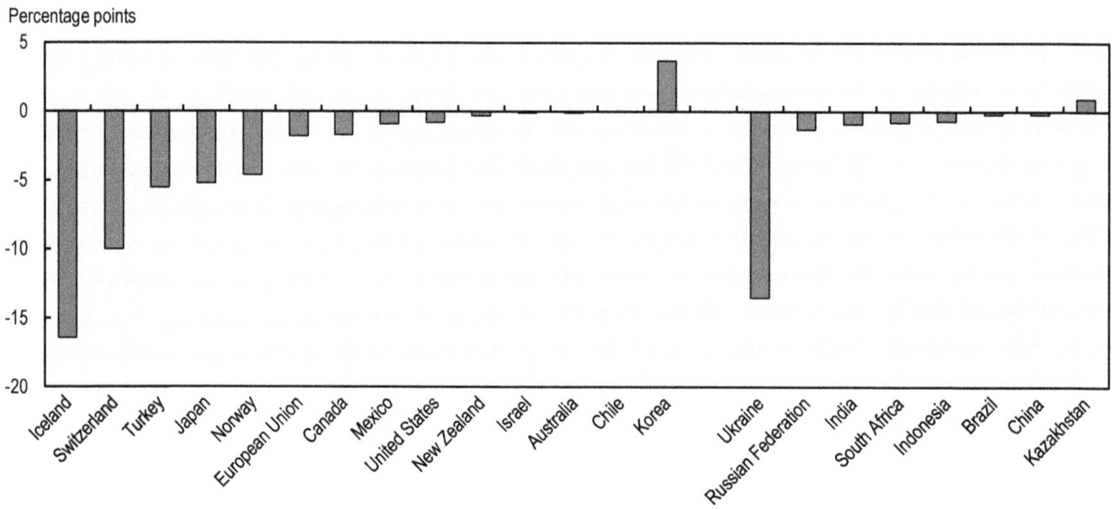

Source: WTO, ITC, UNCTAD (2008), and author's calculations.

In addition to such *ad hoc* changes in import regimes, governments can take recourse to various types of trade remedies. One is the safeguard generally available under WTO rules. For example, between October 2012 and October 2013, there were six cases in which WTO members initiated safeguard investigations, four cases in which provisional safeguard measures were adopted and one case in which definitive safeguard measures were adopted regarding agricultural products (WTO, 2013a). In addition, where countries have reserved the right to use the Special Agricultural Safeguard (SSG) under the AoA, they can take recourse to that mechanism. For example, Korea has frequently implemented SSG action, mainly on ginseng imports but also on a number of other products, and the United States has made use of the price-based SSG mainly on dairy products and typically for limited quantities of individual shipments. Moreover, anti-dumping and countervailing duties can be used in appropriate cases. For example, in March 2009 the European Union imposed anti-dumping duties and countervailing duties on biodiesel imports from the United States for a five-year period set to expire in July 2014. In November 2013, the European Union also imposed anti-dumping duties on biodiesel imports from Argentina and Indonesia.

Tariffs constitute only one category of the host of "traditional" border measures (as opposed to non-tariff measures such as sanitary and phytosanitary restrictions). Tariff rate quotas (TRQs) are another category of import barrier in agriculture that is frequently used. Many TRQs resulted from the process of tariffication in the Uruguay Round. Combined, WTO members maintained 1 094 TRQs for agricultural products in 2011 (WTO, 2013b). This number, which is somewhat lower than the 1 430 TRQs in 2002, has remained nearly unchanged since 2007. Fill rates of these TRQs vary across countries, products and methods of administration. On average (unweighted), the fill rate over the 2002-2011 period was 61%, with little variation from year to year.[12]

Market access is also greatly influenced by regional trade arrangements (RTAs). The prevalence of RTAs has grown significantly in recent years. As of mid-2014, 283 RTAs were in force (WTO, 2014c).[13] From 2001 to 2013, some 13 new RTAs entered into force on average every year. In 2008, slightly more than one-third of all world merchandise trade (excluding intra-EU trade) was conducted within RTAs, up from 18% in 1990 (WTO, 2011: 64). The share of global trade in agricultural products flowing between countries connected through RTAs has grown from slightly above 20% in 1998 to nearly 40% in 2009 (Bureau and Jean, 2013a).

Over time, the share of agricultural tariff lines has grown for which partner countries of new RTAs have agreed complete tariff elimination, though there is still considerable variation across RTAs. The share of duty free tariff lines in agriculture at the end of an RTA's implementation period may be as low as 32.3% (e.g. Switzerland in the Japan-Switzerland RTA; Japan is to eliminate 62.0% of all agricultural tariff lines by 2014) or as high as 100% (e.g. both parties in the Thailand-New Zealand RTA) (WTO, ITC and UNCTAD, 2013). Another category of preferential trade is conducted under non-reciprocal preferences, in particular those extended by developed country importers to developing country exporters. In 2008, such non-reciprocal preferences covered another 17% of all merchandise trade (calculated from data in WTO, 2011). Of all agricultural trade conducted under both of these categories of preferential arrangements in 2008, 24.1% benefitted from tariff preferences, 36.4% was non-preferential trade, and 35.1% had MFN duties that were zero (WTO, 2011: 79). The trade-weighted preference margin on all agricultural trade under preferential regimes was 4 percentage points (*ibid*). In North-South RTAs, South countries receive a notably larger preference margin than North countries (Bureau and Jean, 2013b). RTAs have generally resulted in a significant expansion of agricultural trade among the partner countries, both in terms of already-existing trade flows and in new trade in products not originally exchanged (Bureau and Jean, 2013b).

Export measures

An important exception for agriculture in the WTO is that ***export subsidies*** are still legal, though only within the country- and product-specific constraints agreed in the Uruguay Round. In the Doha Round negotiations, one aim is to eliminate that exception. At the Bali Ministerial Conference of the WTO, Ministers declared:

> We recognise that all forms of export subsidies and all export measures with equivalent effect are a highly trade distorting and protectionist form of support, and that, accordingly, export competition remains a key priority of the agriculture negotiations in the context of the continuation of the ongoing reform process set out in Article 20 of the Agreement on Agriculture, in accordance with the Doha work programme on agriculture and the 2005 Hong Kong Ministerial Declaration.
>
> In this context, we therefore reaffirm our commitment, as an outcome of the negotiations, to the parallel elimination of all forms of export subsidies and disciplines on all export measures with equivalent effect, as set out in the 2005 Hong Kong Ministerial Declaration. We regret that it has not been possible to achieve this objective in 2013 as envisaged in that Declaration.
>
> [...]
>
> We recognize the decrease in recent years in the use of export subsidies subject to reduction commitments under the Agreement on Agriculture, as indicated by information contained in

> Members' notifications to the WTO, and the positive developments that have also taken place in other areas of the export competition pillar. (WTO, 2013c)

Following that declaration, the WTO Secretariat sent questionnaires to all members in order to collect information on export competition policies. The results were compiled in a Secretariat background document (WTO, 2014d and addenda), providing up-to-date information on export subsidisation and equivalent measures.

Actual use of export subsidies has declined notably in recent years, in part as a result of high prices on international markets, but in part also due to policy reforms. Of the 18 WTO members (counting all EU member countries as one) that had agreed non-zero export subsidy commitments in the Uruguay Round, ten countries[14] have not used export subsidies in all years notified since the beginning of the Doha Round in 2001.[15] Two countries have not submitted notifications since the Doha Round began.[16] The remaining six WTO members can be grouped into three classes. Canada, Switzerland-Liechtenstein and Norway have continued to make ample use of export subsidies in the most recent years notified (up to 2011 or 2012): as much as about 20% of their aggregate budgetary outlay commitments (across all commodities) for Canada and Switzerland-Liechtenstein, and about 50% for Norway. The United States has made zero or only marginal use of its commitments since 2003 (2010 being the last year notified). The European Union used no more than 2% of its outlay commitments in 2011, the most recent year for which the European Union notified export subsidisation. When the Uruguay Round implementation period began, the European Union held by far the largest share of all export subsidy commitments in the WTO (nearly 70% of all "rights" to budgetary outlays in 1995), and granted the overwhelming share (90%) of all export subsidies that were paid in 1995 (Tangermann, 2002). In the first years of the Doha Round, the European Union still utilised about 40% of its outlay commitments. Since 2004, the European Union's export subsidies have declined significantly. In 2013, the European Union stopped using export subsidies, and under its new policy framework for the 2014-20 period, it has given up on using export subsidisation as a systematic tool of its market policy, though it can still use export subsidies as an "exceptional measure".

While use of direct export subsidies has declined significantly, the picture is less clear regarding other export measures "with equivalent effect", such as export financing, food aid and state trading enterprises. In particular, in the absence of data on the subsidy equivalent of export measures that are not direct subsidies it is not possible to gain an impression of the overall magnitude of the measures concerned and their evolution over time. The data provided by the 12 WTO members that submitted information (WTO, 2014d, Add.2) suggests that no major change in ***export financing support*** (export credit, export credit guarantees and insurance programmes) has occurred since the Doha Round began. The information submitted by members granting ***food aid*** (WTO, 2014d, Add.3) suggests that most food aid is provided in cash form, and where in kind aid was delivered, it went mostly to the World Food Programme or to recipients in an emergency situation. In their notifications and questionnaire responses, 20 WTO members reported that they had a total of 77 ***state trading enterprises*** (STEs) dealing with agricultural exports (WTO, 2014d, Add.4). China, Colombia and India reported the largest numbers of STEs, accounting for a little more than two-thirds of all reported STEs. A few STEs have been abolished since 2001, but other countries also established new agricultural exporting STEs.

Commenting on the information provided in the WTO Secretariat's background note, the Cairns Group summarised the picture as follows:

> Despite some of the information gaps, the Secretariat's report reaffirms the fact that since the launch of the Doha Round there have been positive developments in the export competition pillar. In particular, export subsidy expenditure has fallen significantly and there are examples of individual Members' reforms in the other pillars. This generally positive trend however is not without exception as not all Members have reformed and some have introduced new export competition policies since the beginning of the Doha negotiations and in recent years. (WTO, 2014e).

In the past, relatively little attention was paid to ***export restrictions***, though there have always been occasional instances of governments blocking exports so as to maintain domestic food supplies in moments of acute shortages. Moreover, some countries have long tended to tax exports of raw materials in order to support availability to domestic consumers and processors, to collect fiscal revenue or for other reasons.[17] However, when agricultural product prices on world markets spiked in 2007-08 and a number of exporting countries imposed export restrictions, placing priority on domestic food security, the international community began to pay much more attention to the implications of export restrictions in the food sector. The issue of how to deal with export restrictions in the international trading regime became an agenda item in various fora.

In the framework of the WTO, information on which country has adopted which type of export restrictive measures for which good is scarce. Anania (2013: 17) observes that:

> In fact, the WTO notification and consultation record on export restrictions is disappointing. It appears that ... between 1995 and March 2013 only eight members submitted notifications for the introduction of 14 export restricting measures under Article 12 of the AoA, and only one country, the Kyrgyz Republic, notified export restriction measures at the time of the 2007-08 price spike.

In reality there was a large amount of activity regarding export restrictive instruments in 2007 and subsequent years. Liapis (2013) provides an overview based on an inventory maintained by OECD. The measures used by the 16 exporting countries covered in the inventory include export duties, tax rebates on exported goods, quotas, bans, licensing requirements and minimum export prices. In his Table 2.1, Liapis specifies the number of measures taken on four groups of agricultural products in the years 2007 to 2011 (his summary is presented in graphical form in Figure 2.10). Liapis's count includes all measures taken, whether more restrictive or more liberalising (following a restrictive measure), and each specific agricultural product affected counts as one measure. The height of activity regarding export restrictive measures was in 2008, with more than 900 measures taken. The largest number of measures was taken in the sector of semi-processed products such as vegetable oils, live animals, or hides and skins, followed by the bulk products such as grains and oilseeds.[18] Depending on the year

Figure 2.10. Export measures affecting agricultural products: Number of measures taken, 2007 to 2011

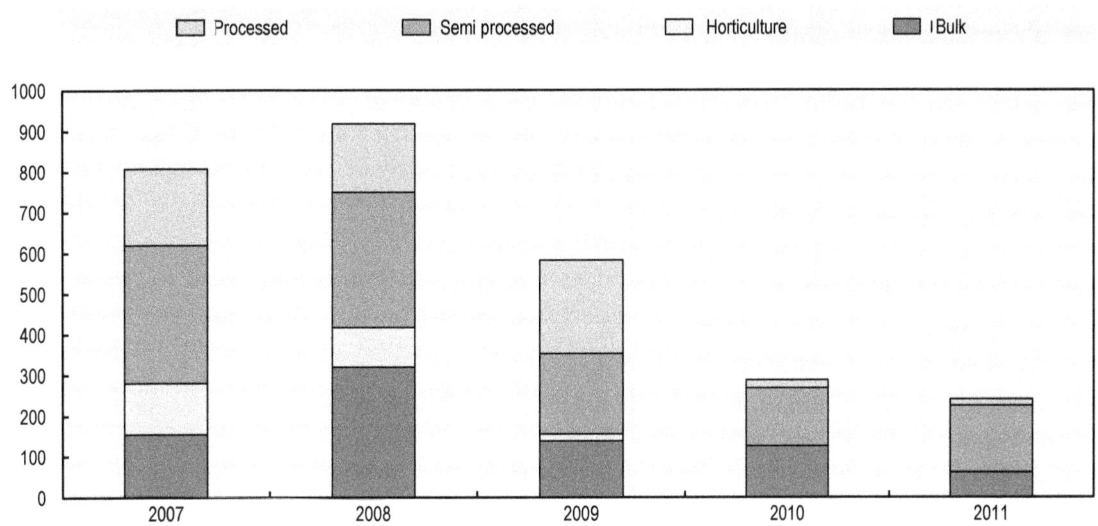

Source: Table 1 in Liapis (2013).

concerned, between 20 and 16 countries took export restrictive measures, although this number includes some double counting as some of the 16 countries covered had obviously adopted measures in more than one sector. Regarding the type of measures taken, Liapis found that "thirteen of the 16 countries banned exports of at least one product in at least one of the five years between 2007 and 2011. Export taxes were used by nine countries while export quotas were used by eight."

Based on this information, it appears that at the same time that export support through export subsidies and equivalent measures was declining, there was significant activity in export restrictive measures.

How restrictive are WTO disciplines?

Since the Uruguay Round, there is a firm set of rules and quantitative commitments for agricultural policies of WTO member countries, as defined by the AoA and specified in countries' schedules. The evolution of both policy settings and market conditions can change the extent to which a country's commitments under the AoA impose effective constraints on its policy pursuit in market access, export competition and domestic support. The extent to which existing bindings are already restrictive will also have some impact on governments' willingness to accept a further tightening of constraints in ongoing negotiations.

Considering ***market access,*** the current situation in many countries is such that MFN tariffs actually applied for most products are below, sometimes significantly below the tariffs bound in the WTO, at least for the average of all agricultural tariff lines (Brink, 2014). That average may, however, hide several cases where tariffs applied for individual products make full use of the respective binding. This is likely to be the case for products that are considered particularly sensitive. Moreover, some countries have set their applied tariffs very close to or exactly at the bound rates (Figure 2.9). Among OECD countries, this is true for Canada, the European Union and the United States. Among emerging economies to the same is true of China, the Russian Federation and Ukraine. In cases where currently applied tariffs do not leave a binding overhang, any commitment to reduce tariffs that may result from the ongoing Doha negotiations will require actual tariff cuts. On the other hand, where the binding overhang is large enough, no changes in tariffs actually applied will be necessary. Given the large number of tariff lines in agriculture in most countries, only a highly detailed analysis could show to what extent alternative tariff cutting formulae would bring about actual reductions in tariffs applied.

The situation is somewhat similar in the domain of ***export competition***. Overall it can be said that actual use of overt export subsidies has declined very much, if not actually disappeared, in many countries for many products (Brink, 2014). This leaves much "unutilised" scope in a large number of currently existing export subsidy commitments under the WTO. Yet, in this domain, too, only a detailed analysis of individual countries and products, and of both quantity and expenditure commitments, can show where an elimination of export subsidies would require noticeable changes. More data and research would be necessary to assess the situation regarding other forms of export support (financing, state trading and food aid). Yet, overall it appears that an agreement to eliminate all export subsidies and to introduce equivalent disciplines for other forms of export support would now require much less change in actual policies than ten years or so ago.

For ***domestic support***, Brink (2014) provides a careful analysis of the extent to which existing commitments are binding, and of the room for manoeuvre, if any, that commitments as envisaged in the Doha negotiations under Rev.4 would leave for individual countries' policies. His study examines the situation of 19 countries, 7 developed and 12 developing. It compares the support levels reported in the latest domestic support notifications submitted by these countries with both their commitments under the existing AoA and the new commitments that would result if the rules and parameters suggested in Rev.4 were to apply. This study takes into account, in a detailed way, the varying reduction commitments under Rev.4 that individual countries would have to respect based on factors such as their base levels of support, whether or not they have a commitment on Aggregate Measurement of Support (AMS), whether a developed or developing country, and whether or not having recently acceded to the WTO. One of Brink's general findings on domestic support is that Rev.4 would establish "a set of rules and commitments that varies greatly among countries" (Brink, 2014: 67).

Brink finds that as a result of market developments and the evolution of policies, as reflected in the most recent available notifications of domestic support, an agreement on rules and parameters as suggested in Rev.4 would not noticeably restrict agricultural support policies in most of the 19 countries covered in his assessment. This is particularly the case for the new bindings on Overall Trade Distorting Support (OTDS) that would be introduced if Rev.4 were to be implemented:

> Most countries – possibly all except one in this study – would have a comfortable margin between applied trade-distorting support measured as OTDS and the new Bound OTDS under Rev.4. The same can be said about the new limits on total and on product-specific blue box payments. (Brink, 2014: 68)

Norway is the one country that might have difficulties: Brink finds that its Current OTDS (calculated from its notification for 2011) is about 50% above its Bound OTDS under Rev.4, requiring potentially significant policy adjustments. A number of other countries might find that their final Bound OTDS leaves "a very large margin above Current OTDS", namely Argentina, China, Indonesia, Korea, Mexico, the Philippines, South Africa, Thailand and Viet Nam. Brink found a "smaller but still sizeable" margin for Brazil, Canada, the European Union, Japan, and Switzerland. In the case of India, the result would depend on whether its "large input subsidies claimed under [AoA] Article 6.2" must be included in the Current OTDS – an issue that is, according to Brink, not entirely clear from the wording of Rev.4. The United States was found to be very close to exceeding its Bound OTDS based on its 2011 notification. The policies introduced in the United States with the 2014 Farm Bill, including elements of support that vary inversely with prices and revenues, may have increased the likelihood of the United States exceeding its OTDS limit when market prices decline.

Regarding the AMS bindings under Rev.4, Brink points out that most countries would not have major difficulties meeting this constraint. Two factors have contributed to this situation: the elimination of "administered prices" in several cases, resulting in a decline of notified Current Total AMS; and the increase in world market prices, reducing those payments that depend on price gaps. There are, though, a few special cases where the AMS constraint under Rev.4 could turn out to be binding. Brink also suggests that there may be several cases where product-specific AMSs exceed the new limits that would be set if Rev.4 were to be implemented. Finally, the blue box constraints under Rev.4 would require policy adjustments in Norway, and their product-specific version could constrain rice support in Japan.

Brink summarises his findings regarding the extent to which Rev.4 would constrain current policies by suggesting that:

> [F]ew countries would need to change their settings very much if at all in order to conform with the rules and commitments of an agreement corresponding to Rev.4, if implemented immediately. This is the combined result of policy settings having already been changed since the drafting of Rev.4, the rules and commitments of Rev.4 being generous enough and/or tailored to accommodate the situations of individual countries, and international prices of many agricultural products generally having increased since the time of drafting Rev.4. (Brink, 2014: 77)

When drawing conclusions from Brink's findings, it is useful to keep in mind that they are based on policies as reflected in the most recent available notifications, some dating back to 2008 and none more recent than 2012. In reality, of course, actual policies in future years, possibly for a long time, will have to be set against any new commitments that would be agreed in the Doha negotiations. Moreover, future inflation can drive up levels of support to be notified and thus make any commitments agreed, which would probably be defined in nominal terms, as under the AoA, appear more restrictive. Yet, as shown by Brink, in most cases commitments following from Rev.4 would, for the time being, contain considerable amounts of water. This means that quite some time could pass before the commitments begin to bite – if they ever do.

2.4. Market and trade impacts of agricultural policies

Agricultural market and trade policies pursue a number of objectives, ranging from supporting farm incomes or improving food security to correcting for market failures, for example regarding the sustainability of resource use (OECD, 2008a). Often an individual policy instrument such as market price support provided through tariffs and export subsidies is supposed to achieve a combination of several agricultural policy objectives simultaneously. At the same time, society envisages many other objectives outside the realm of agricultural policies. In an institutional sense, these non-agricultural objectives are typically catered for by government departments other than the ministry for agriculture. Nevertheless, most agricultural policy measures also affect such non-agricultural objectives. Moreover, policies pursued in one country may affect the situation of people in other countries, and among the aims pursued by friendly governments there is also the objective to minimise any negative implications their policies might have on the rest of the world. Where agricultural policies are planned and designed with a view to their effectiveness and efficiency, the whole variety of these multiple objectives is taken into account.

The dominant part of agricultural policy measures focuses on either of two categories of objectives: redistribution of income or provision of public goods. Examples of the first category are support and stabilisation of farm incomes or improvement of access to food among low-income households. An illustration of the second category is the protection of biodiversity. Objectives in both categories do not typically include any deliberate aims regarding quantities produced or traded.[19] However, many agricultural policy measures have side effects that affect markets and trade. While they may not form a part of the stated set of agricultural policy objectives, these market and trade impacts are still highly relevant as they affect a government's non-agricultural objectives, such as improving overall economic wellbeing of the country. They are also relevant as they may have adverse or positive implications for people in the rest of the world. It is, therefore, relevant to take a careful look at the market and trade impacts of agricultural policies. Work done in the OECD has provided insights into these impacts, some of which will be summarised here.

Production and trade impacts of reforming domestic support through decoupling

In many developed countries, government support to agriculture has traditionally relied heavily on market price support, provided either through border measures such as tariffs and export subsidies, sometimes combined with domestic market interventions, or through payments per unit of output such as deficiency payments tied to given target prices. In the second half of the 1980s, more than 80% of all producer support in the OECD area was given in this form of support based on commodity output. Over time, the importance of this type of agricultural policy has declined and it now accounts for less than 50% of all producer support. While the share of support based on commodity output decreased, the share of other forms of support that are more decoupled from agricultural output, in the sense of not being based on nor requiring production, has grown. This was particularly true, in terms of the OECD's classification of policy instruments in measuring PSEs, for payments based on non-current criteria without requirement to produce, and payments based on non-commodity criteria. The sum of these two policy categories, which accounted for less than 2% of all producer support in the second half of the 1980s, now amounts to more than 25% of PSE in the OECD area.

In other words, a significant development in agricultural policies among developed countries over the last two and a half decades has been the process of increasingly decoupling agricultural support from production. The evolution of farm policies in this direction has sometimes been referred to as being driven by the "paradigm" of decoupling, reflecting a growing awareness that it is desirable to improve policy performance, both from a domestic perspective and with regard to reducing unintended international spillover effects.

Work done in the OECD's Committee for Agriculture has greatly contributed to this development through analysis and policy dialogue. The analytical studies were done by both the OECD Secretariat and consultants from academia, and they involved theoretical considerations as well as empirical research. They yielded insights into channels of influence that alternative policy instruments can have on farmers' decisions, and on that basis they helped to understand the market and trade implications of more or less decoupled support measures. The most important results of the suite of studies on decoupling and their policy implications were summarised in *Decoupling: Policy Implications* (OECD, 2006a).[20]

It is possible, in theory, to define the properties of an agricultural policy measure that is fully decoupled in the sense of having no link whatsoever with input or output quantities and hence has not effect at all on production and trade. However, OECD research has yielded the crucial finding that even the most decoupled instruments in agricultural policy making have at least some market impacts. Hence "decoupling" should be seen as a matter of degree, rather than an absolute concept: policies are more or less decoupled. At the same time, it has also become clear that the continuum between more and less decoupled policies spans a wide range, extending from rather strong interference with market forces to measures that have only minimal impacts on production and trade. The background to these findings is that various mechanisms are at work that determine the way in which agricultural policy measures affect farmers' decisions and hence on production and trade. OECD research has identified three categories of effects that are relevant in this context.

First, policies can have static effects that can be seen more or less immediately when a given instrument is implemented. Typical examples are the impacts of policy-induced changes in output or input prices. When a policy raises the price of an agricultural product, it is profitable for the farmer to produce more of it. When an input is subsidised, the farmer is induced to use more of it. Static effects also include the impacts of quantitative constraints such as production quotas or compulsory land retirement. One of the most important findings of OECD research on the static effects of alternative support policies confirms the hypothesis that area-based payments have less impact on output, and hence trade, than price support and output-based payments, mainly because yields respond more strongly to output prices than to area-based payments. It was also confirmed that area-based payments without an obligation to produce have even less influence on output. Other findings that were perhaps less commonly expected include the result that subsidies on variable inputs are the most production- and trade-distorting among all measures analysed, and that area-based payments can induce significant cross commodity effects.

Second, policies can affect production decisions through risk-related effects. Where a policy instrument reduces the variability of farm income, it acts like an insurance. At the same time a policy that increases expected farm income, and hence raises implicit farm wealth, may lead the farmer to adopt riskier behaviour. Both the insurance and the wealth effect can result in an expansion of production if farmers are risk averse – an attitude that is found in many empirical studies. Thus, even if a given payment to farmers were to be designed so as to have the smallest conceivable static effects on production (e.g. a lump sum payment without any relation to given outputs or inputs), it is still likely to induce additional production because of its risk effect. Perhaps one of the more surprising results was that risk effects, often disregarded in policy debates, can be significant in quantitative terms, in some cases even larger than the traditional relative price effects. One implication of the analysis of risk effects is that insurance subsidies and other measures intended to reduce the variability of farm revenue or income may have strong impacts on production and trade. It was also found that policies that have the effect of smoothing the variability of domestic prices relative to fluctuations of world prices may have a large impact in increasing the variability of world prices. Thus there is a clear trade-off between reducing risk for domestic farmers and increasing risk faced by farmers and consumers in the rest of the world.

Third, policies can have dynamic effects, for example through investment decisions. Additional farm incomes and less variability of returns can lead farmers to make larger investments, raising output potential in the future. While relevant, such investment effects tend to be smaller than the more direct relative price or risk related effects. More important may be another type of dynamic effect: expectations regarding future policy conduct. For example, where farmers expect that base area or yields may be updated from time to time, with consequences for future payments, they are likely to respond with current production decisions. Where such expectations are created and confirmed, strong production responses may be generated.

A central outcome from the OECD work on decoupling was a summary of the results provided by various quantitative studies regarding the comparative production impacts of alternative types of agricultural policies. The results were presented in terms of the production impact of one additional dollar spent on each of the different types of policy instruments, relative to the production impact of an additional dollar provided through market price support, this being set equal to one. These relativities were dubbed "production impact ratios". Figure 2.11 provides a graphical representation of the results, showing for each of the policies analysed the highest and lowest production impact ratio found among any of the studies reviewed. It cannot come as a surprise that results differed notably across studies, depending on the analytical methodology applied, the particular empirical case studied and the data used. The studies were therefore not strictly comparable, and comparison of results across the alternative policy instruments analysed must be interpreted with considerable caution. Also, since only a limited number of concrete policies were analysed, the results should be considered no more than illustrative.

Figure 2.11. Production impact ratios of alternative agricultural policies: Highest and lowest results of various OECD studies on decoupling

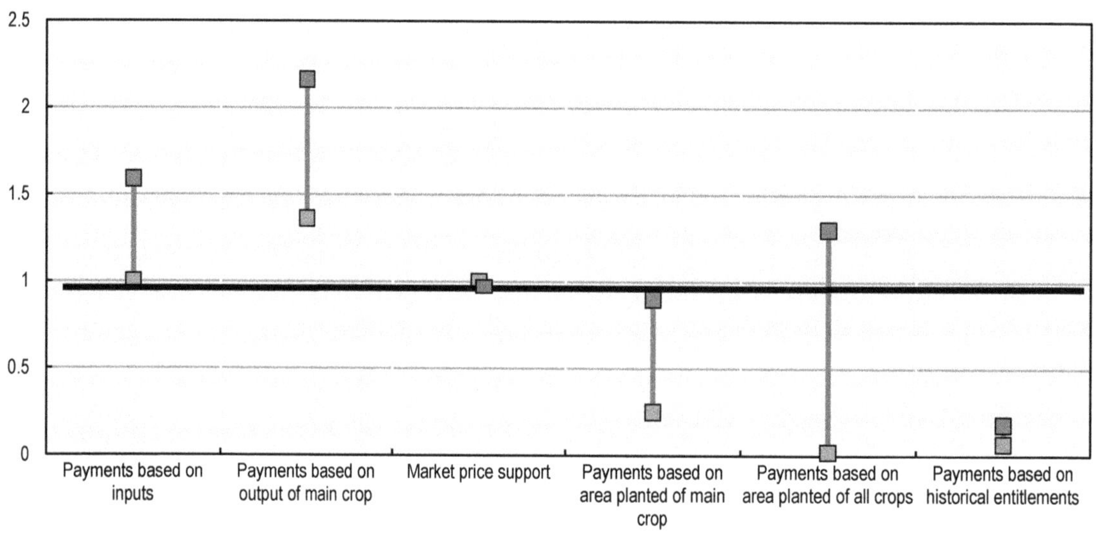

Source: Table 1 in OECD (2006a).

In spite of these caveats, a few general conclusions emerge. Input payments and payments per unit of the main crop tend to have the largest impact on production.[21] One study found that one dollar spent on input payments could have a production impact nearly 60% larger than one dollar spent on market price support (production impact ratio 1.59). The lowest production impacts, on the other hand, were found for area-based payments. The agricultural policy category with the lowest production impact by a wide margin is that of payments based on historical entitlements (criteria that recipients cannot change). Such payments are therefore the most decoupled policy. Yet, even payments based on historical payments were found to have some impact on production.

The fact that even some of the most decoupled agricultural policies were found to have some effect on production is mainly explained by their risk-reducing effects. One important implication of the finding is that the level of support provided matters. Where large amounts of money are spent on payments that are, in principle, strongly decoupled, there may well be a significant impact on production and trade. However, this finding does not change the relativities across the policy alternatives. A given (potentially large) sum of money transferred to agriculture through market price support has a much stronger impact on production and trade than the same transfer made through payments based on historical entitlements.

Another important finding of OECD work on decoupling relates to transfer efficiency, which is the share of policy-induced transfers to agriculture that actually adds to farm household income. It was found that one dollar spent on payments based on historical entitlements raises farm household income about twice as much as one dollar transferred to agriculture through market price support (OECD, 2001 and 2003a). Thus, if a government had the objective of raising farm household income by a given amount of money, its policies would need to transfer only half the sum to agriculture through well decoupled payments than through market price support. Considering also that a dollar spent on payments based on historical entitlements has only, say, one-fifth of the production and trade impact that a dollar spent on market price support can have, then reforming agricultural policy by moving from market price support to the most decoupled form of payments can reduce the distortion of production and trade by a factor of ten without decreasing the intended support to farm household income.

Trade impacts of improving market access

As seen above, import tariffs on agricultural goods are still relatively high in several countries, specifically on some "sensitive" goods. Moreover, TRQs play a significant role in agricultural trade. In consequence, domestic market prices are kept above international levels, as reflected in NPCs. One objective of the Doha Round negotiations on agriculture is to improve market access by reducing tariffs and relaxing TRQs. OECD research has analysed the implications such improvements might have. In particular, the same partial equilibrium model that is used for the OECD's work on the *Agricultural Outlook* for markets (i.e. AGLINK) was employed, with necessary modifications, to study the impact on world market prices. The analysis was done by using the most recent *Outlook* market projections for coming years as the baseline for comparison with scenarios in which market access conditions were improved through gradual policy changes from year to year to an assumed final level.

A first study (OECD, 2002b) looked at scenarios implying (i) an expansion of TRQ quantities by eventually 50%; (ii) an additional reduction of within-quota tariffs by 36%; (iii) a cut of out-of-quota and non-quota tariffs by 36%; and (iv) a combination of (ii) and (iii). The somewhat sobering result was that the impacts on world market prices were rather small. Even for scenario (iv) – the combination of all improvements of market access analysed – it was found that international market prices for most agricultural commodities included in AGLINK increased by no more than about 1% in the final year of the five-year projection period. Dairy products was only product category where larger price increases were found, with the butter price rising by nearly 10%, the price of cheese by about half that much and the price of skim milk powder by close to 2%.[22] A subsequent study (OECD, 2007a) working with updated market and policy data, including a larger set of individually modelled countries (e.g. Brazil, China and the Russian Federation) and a ten-year projection period, analysed essentially the same scenarios except that the tariff reductions assumed were 50% for both within and above quota tariffs. The finding was again that such tariff reductions and quota expansions might have only relatively small impacts on world market prices for most agricultural commodities, in the same order of magnitude found in the earlier study.[23] In both studies it was found that world prices of some agricultural commodities might decrease when barriers to market access are relaxed, due to substitution effects. Both studies also found that impacts on domestic market prices remained relatively small in most cases, with the major exception being the dairy sector, where domestic prices in some countries with relatively high levels of protection came under more pressure.

These OECD studies found that there are mainly three reasons why market impacts may remain rather small when barriers to market access are relaxed by orders of magnitude, as was assumed under the scenarios studied. First, the tariffs assumed to be reduced were, as customary in international trade negotiations, the bound tariffs. In many cases, this results in no reduction or only small reductions in tariffs actually applied because there is significant binding overhang in several countries, as discussed above. Second, a similar situation exists regarding TRQs, many of which are not filled, as highlighted above. Where that is the case, an expansion of the quota volume has no market effect. Third, many

TRQs are rather small relative to the size of the domestic market of the importing country, and even smaller relative to the quantity traded internationally. Even an expansion by 50% does not add much to actual market access where a TRQ is small in the first place.

Trade impacts of reducing export subsidies and equivalent measures

As discussed above, use of ***export subsidies*** has declined significantly since the turn of the century, in several countries to the point where they have virtually disappeared. For the time being the European Union, by far the largest user of export subsidisation in the past, has discontinued granting export subsidies though in its market policy rules, although it has maintained the possibility of re-introducing them in "emergency cases". Given the low current use of export subsidies, their complete elimination, desirable as it would be in terms of aligning WTO rules for agriculture with those for other sectors, would not have much effect on actual market conditions. This differs from the past, when agricultural exports were still subsidised at a much larger scale by some countries. The two OECD studies mentioned in the previous section have looked not only into the impact that improvements in market access might have, but also analysed the market impacts of eliminating export subsidies. In the earlier study (OECD, 2002b), it turned out that impacts on world market prices for crops (wheat, coarse grains, oilseeds) and beef were minimal (between -2% and 1% in the final year of the five-year projection period). The major reason found for these limited impacts was that export subsidisation for these products implied in the base line projections was relatively small due to projected increases in world market prices and policy reforms, in particular in the European Union.[24] For dairy products, however, the effects were found to be much larger: 9% in the final year for skim milk powder, 15% for whole milk powder and as much as 26% for butter. At the same time, it was found that domestic prices in the countries eliminating export subsidies declined significantly, even for crops. For example, the European Union's domestic price for coarse grains decreased by 14% in the final year. Domestic milk prices were found to decline even more, by 18% in Canada in the final year, and by 10% in the European Union.

In the more recent study (OECD, 2007a), the change in export subsidisation was not analysed separately, but was added to a scenario that also included the improvement in market access discussed above. Moreover, it was assumed that export subsidies would not be eliminated completely, but that the volume commitments countries have under the AoA were to be reduced by 50%. Adding this export subsidy reduction to the market access scenario had an even smaller incremental effect on world market prices than had been found in the earlier study. Again, dairy products was the only sector where impacts were more noticeable, though even there the largest world market impact found was a price increase of 7% for whole milk powder. In interpreting these results, it should be considered that in the projection period (2004-13), actual export subsidisation was already low and hence a good part of the assumed reduction in allowable volumes of subsidised exports did not achieve any more than squeezing out the "overhang" of commitments.

As mentioned above, the Doha Round negotiations in agriculture deal not only with direct export subsidies, but also with "all export measures with equivalent effect", i.e. ***export financing, exporting state trading enterprises and food aid***. The OECD has invested significant efforts in conducting analysis of these "indirect" forms of government support to agricultural exports. However, due to the political sensitivity of both the issues involved and the data required, that work had to be discontinued and the documents drafted were not declassified. A central focus of that work was to develop analytical approaches to investigate the impacts of these rather different types of export support in a comparable way.[25] Two benchmarks for comparison were shown to be relevant (OECD, 2004).

As a first benchmark, it is sensible to look at the extent to which the cost to foreign buyers is reduced. In the case of a direct export subsidy, this is the subsidy granted. In the case of government supported or guaranteed export credit, the cost reduction can result from lower-than-market interest rates, a longer duration of the credit, lower fees or other conditions that provide benefits to the importer. The magnitude of the cost reduction can be calculated from these variables. For food aid (when used as an instrument of commercial policy), the cost reduction follows from the degree of concessionality. For example, where food aid is provided in fully grant form (i.e. 100% concessionality), the cost reduction is equal to the full price paid for the respective commodity when it is procured by the institution providing the food aid. Exporting STEs can benefit, for example, from government guarantees of their financing, their ability to set initial farm prices below expected prices, their control over planting, tax exemptions or from rents that accrue to them when they sell to markets where they enjoy preferentially low import tariffs. All of these conditions can be taken into account when estimating the cost reduction. In addition, exporting STEs with monopoly powers may be able to price discriminate between different markets to which they sell. Where that is the case, they can derive an extra benefit over and above the cost reduction resulting from the other factors. Where appropriate and reliable data are available, the cost reductions resulting from given forms of government support to the "export measures with equivalent effect" can be estimated in a reasonably straightforward manner. They can be expressed as a total sum or per unit of the product concerned, dividing the total by the quantity of either the targeted exports or of all exports. To illustrate this approach, tentative estimates were provided for measures applied in the wheat market in 1998. The total cost reduction generated by the 30 selected export competition measures covered in the analysis (including some direct export subsidies and some output payments) varied between USD 10 000 and USD 556.50 million per programme. The per unit cost reduction for the average of all exports was between zero and USD 1 145 per tonne.

The second relevant benchmark is the market effect of a given export support measure. It needs to be investigated in its own right as there is not a simple one-to-one relationship between cost reduction and market effect. For example, where a measure is implemented such that the cost reduction is fully transferred to the buyer as a pure rent (for example, food aid to recipients who could otherwise not buy any food in the market), it does not change conditions in the rest of the market. In this context it was emphasised that the concept of "additionality" is crucial. It was shown, for example, in an illustrative quantitative exercise based on the OECD's Policy Evaluation Model (PEM) how the additionality of given quantities of food aid provided could be estimated for selected countries based on particular assumptions and parameters. That exercise showed that 63% of the overall amount of food aid resulted in additional imports, while the remaining 37% replaced commercial exports. Using the same analytical framework, it was also demonstrated that plausible estimates of the comparative world market price impacts of eliminating alternative export support programmes could be determined. The policies included in this illustrative analysis comprised selected countries' existing measures in the form of direct export subsidies, government supported export finance, certain benefits to exporting STEs and food aid. This demonstrated that the matter of "equivalent effects" can be dealt with in an operationally effective way if the necessary data are made available and analysts are given leeway to engage in the necessary research.

Welfare impacts of agricultural policy reform

Impacts of reforming agricultural and trade policies were also analysed by the OECD in the framework of a computable general equilibrium model, including the overall economy, macro-economic relations and feedbacks between income generation on factor markets and consumer spending (OECD, 2006b). For that purpose, the new GTAPEM model was employed, modifying the widely used GTAP model so as to include a number of features relevant for analysing agricultural policies by adopting them from the PEM. The policy scenario investigated was a 50% reduction in (rates of) tariffs in both agriculture and all other sectors, combined with 50% reductions in (rates of) all budgetary payments to agriculture and export subsidies.

It was found that such an agricultural policy and trade reform could raise global welfare by USD 44 billion per year, or 0.1% of world GDP. Nearly 60% of that global gain resulted from reforms in agriculture. Reductions in tariffs and export subsidies were found to be particularly important, accounting for 80% of the global gains to be reaped from reforming agricultural policies. As far as country groups were concerned, three-quarters of the global welfare gains accrued to OECD countries, half of which stemmed from these countries reforming their own agricultural policies. Non-OECD countries were also found to gain slightly from agricultural policy reforms in the OECD area, though a much larger part of the welfare gains reaped by these countries originated from the liberalisation of imports of non-agricultural products into the OECD countries. The sources of welfare gains, however, differed significantly across the non-OECD countries. For example, the greatest gains for Brazil came from agricultural policy reform in the OECD countries, whereas China was found to gain most from the opening of OECD markets to non-agricultural goods, while India and South Africa benefitted most from non-agricultural reforms outside the OECD area.

In conjunction with the global analysis, the distributional implications of such policy reforms were also analysed at the household level through country case studies for Brazil, Italy, Malawi, Mexico and the United States. Each of the case studies worked with its own modelling framework, generally a computable general equilibrium model with disaggregate representation of various groups of households within agriculture and in the rest of the economy. As expected, the results differed very much from country to country, depending in particular on the direction of price changes resulting from reforms and the nature of the linkages between factor income and market developments in the individual categories of households. It was important, though, that the analysis demonstrated that the welfare implications of a global reform of agricultural and trade policies can be traced all the way down to the level of wellbeing in different types of families.

Impacts of export restrictions

As discussed above, export restrictions were an important element of the picture when food prices spiked in 2007-08 and subsequent years. The OECD's work has aimed to throw light not only on the policy actions taken at that time, but also on their market and trade impacts. In an econometric exercise (Liapis, 2013), the question was asked whether exports of rice, wheat and maize from countries that imposed export restricting measures had remained below their otherwise explainable level[26] in years when such measures were taken. It was found that export-restricting measures had a statistically significant restraining impact on exports only in the case of rice, but not for wheat and maize. This same study, using a similar econometric approach and looking at the same three products, asked whether export restrictions had reduced the volume of imports into countries sourcing their imports from exporting countries imposing restrictions. No statistically significant effects were found.

As suggested in the study, these results need to be interpreted with considerable caution. Trade data used in the analysis were available only on an annual basis, and hence the short-term and immediate impacts that export-restricting measures can have on market conditions could not be traced. Moreover, because of the annual periodicity of the analysis, no distinction could be made between different types and intensities of the export restricting measures included in the inventory (from which some information was presented above). All export-restricting measures were represented in the regression equations through a zero-one dummy, and thus a small export tax was represented in the same way as a complete ban of exports.

The limitation of annual periodicity was overcome in an earlier OECD study (Jones and Kwiecinski, 2010) which used quarterly data for exports of wheat, maize, rice and soybeans from major exporting countries in the period 2006 to 2009. It was found that export restrictions were mostly effective and kept quantities exported well below the levels that would otherwise have been expected. The timing of these export constraints was also crucial to their world market impact because export volumes were reduced at precisely the moment when the price rise on world markets was already accelerating. This study, therefore, confirmed the findings of several other authors who had concluded that export restrictions contributed decisively to driving up international market prices further in the price spike episode of 2007-08 and subsequent years.[27]

The beggar-thy-neighbour implications of export restrictions (and import tariff reductions), i.e. the upward price pressure imposed on international markets by countries aiming to keep domestic prices low in times of scarcity, was also demonstrated in an OECD study that simulated alternative policy responses to price spikes (Thompson and Tallard, 2010). Using AGLINK and exposing international markets for wheat and rice to a simulated exogenous shock that drove up prices, it was shown, among other findings, that in a tight market situation world prices rise even further if major exporters try to stabilise domestic prices through export restrictions (and reduced import tariffs). The study concluded:

> Policies that insulate domestic consumers or producers from responding fully to an international price surge exacerbate the world price increase and force greater adjustments on producers and consumers in other countries to sell even more or buy even less in order for supply and demand to adjust to the higher peak prices. (Thompson and Tallard, 2010)

Impacts of non-tariff measures

Given the importance of non-tariff measures (NTMs) in food and agricultural trade, the OECD has engaged in several studies on aspects related to such regulatory measures. Particular attention was paid to the implications of the WTO Agreements on Technical Barriers to Trade (TBT) and Sanitary and Phytosanitary Measures (SPS). Based on these, more general conclusions were drawn regarding analytical and implementation aspects of NTMs (for example OECD, 1999 and 2003b). A conceptual framework was developed that systematically accounts for the economic costs and benefits of imposing given NTMs, thereby presenting a reasoned choice among alternative ways of dealing with the market failures that NTMs are supposed to correct (OECD, 2008b). This framework's usefulness, flexibility in analysing different sets of issues, information requirements, and limitations were then demonstrated by applying it to the analysis of three concrete examples of NTMs introduced to deal with specific matters regarding sanitary and phytosanitary issues (van Tongeren et al, 2010). Another OECD study (Korinek et al., 2008) reviewed methods to quantify the trade effects of NTMs in the agri-food sector, producing an assessment of which approaches might be particularly appropriate for which types of measures.

An attempt was also made to investigate the trade effects of changes to NTMs in SPS measures that may have been brought about by the rules established under the WTO's SPS Agreement (OECD, 2002b). The conceptual difficulties of pursuing an analysis of that type were highlighted, with a particular emphasis placed on identifying concrete changes in SPS measures that were made in response to requirements emanating from the SPS Agreement. The study also aimed to establish clear cause-effect linkages between modifications in SPS measures and changes in trade flows. To illustrate the issues, the study looked at five concrete cases of changes in SPS measures and the changes in the respective trade flows in subsequent years. It was found that each case had idiosyncrasies that made it difficult to draw general conclusions.

An interesting aspect is the treatment of NTMs, including SPS measures, in RTAs. Most RTAs include provisions not only for tariffs, but also for NTMs, but the extent to which they are specific and geared towards facilitating trade in agricultural and food products differs very much from case to case (Fulponi et al., 2011). In some cases, the arrangements found in RTAs do not go beyond confirming rights and obligations under the relevant WTO rules; in others, they have the character of "WTO-plus" provisions. The specific nature of such provisions that go beyond the WTO Agreements on TBT and SPS were analysed by the OECD in selected case studies, with a particular emphasis placed on the procedural aspects regarding the establishment and implementation of regulatory measures (von Lampe and Jeong, 2013).

Impacts of stockholding for price stabilisation

The pronounced volatility of agricultural commodity markets has prompted significant efforts to bring more stability to these markets in the interest of reducing risks for both farmers and food consumers. One effort saw the creation of buffer stocks that would take product off the market when prices appeared to decline too much, and to add to supplies when prices shot up. The idea of such buffering stocks appears attractive. After all, there is relatively little that can be done to eliminate output fluctuations due to the vagaries of natural factors such as weather, which is the main source of volatility in agriculture. Using stock changes to compensate for such supply variations, thereby dampening price volatility and associated problems for producers and consumers, looks like a promising avenue. Moreover, it is evident that there is a close relationship between stocks and price changes. In particular, price spikes on markets for storable commodities such as cereals have nearly always been associated with depleted stocks. When prices begin to spike, buffer stocks are the only source of additional supplies that could prevent a price explosion. And accumulating those stocks in periods of particularly low prices would have the additional benefit of avoiding periods of excessive price depression. Therefore, it is no surprise that throughout history there have been frequent attempts to use buffer stocks to reduce price volatility in both international and domestic markets. Yet, success has been rare.

Experiences with international buffer stocks, mostly as elements of international commodity agreements (ICAs), were reviewed in OECD (2010a). The rather clear conclusions are worth repeating here:

> a) They are potentially very costly, in part because public storage crowds out private storage.
>
> b) There is a need to update the stabilisation range in relation to changed market circumstances. This can result in controversy. Formulaic updating, on the basis for example of a moving average of past prices, reduces the potential for stabilisation and hence the value of the intervention, but does offset the costs of intervention.
>
> c) Given sufficient finance, a buffer stock authority can maintain a price above the agreed floor. However, the buffer stock can only sell what it has previously bought so once its stock is exhausted the authority has no further means of defending the ceiling. The consequence is that buffer stock agreements tend to [be] more effective in limiting price falls than in curtailing the incidence and magnitude of spikes.
>
> d) This feature is exacerbated by the possibility of speculative attack. Although attacks can take place either on a floor or a ceiling price, the problem is more serious at the ceiling.
>
> In practice, there is little evidence that buffer stock stabilisation did result in any significant reduction in price volatility.
>
> The substantive lessons from the ICA experience, where relevant to current circumstances, are therefore predominantly negative, informative about what should be avoided and not what should be done. (OECD, 2010a)[28]

The performance of national buffer stocks in reducing price volatility on domestic markets of the countries concerned is reviewed in Chapter 4. Based on empirical studies, the experiences of several African and Asian countries with stock schemes over the last 15 years are assessed. A number of the stockholding policies reviewed did not aim primarily or exclusively at symmetric price stabilisation (i.e. avoiding both too high and too low prices) but pursued other objectives as well, such as providing grains in cases of emergencies, distributing food aid, providing food assistance and managing international trade. In some cases, providing price support to farmers was an (implicit) mandate of the schemes.

Chapter 4 shows convincingly that empirical analysis of the performance of these national stock schemes is fraught with difficulties owing not only to their multiple objectives but also to a complex set of other factors that influence price developments. In particular, prices on domestic markets are strongly dependent on trade policies pursued in the countries concerned. In fact, there is effectively no way that stockholding policies in any country can permanently override the domestic market price effects of its government's trade policy unless the country concerned is either extremely large relative to the world market or has an unlimited budget and storage capacities.

This complexity was not (fully) taken into account in the empirical studies reviewed, many of which concluded that the stock schemes had performed rather well. Chapter 4 found that on closer inspection the track record of the national stock policies analysed was far less convincing. These findings resemble very much those of the earlier OECD review of international buffer stocks.

As for reducing price risks for food consumers, the study finds that:

> [T]here is little evidence of buffer stocks stabilising consumer prices. This is mainly due to the fact that buffer stocks are more adept by nature at preventing price drops than curbing price hikes and are more often used to raise prices. Accordingly, consumer prices often rise as a result of buffer stock schemes. Also, stocks that were bought with the purpose of stabilising prices are not necessarily released with the same purpose and could end up in regular distribution programmes. The fact that it is hard to trace these stocks complicates the analysis. (Deuss, 2015)

Where stock schemes appeared to have reduced domestic price volatility, the actual cause was the impact of trade policy. Stockholding policies that aimed at supporting producer prices seemed to be more successful in reaching their immediate objective. However, there were significant negative side effects, the same side effects associated with price support policies in OECD countries. The overall assessment of Chapter 4 of national stockholding policies concludes that countries are better off without these policies.

It is only where storage policy and trade policy work hand in hand that stock schemes can have a beneficial influence on domestic markets. Fundamentally, the lesson is that trade policy is the most effective and least costly approach to controlling domestic price developments for individual countries.[29] Stockholding policies can play a supportive role, for example to influence prices in locations that are so remote (in economic terms) from international markets that the effects of border policies are not transmitted to them, or as an element of a social safety net regime aimed at food security. Stocks can also play an important role in providing food security for cases in which physical supply chains break down. Yet, the role of food safety net stocks and emergency stocks differs from that of conventional buffer stocks, and their management needs to be planned quite independently from policies pursued to deal with price volatility.[30]

2.5. Achieving optimal policy performance

Based on its analytical work and on policy dialogue with governments, the OECD has gained insights into the performance of alternative policy options. In each particular environment, some policies work better than others. Choosing the specific set of measures that promises optimal policy performance in any given case is not a trivial task, but experience in assessing different policy choices helps to identify the best way forward. This section will first summarise some of the particularly relevant insights into optimal policy pursuit achieved in OECD work. It will then discuss whether these insights may need to be modified in the light of the changing conditions in markets and policies discussed above.

Policy insights generated by OECD

A close look at agricultural policies pursued around the globe indicates that a breath-taking variety of measures and implementation details is available in the arsenal of instruments that can be employed to shape the conditions prevailing in and around agriculture. How to choose the optimal combination of measures from this nearly endless range of instruments available? In principle the answer is easy: policy objectives need to be clearly defined, and instruments then chosen such that the objectives are attained as far as possible without causing undesirable side effects. In practice, however, policy design is significantly more complex given not only the variety of instruments and objectives, but also the conflicting interests of different segments of society, uncertainties regarding cause-effect relationships, path dependencies originating from the historical process of policy evolution, and other complications.

In this complex policy environment, work done for and in the OECD Committee for Agriculture has adopted a method that combines a handful of basic principles with a pragmatic approach based on best practice found in the day-to-day pursuit of agricultural policies adopted by OECD members and other economies. The results of this work have been presented in a host of documents, and occasionally has been synthesised, as in *Agricultural Policy Design and Implementation: A Synthesis* (OECD, 2008a). This booklet presents the most important principles derived from a variety of studies done by the OECD, as well as experiences gained from concrete policies in individual countries and with lessons learned regarding the practical implementation of policies in diverse settings. Another important ingredient in policy design is also discussed: the facilitation of reform where the modification of policy instruments can improve performance. This is where measures such as compensation and adjustment assistance come into play.

An absolutely central principle, running as a red thread through all considerations of policy design, is the importance of ***minimising distortions of markets and trade***. This is sometimes interpreted (if not criticised) as an ideological position representing the entrenched philosophy of economic liberalism (or neoliberalism). Yet, there are very good practical reasons behind that principle. Three thoughts are particularly relevant. First, it is desirable to minimise international spillover effects. Friendly nations are considerate of each others' interests and try to avoid doing harm to other countries' trade flows – not least because they want to see their own trade interests respected by other nations. Second, where policies have unintended side effects on markets and trade, they introduce extra costs to the economy in the form of use of resources that could be employed more productively elsewhere. In the political process, these extra costs are often not directly visible, but they are nevertheless real. For example, where an expansion of agricultural output follows from a policy that is intended to reduce erosion, the extra fertiliser and pesticides applied may use chemicals and energy that could have been utilised more profitably in producing medicines or fuel. Third, in most cases there are alternative policy options that could have achieved the same objective without the negative side effects on markets and trade. They may require the investment of more political capital, but they save trade partners and the home economy from avoidable trouble, and hence they are politically more sustainable in the longer term. The principle of avoiding market distortions wherever possible is thus not ideology, but well considered practical advice.

This general principle is equally relevant in various cases of specific policy concerns in agriculture. In many developed countries, one of the most prominent political priorities in agricultural policy making is support for farm incomes. The traditional response was to provide that support through price policy for agricultural commodities or output-based payments, keeping domestic prices above the level prevailing on international markets. As discussed above, the OECD has engaged in all sorts of analysis showing how such policies distort markets, create trade problems, waste resources and reduce economic welfare. As a way forward, the concept of ***decoupling*** was developed and comprehensively analysed by the OECD (see above). Decoupling provides a prime example of applying the principle of minimising distortions of markets and trade.

Yet decoupling should be seen as only one element in the process of reforming agricultural policy, rather than as a policy approach in its own right. If a new agricultural policy had to be designed from scratch, "decoupled" payments of the sort employed in some OECD members' policies would not have a place as there are more efficient and effective measures to achieve a given set of objectives. In particular, where it is felt that farm households' incomes need to be supported, measures that target families – as are used in social policies for other sectors of the economy – rather than policies tied to agricultural land (which are still the basis of most "decoupled" payments) should be used (OECD, 2003a). Hence, a blueprint for a synthetic new agricultural policy would not include "decoupled" payments. However, where reform is initiated to improve policy performance, decoupling can play a useful role in reducing market and trade distortions while providing compensation to farm families that might otherwise come under socially unacceptable income pressure. Decoupling is, therefore, an alternative to removing past price support without providing any accompanying assistance to farmers: it is not a policy instrument to be introduced in the first place. Decoupling buys time during which farmers can adjust. Adjustments needed in response to policy reform can and should also be actively assisted through government policy, and there are good examples of best practice in terms of adjustment assistance provided by a number of governments in OECD countries (Kubota, 2007). As a method to provide ***compensation*** in the process of policy reform, decoupling can play a subsidiary role until adjustments have taken place. Compensation is justified only for some time (OECD, 2007c), and hence there is no permanent function for "decoupled" payments.

"Decoupled" payments are sometimes saddled with ***cross compliance*** requirements. That is, in order to be eligible for the payments, farmers must comply with given regulations, typically related to environmental and sustainability criteria. This may be a practical approach as it can save the transaction costs involved in setting up a separate system of sanctions for non-compliance. However, it remains a blunt approach as there is no one-to-one relation between the cost of compliance with existing regulations and the level of payments that resulted from past reforms. Compliance costs differ from location to location, and in many cases also from farm to farm. Moreover, environmental conditions, and hence the need for environmental protection activities, also differ from place to place. Requiring all farmers to comply with the same criteria in order to receive the "decoupled" payments, is therefore neither efficient nor effective. Finally, the concept of cross compliance loses all rationality if the logic is turned around and, rather than adding cross compliance requirements to existing direct payments, the cross compliance criteria are utilised as justification for continuing to make direct payments. Environmental and similar needs may well require government action. But they cannot provide *ex post facto* justification of payments that were introduced for a different reason and whose level has nothing to do with the cost of the environmental action required.

This is where ***targeting and tailoring***, the second fundamental principle of effective and efficient policy design, becomes important. Well-targeted measures are those that address the operational policy objectives as directly as possible, and the measures are well tailored if the rate and duration of support are commensurate with the cost of providing the expected outcomes (OECD, 2007b and 2008a). Again, this is not abstract theory or wishful thinking, but very practical policy advice, illustrated by the OECD with several examples of best practice in the form of concrete policies pursued in individual OECD countries.

There are, however, cases where it may appear that targeting is neither possible nor necessary because some relevant variables are closely tied together. Such cases have been considered in the long debate about the ***multifunctional character*** of agriculture and its potential implications for policy design. The OECD has conducted a suite of studies in this domain.[31] The issue is that while producing commodities, agriculture may also generate non-commodity outputs (NCOs) such as rural development, environmental amenities or food security. Where these NCOs are desirable public goods or externalities, governments are called upon to provide them. If the NCOs concerned are strictly "joint products", then two implications would appear to follow. First, rather than looking after the provision of these NCOs directly, governments could support the production of agricultural commodities and in that way make sure that the desirable NCOs are also supplied. Second, because of the "jointness" in production, it is impossible to provide the desirable NCOs without affecting trade flows. Trading partners would then have to accept that interference with their trade interests in an unavoidable implication of the legitimate pursuit of domestic interests by governments taking action to provide desirable NCOs.[32]

In its work on multifunctionality, the OECD has considered in much detail the wide variety of issues, both from a theoretical perspective and with a view to concrete and practical policy matters in many countries. Several policy implications emerged (OECD, 2003b and 2008c). One is that strict "jointness" between agricultural commodity output and NCOs is rare. For example, environmental benefits may accord with agricultural production at low levels of intensity, but typically have an inverse relationship at higher levels of intensity. Furthermore, practical experience during World War II and after showed that there is little jointness between public support to agriculture in normal times and food security in times of crisis. Another policy implication is that the demand or need for given NCOs tends to be region-specific or even site-specific. For example, improved biodiversity may be needed for fauna in some places, while flora is more threatened in other locations. Broad-based policies such as price support to agriculture are not only inefficient in such cases, they may also be ineffective, if not actually counter-productive. The general conclusion from the OECD's work on multifunctionality is that in essentially all cases that studied targeted policies, pursuing NCOs directly is more efficient and effective. That such targeted measures also minimise distortions of markets and trade is an additional benefit.

One important area of policy making in which these considerations can be fruitfully applied is that of ***environmental policies***, a domain where OECD work on agriculture has been very active. Most environmental variables in agriculture are only loosely connected – or even negatively connected – with the volume of agricultural output. Moreover, many environmentally relevant conditions are location specific, and any environmental protection and improvement needs are, therefore, equally location specific. This means that policies based on agricultural output cannot do an efficient and effective job in pursuing environmental objectives. Instead, environmental policy measures need to be targeted. There is a variety of both market-based instruments (such as taxes and subsidies) and regulatory measures that are well targeted and can therefore make cost-effective contributions to achieving environmental objectives in agriculture while minimising distortions of markets and trade (OECD, 2013a).

An important area of OECD work on agriculture in recent years dealt with ***risk management***, an issue that has become increasingly relevant in both policy debates and actual policy pursuit as markets have exhibited heightened volatility.[33] A number of highly relevant policy insights have resulted from this work stream. To begin with, it is important to develop a holistic approach, taking into account the various types of risks facing farmers and the relationships among them. For example, price risk may or may not be (partially) compensated by output variations: hence, focusing on prices alone is not effective. What counts is the eventual impact of risk on farm income, and hence all factors affecting farm income should be taken into account when dealing with risk management.

OECD analysis has also shown that it is useful to distinguish three different layers or risk and their relevance for policy action. Limited fluctuations of output or prices are normal business risks that can be managed privately by farmers. In fact, policies that aim at counteracting such risks, for example through intervention prices or equivalent measures, can be counterproductive and result in greater risk exposure. However, catastrophic risks such as extreme and infrequent events that affect a large number of farmers and inflict significant damage exceed the capacity of farmers and markets to cope. They may, therefore, require government action. Examples include severe and widespread drought or outbreaks of a highly contagious and damaging disease. The third category is marketable risk, which falls between normal and catastrophic risks. Normal price fluctuations and hail damage are examples of this type of risk. Farmers can deal with these intermediary risks through market instruments such as insurance, futures markets or co-operative arrangements. Governments are well advised to create the institutional framework under which such market approaches can develop. However, governments are less effective and efficient than private agents at dealing with such risks through public policy measures. In addition, where government policies cover such marketable risks they are likely to crowd out private activities.

In essence then, an important finding of OECD research in the domain of risk management is that well-performing government policies focus on assisting farmers in cases of catastrophic risks, and on creating optimal conditions for the market to respond to other risks. As far as catastrophic risks are concerned it is preferable not to rely on *ad hoc* responses after disastrous damage has occurred: it is better to develop contingency plans that specify in advance the responsibilities and procedures for providing assistance, and the limits of government action. Explicit criteria for triggering government action are helpful, as is a predetermined definition of the types and maximum volumes of assistance. It is important to avoid moral hazard on the side of farmers. Where subsidies are granted for crop insurance against disasters, it is important to avoid granting *ad hoc* assistance over and above the insurance subsidies.

Creating optimal conditions for private activity includes providing education and training for farmers so they are well prepared to manage their normal business risk. The tax system can also help, for example by allowing producers to average taxable income across a number of years and by providing incentives to save. A legal system that provides sufficient flexibility for production and marketing contracts between farmers and downstream agents can help to spread price risk across the supply chain and to other agents, for example on futures exchanges. Experience gained in a number of OECD countries shows that income stabilisation and counter-cyclical schemes are not efficient tools to manage risks. In this context, it is also important to remember that risk-reducing forms of support can result in pronounced distortions of markets and trade, and hence cause large welfare costs to the domestic economy and negative international spillover effects.

A controversial subject is the most appropriate response of agricultural policy makers to ***societal concerns***. It is somewhat similar to the issue of multifunctionality because concerns often have to do with NCOs related to agricultural production. Animal welfare, environmental implications, genetically modified organisms, the quality and safety of food products, and the social conditions of production are just a few examples of issues where modern societies have concerns, often arising out of widely diverging views on what is right and wrong. Responding appropriately to such societal concerns and identifying the "best" policies to address these issues has often proven difficult for policy makers. The OECD has, therefore, dealt with such societal concerns and their policy implications in a number of activities (for example Tothova, 2009, and OECD, 2010b).[34] Given the rather different nature of the various societal concerns, the optimal policy responses differ very much. One generalised conclusion is that appropriate measures are targeted rather than being broad based, and that they do not include support to agricultural output. In most cases, some form of regulation or tax is most effective, for example in responding to concerns about animal welfare. Food safety concerns are best taken into account through SPS measures. Asymmetric consumer information and concerns regarding social conditions in production may require labelling. In this domain, though, it can be difficult to avoid trade implications. Where the societies in trading partners have different preferences and concerns, governments may adopt different regulations regarding processes and production methods (PPMs), or promote a given PPM through subsidies and discourage undesirable PPMs through taxes. When these instruments are also applied to imported products, they may conflict with the principle of non-discrimination. In some cases, such conflicts can be avoided or mitigated through other approaches such as labelling or agreements on equivalence or mutual recognition. In other cases, however, the matter will have to be discussed with trade partners.

There is no doubt that well-targeted and well-tailored measures require much administrative effort in the form of information collection, decision making, implementation and monitoring. They are, therefore, likely to involve higher ***transaction costs*** than broad-based measures such as price support. This is often held against targeted measures. The OECD has looked carefully into the issue of policy transaction costs, including empirical case studies of administrative costs resulting from real world agricultural policy measures (OECD, 2007c). It concluded that the transaction costs of targeted policies can indeed be high, but that the resource savings to be made when policies are well targeted rather than broad based are significantly larger than the extra costs involved in moving to better-targeted measures.

The fundamental policy principle of addressing issues at the source rather than intervening in markets applies not only to industrialised economies. It is equally valid for developing countries, as several OECD studies have demonstrated. It may be tempting to think that ***rural development*** and ***poverty reduction*** in rural areas, where over two-thirds of the world's poor live, can most easily be achieved through agricultural price support, for example by imposing tariffs on products considered relevant for livelihood security. Similarly, input subsidies are often considered an instrument that can support both rural incomes and productivity improvement. Yet, as shown in Brooks (2012), both of these types of measures are too blunt. Price support is not only inefficient, resulting in market distortions and a consequent waste of resources that poor economies cannot afford, it is also ineffective, if not counterproductive, because many rural households are net food buyers and are worse off when they have to pay higher prices. Input subsidies have often provided gains to unintended beneficiaries, undermined the development of private market channels and resulted in a heavy burden on the government budget. There are more effective and efficient instruments available. In the short term, well-targeted social safety nets can assist the poor. In the medium and longer term, it is important to raise productivity and create employments opportunities. A good part of the measures needed are not necessarily agriculture specific. Improvements in primary healthcare and education, investments in infrastructure, secure property rights, sound macroeconomic conditions, good governance – all of these measures contribute to creating conditions for economic growth. As not all families living in rural areas will find gainful opportunities in agriculture, an important form of supporting rural development, paradoxical as it may sound, is the creation of jobs outside agriculture. Effective measures include agricultural research, technology transfer, and extension and advisory services.

Similar conclusions can be drawn from OECD work on improving ***food security***, comprehensively presented in *Global Food Security: Challenges for the Food and Agriculture* System (OECD, 2013b). Food insecurity is a consequence of poverty, except in emergency situations where physical supplies break down. Tariff protection for staple foods, which is sometimes suggested as a means to improve food security, may expand domestic output and hence raise the *availability* of food, but it does not help poor consumers to gain *access* to the food they need. On the contrary, tariffs raise food prices and hence reduce the purchasing power of consumers. In the short term, social safety net policies targeted to the poor can improve their access to food. In the longer term, measures that improve the income situation of the poor are needed. Everything that can help to eradicate poverty enhances food security much more effectively than measures operating on food markets. Fostering agricultural development is an important ingredient in a strategy to improve food security, not so much because it improves the domestic availability of food, but because it improves the income situation of families living in rural areas where a large proportion of food insecure households are located. But there are also many other initiatives, sometimes seemingly distant from the food sector, that can effectively improve food security. For example, providing safe water supplies and sanitation, and the resulting health benefits, is a much more effective approach to enhancing food security than imposing tariffs on staple foods. Initiatives to raise awareness about adequate nutrition and childcare can help to overcome nutritional deficiencies. Using international trade to make food available and affordable on domestic markets is beneficial for food consumers, while negative implications of open trade for producers and for market stability can be counteracted through appropriately targeted policies. Developed countries can contribute to well-functioning international food markets by reforming distortive policies and abstaining from policies that add to the volatility of world markets. Doing away with support for the production and consumption of conventional biofuels would contribute to making more food available at lower prices to the poor in developing countries.

The world has changed: Are past findings still relevant?

The evolution of actual policies in the OECD area described above can be briefly characterised as a gradual decline in the level of farm support and an ongoing shift towards less distorting policy measures. These trends are clearly more noticeable in some countries than in others, but overall the development has gone in this direction. This evolution of policies among developed countries is basically in line with the OECD's insights regarding well-performing policies, and as such it does not require fundamental reconsideration of the policy messages developed in the past. Recent developments have, though, raised a number of issues, three of which appear to be particularly relevant.

First, the decline in the level of farm support is in part the result not of deliberate changes in policy settings but of rising prices on international markets. This is not a problem per se. When governments feel that more favourable market conditions provide the opportunity to reduce transfers to farmers, in particular those transfers that are not well targeted, then this is a welcome development. However, the flip side of that coin may turn out to be that farm support rises again if market prices decline. If and when that happens, the question to be considered is to what extent well-performing policies should shield farmers from changing market conditions. This question will be taken up below in the context of risk management. Another directly related, but also distinct, question is whether and how policies can be structured in such a way that they are reasonably immune to ups and downs in international market prices in terms of their budgetary implications and the government's capacity to comply with international commitments.

Second, a number of issues can be discussed regarding the overall trend towards more decoupled and less distorting policies. For example, it is not clear that all governments embrace the view that compensation for policy reform, if granted through direct payments, should support adjustment and be limited in time. It can equally be asked whether the large amounts of public money spent on transfers to farmers are sufficiently targeted to well-defined objectives. Where direct payments that had been introduced in the context of policy reforms were terminated recently under favourable market conditions, the question arises whether this was based on the view that compensation for past policy reforms was no longer needed and justified, or whether a re-instrumentation was chosen that promises larger benefits for farmers when market prices decline. In other words, behind the apparently positive trend towards lower support levels and less distorting policy structures there may be developments that are not in line with a desirable progression towards better-performing agricultural policies.

Third, with a declining level of farm support and less distortionary policies in the OECD area, the traditional concerns regarding the price-depressing implications of rich countries' policies on international markets for agricultural commodities, and the consequent calls for reforming these policies in the interest of well-functioning global markets, are less urgent now than in the past. At the same time, government support for the production and consumption of biofuels in the OECD area and the resulting policy-induced additional use of agricultural raw materials as feedstocks has had the opposite effect of raising world market prices of these commodities (OECD, 2008c), possibly by more than the price-depressing effect of the traditional support policies. Given that the price level on world markets for agricultural products is higher now than in the past, the price-lifting impact of biofuel support policies has, among other things, raised concerns regarding implications for food security in poor countries. It has been commented that critiques of such price-raising policies and their impact on food security, by the OECD as well as other international organisations and of a number of non-governmental organisations, appears to be inconsistent with past critical comments regarding depressed prices (Swinnen and Squicciarini, 2012). However, the OECD's policy analysis has not been concerned with identifying a "desirable" level of international market prices for agricultural products but with assessing any potentially distorting implications of policies, irrespective of whether the resulting bias is downward or upward. From that perspective, the changes in the policy landscape and on markets do not require the development of a fundamentally new way of looking at things.

While support levels have declined in the OECD area, the evolution of policies in major emerging countries has gone in the opposite direction. As shown above, their levels of farm support are rising, and there has also been a tendency to resort to more distorting policy measures. As a result, the centre of gravity in global farm support is shifting from the OECD area to the emerging economies, and possibly also to less developed countries. In addition, some of the emerging economies are large and have sizeable agricultural sectors. This means that substantial sums of money are transferred to agriculture in some of the emerging economies. China's absolute PSE (in USD) is now more than 50% larger than that of the European Union, and Indonesia's farm support comes close to that of the United States. At the same time, some emerging economies are large participants in international trade with agricultural products, either as exporters or importers. It is conceivable that agricultural policies in emerging and developing countries now affect price formation on international markets at least as much as do OECD countries. For all of these reasons, the nature and evolution of agricultural policies in emerging and important developing countries has become a focus in the OECD's work.

Policy concerns and objectives in emerging economies in part overlap with those of rich countries, but also entail different priorities and specific weights. For example, food security among poor consumers is a more pressing concern than in most developed countries. General services and development of infrastructure require particular attention. Policy reforms may be needed in several cases, but their nature differs from the reforms initiated in many developed countries in past decades, where much of the focus was on redressing excessive price support. Moreover, the conditions under which policies can be pursued in emerging and developing countries differ from those in rich countries. All of this does not mean that the general orientation of the OECD's policy analysis and the insights generated are obsolete and must be replaced by new paradigms. In particular, the fundamental principle that market distortions should be avoided as far as possible is equally relevant outside the OECD area. In fact, the lower the standard of living is in a given country, the more important it becomes to avoid the extra resource costs and consequent welfare losses resulting from policies that unintentionally distort markets . Markets are more distorted the less well policies are targeted and tailored – another important policy principle that has emerged from OECD work. There is no doubt that this principle applies to emerging and developing countries with equal force. The same can be said about other findings from OECD work even if the policy issues and empirical cases to which the analysis is applied differ from those in the OECD area. OECD work on agricultural policies in emerging and developing countries has demonstrated that insights from the work done earlier on OECD countries can be transferred and adapted to the conditions prevailing in other parts of the world. Thus, the shifting centre of gravity in global farm support does not appear to demand a reorientation of the fundamental findings in past OECD work; instead, it calls for a continuation of what has been done with more and more attention given to the policy issues of emerging and developing countries and to the types of policies these countries pursue.

Do changes in global market conditions for agricultural products in recent years require a reconsideration of the insights gained in past OECD work? Do the higher international prices now prevailing warrant a modification of major policy principles? Most of the findings regarding well-performing policies relate to the domestic functioning of alternative measures and therefore do not depend on the level of prices on international markets. The desirability of avoiding market distortions and the benefits of employing measures that directly target well-defined and carefully tailored objectives do not depend on high or low world market prices. The conclusions drawn from work on decoupling and multifunctionality are not affected by changes in market conditions. The need for many measures aimed at providing NCOs, in particular environmental protection, to be site specific rather than broad based is relevant irrespective of market prices for commodities. What may have changed is the urgency of the need for, and the political economy of, agricultural policy reform. In most OECD countries, price-supporting policies and directly output-related payments play a somewhat reduced role under current market conditions. How to reform these policies is therefore perhaps less pressing than in the past. However, growing attention may now need to be paid to policy regimes that more or less automatically re-introduce price supports or equivalent measures if market prices decline again.

Policies that have become more critical now under market conditions with high prices are those that tend to raise, rather than depress, international commodity prices. Two outstanding examples are government support for biofuels and all forms of export restrictions. The OECD has already done important work in both areas. However, given the importance of these policies for the functioning of world markets, and in particular for food security, there are good reasons to remain active in analysing such policies, if not investing more resources in them. A few comments on OECD analysis of export restrictions have been made already. As far as biofuels are concerned, there is still a need for more and better information on the nature and levels of government support in this domain. The database on biofuels policies created by the OECD is a good start. However, there are still many blanks in the data supplied by OECD members. Missing also is an OECD estimate of total levels of support in the biofuels sector, similar to that of the PSE, perhaps even integrated into the PSE. It is clear, though, that significant conceptual problems would have to be overcome in order to produce such estimates. In particular, when estimating transfers to farmers resulting from biofuels policies, it is necessary to estimate their impact on price formation in markets for the feedstocks concerned. This is possible in principle, as shown in past OECD work (OECD, 2008c). There are, however, conceptual problems that have to be considered. Specifically, support for the use of agricultural commodities in biofuel production in a given country provides benefits not only to the farmers in that country, but also to those in other parts of the world. Moreover, price effects on commodity markets can be estimated only based on modelling approaches – an element that has, for very good reasons, never been introduced into PSE work (Tangermann, 2005). Yet, given the heightened importance of price-raising policies under current market conditions, it is perhaps time to confront such conceptual issues.

In a high-price environment, there is also a need for intensive work on food security issues in developing countries. The OECD has been very active in this domain, and current market conditions do not warrant a reconsideration of the policy conclusions drawn, not least because a good part of that work was accomplished at a time when food prices on international markets had already reached high levels. It appears desirable to continue, if not intensify, that work. The comparative performance of alternative policy approaches in emerging and developing countries remains an issue that might benefit from more analysis. For example, India and some G33 countries have expressed pronounced concerns regarding WTO disciplines related to public stockholding for food security purposes. This has been a controversial item both at the Bali Ministerial of the WTO and in the subsequent negotiations in the summer of 2014. To what extent and under which conditions is stockholding of staple foods a well-performing ingredient in a country's strategy to improve food security? Another dimension is the contribution that agriculture and agricultural policies in rich countries can possibly make to improving global food security. OECD work has already thrown light on this issue, but its continued prevalence in policy debates in the OECD area[35] suggests that continued work might be useful.

The pronounced volatility that international markets for agricultural products have exhibited in recent years and that may continue is an important concern for agricultural policy makers. It does not affect the validity of the central OECD findings regarding well-performing agricultural policies. It does, however, highlight the importance of the results generated by OECD work on risk management, as summarised above. However, actual risk-related policies in several OECD countries appear to diverge significantly from the policy messages derived from OECD analysis. Perhaps this situation can be compared with the case of price support policies a few decades ago. In a situation where price support and equivalent measures largely dominated agricultural policy structures in the OECD area, OECD research and its effective dissemination in policy dialogue contributed greatly to helping governments understand the nature of their policies and their undesirable implications. Early work on the benefits of decoupling support from production showed that there was a way out. Many governments finally embarked on that route and engaged in policy reform. As a result, policy structures in the OECD area are now far less dominated by price support and similar measures. Meanwhile, volatility has become a dominant policy concern in several countries in recent years, and inefficient risk management policies are widespread. Perhaps the case can be made that analytical work and policy dialogue in the OECD on well-performing risk management policies is as important now as work on reforming price support policies was in the past.

2.6. Implications for agricultural trade negotiations post-Bali

After the failed attempt in 2008 to agree on modalities for new commitments in agriculture and the other subjects of the Doha Round negotiations, the fact that the Bali Ministerial of the WTO in December 2013 managed to arrive at a number of positive decisions ended five years of widespread frustration over a lack of progress in the multilateral trade talks. The most important achievement at Bali was the agreement on the package of trade facilitation measures that had been negotiated over the years, an accomplishment that, if put into practice, promised to result in rather practical improvements in trading conditions and corresponding welfare gains in the global economy. However, that Bali achievement fell apart when it proved impossible to find a way of bringing all WTO members to adopt the protocol on the Trade Facilitation Agreement by 31 July 2014, the deadline agreed by Ministers at Bali. This was another case where disagreement over agricultural matters got in the way of overall progress in WTO negotiations. India and a few other countries would not let the trade facilitation package go forward as long as they felt there was not sufficient progress towards a permanent solution that would address their concerns regarding public stockholding of food, another item on which Ministers had taken a decision at Bali. Thus, a few months after optimism had been rekindled among WTO members, the mood has suddenly and dramatically turned into deep pessimism. Like the WTO Director-General, many participants in WTO business have made it known that they are "very, very concerned". What this will mean for the future of the DDA negotiations is difficult to assess before the WTO's work has come into full swing again after the 2014 summer break. But it appears unlikely that the negotiations, including those on agriculture, will be any easier in the future than they were before Bali.

On the other hand, it could be argued that the fundamentally changed market conditions should now make it easier than in in 2008 to find agreement on the core of the draft modalities for reduction commitments suggested in Rev.4. The negotiations from which these parameters resulted were conducted in the years before 2008, when the price spike on world markets for food and agricultural products had not yet occurred and, more importantly, when it did not yet appear that the world had entered a phase where prices will remain higher for some time to come.

This is at least the impression one gains if comparing, for example, the tariff reductions suggested in the successive draft modalities tabled in 2006, 2007 and 2008 (Figure 2.12). By 2006, the approach considered for tariff reductions in agriculture had stabilised to a tiered formula, with four tiers. The draft modalities tabled in 2006 still contained ranges of suggested reduction rates for each of the tiers (in squared brackets). In the 2007 draft, these ranges were narrowed considerably, and the 2008 Rev.4 had advanced to the point where only one reduction rate was still suggested for each of the four tiers. In terms of the negotiating dynamics, this evolution indicated good progress towards a common view. However, the orders of magnitude considered for tariff cuts did not change in response to market developments occurring at the time. As reflected in Figure 2.12, there was perhaps a slight increase in the magnitude of cuts considered between 2006 and 2007, but the reduction rates suggested in Rev.4 in 2008 when the price spike had already caused much excitement in the "real world" outside the negotiating rooms, were more or less precisely the mid-points of the ranges that had been considered in July 2007 before food prices began to rise dramatically.

Figure 2.12. Ranges of reduction rates for agricultural tariffs in developed countries suggested in the successive draft modalities of 2006, 2007 and 2008

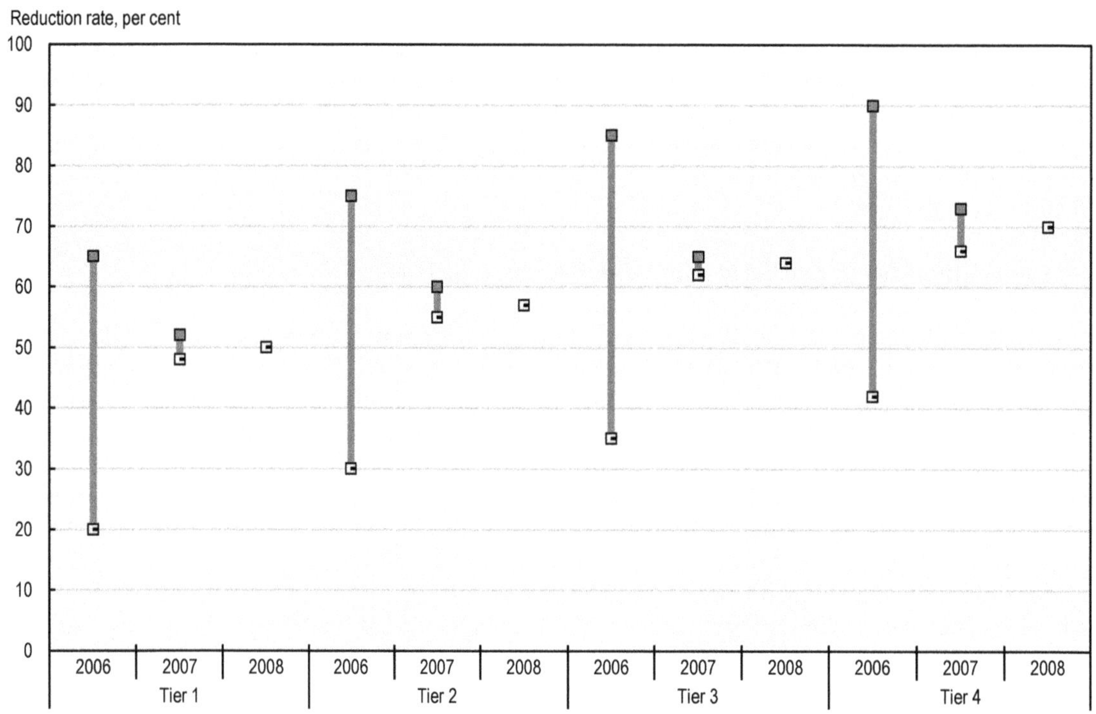

Note: In the 2006 document TN/AG/W/3, the tariff ranges suggested for tiers 1 to 4 were still 0%-[20-30%]; [20-30%]-[40-60%]; [40-60%]-[60-90%]; >[60-90%].

Source: WTO documents TN/AG/W/3; TN/AG/W/4; TN/AG/W/4/Rev.4.

This has implications for the Doha negotiations on ***market access*** in agriculture. Tariffs generate a given margin between domestic and international prices. Yet, from the perspective of pursuing a set of well-defined agricultural policy objectives, that margin appears less relevant than the level of domestic prices in relation to other domestic variables. More specifically, when a government sets a given tariff level, it must at least implicitly have some idea of what a "satisfactory" domestic market price should be. What is considered a "satisfactory" domestic price may depend on views regarding such matters as a target level of producer income, a desirable degree of self-sufficiency or a minimum producer revenue believed to be necessary to achieve survival of a domestic industry. If it later turns out that the international market price attains a higher level than expected, then the "satisfactory" domestic price can be achieved with a lower tariff. From that perspective, if the level of world market prices for agricultural commodities turns out to be around 30% higher than originally expected, then *ad valorem* (equivalents of) tariffs could be reduced by around 30 percentage points without threatening the attainment of "satisfactory" prices on domestic markets. On that basis, it could be argued that the now higher level of international prices should reduce the perceived "need" for tariff protection – and hence facilitate agreement on the tariff cuts considered in 2008. In fact, with international market prices about one-third higher than probably expected in 2008, tariffs could even be cut by rates larger than what appeared potentially acceptable in 2008.

This argument does not, however, take into account that some of the same factors that have pushed up international market prices may also have raised the target level of domestic prices. As suggested above, one reason behind the step increase in world market prices for agricultural commodities that appears to have occurred since 2006 was a cost push caused by rising energy prices. One can probably argue that this cost push has also raised the target level of domestic prices by the same order of magnitude. Other factors behind the increase in international market prices (such as resource constraints, a slowing in productivity growth, demand expansion) should not have changed the level of domestic prices that is considered "satisfactory" from a producer point of view.[36] Thus, if one assumes that the cost-push element was responsible for about two-thirds of the around 30% increase in the global level of agricultural commodity prices experienced after 2006[37], then tariffs could be reduced by about 10 percentage points and still achieve the original target level for domestic prices.

Another issue in the DDA negotiations on market access in agriculture is the large binding overhang of tariffs that has accumulated in several countries (see Section 2.3). On a global scale, tariffs applied for agricultural products have come down to about one-half of the tariffs bound (Bureau and Jean, 2013b). Tariff cuts that do not go beyond 50% would, therefore, in many cases would only eliminate the binding overhang without improving market access. Another factor in favour of considering relatively large tariff cuts in the DDA negotiations is the growing significance of RTAs. A disadvantage of these preferential arrangements is their discriminatory nature, potentially resulting in trade diversion at the cost of third parties. The lower the level of non-preferential tariffs, the less danger there is of this happening.

The changes in market conditions since 2008 should also facilitate the DDA negotiations on ***export subsidies and equivalent measures***. The higher the level of world market prices, the less the "need" for supporting exports. The decline in export subsidisation actually observed in recent years (discussed above) is in line with that view. It should, therefore, be easier now than it was in 2008 to find agreement on eliminating export subsidies and equivalent measures.

The situation is somewhat different when it comes to the ***domestic support*** commitments that would result from the rules and parameters suggested in Rev.4. One important element of domestic support in several countries is market price support (MPS). Under the AoA (and under Rev.4), MPS is defined relative to fixed external reference prices: thus, the increase in actual world prices has not reduced the calculated level of MPS. Where governments raised applied administered prices in response to rising international market prices, the MPS relative to WTO commitments has actually increased, even if the applied administered prices were increased less than the rise in world market prices. This is an issue of concern, for example, to India and is (indirectly) reflected in the Bali decision on public stockholding for food security purposes.

The rationale for including the MPS element in the WTO rules for domestic support, in addition to tariff bindings, was debated early on, as was the use of fixed external reference prices (see, for example, Josling et al., 1996). With the significant increase in the level of world prices in recent years, the external reference prices based on the situation in 1986-88 have become entirely outdated. The situation is particularly problematic where countries maintain applied administered prices that are below currently prevailing world market prices but above the fixed external reference prices. In such cases, price support is not provided in an economic sense, but the countries concerned may still be in violation of their domestic support commitments under the WTO. This is one dimension of the food security stocks issue pursued by India and a few other countries at Bali and in subsequent negotiations.[38] At some point, the use of MPS based on fixed external reference prices will have to be reconsidered in the WTO.

In some other regards, the changes that have taken place in recent years and which have been discussed above should now make the rules and parameters reflected in Rev.4 appear less restrictive, and hence more easily acceptable, than in 2008. Where countries use deficiency payments towards a given target price (or other payments of a similar nature), the level of domestic support is related inversely to the movements of world prices and hence has decreased as a result of the increased price level on international markets. Several countries, in particular in the OECD area, have also continued to reform their policies and in the process reduced levels of support. Moreover, in a number of cases countries have trimmed their notified levels of MPS by eliminating the notion of administered prices.

When looking at the combined implications of these and other factors for domestic support levels notified recently to the WTO, Brink (2014) finds that the agricultural policies in most of the 19 countries (both developed and developing) included in his study would not have to be changed if an agreement along the lines of Rev.4 were to be concluded. This means that the domestic support provisions suggested in Rev.4 should not be too difficult to accept in the negotiations.

An issue that may need more attention than so far reflected in Rev.4 is the treatment of ***export restrictions***. In the Doha negotiations up to 2008, this issue played no more than a limited role. In 2008 and subsequent years, use of export restrictions expanded very much (see above), and it became obvious how detrimental export restrictions imposed in a period of spiking prices can be, in particular for food security in poor countries. The draft modalities tabled in 2008 do not appear to have responded to that experience.

It can also be argued that the greater volatility of agricultural markets and, in response to it, the rising importance of policies aimed at ***risk management*** may require consideration in the Doha negotiations on agriculture, over and above of what is already reflected in Rev.4.

2.7. Conclusions

When the Doha negotiations resumed after the December 2013 Ministerial at Bali, one of the major questions considered in agriculture was whether global conditions had changed so much that Rev.4 draft modalities could no longer serve as a useful reference for the talks. Indeed, as shown in this chapter, the agricultural world has changed significantly since 2008. In short, international market prices of agricultural commodities have exhibited a step increase in the order of magnitude of one-third, and there is some likelihood that they will continue to exhibit more volatility than in the past. Farm support has declined in the OECD area, and the policy structure has shifted towards somewhat less distorting policies. Among emerging countries, on the other hand, farm support is on the rise, and it also appears to have become more distortionary. Tariff structures in many countries are characterised by a noticeable degree of binding overhang. Export subsidies have come down significantly, and other export support measures with equivalent effect appear to have also been cut back. In other words, in the domain of export competition there is also a large degree of binding overhang relative to WTO commitments. As far as domestic support commitments under the AoA are concerned, not only is there binding overhang relative to existing AoA commitments, but even the reductions implied in Rev.4 would leave considerable amounts of water in most countries' schedules.

For the WTO negotiations on agriculture, this means that the "continuation of the reform process" mandated in the AoA and folded into the Doha talks is not only more important now than it was in 2008, but that from a policy perspective it should also be more easily achieved. More specifically, the rule changes and reduction parameters suggested in Rev.4 should appear more easily acceptable now than they may have been in 2008. In fact, larger reductions may now be needed to squeeze enough water out of the resulting commitments.

The changes that have taken place since 2008 and the experiences made in the last few years suggest that two issues need more attention than they had received in the negotiations up to 2008. First, export restrictions have not only been more frequently used, in particular in response to spiking prices in 2007-08 and subsequent years, but their problematic impact, in particular on food security in poor countries, has also become more apparent. It appears highly desirable to establish more effective disciplines on these measures in the WTO. Second, heightened market volatility has sparked rising interest in risk management policies. Treatment of these policies in the AoA rules on domestic support may have to be reconsidered. An additional reason to do so is the result of OECD work that has shown that such policies can have strong distortionary impacts on markets and trade.

The OECD has done a large amount of work in analysing the impacts of a variety of different policies on markets and trade, and important elements of the findings are summarised in this chapter. Based on that work and on research regarding the effectiveness and efficiency of alternative policies, as well as on best practice among member countries, the OECD has engaged in policy dialogue. Most of the OECD's findings regarding well-performing agricultural policies have not only stood the test of time, they continue to apply under the changed conditions in global agriculture. What might be useful is a somewhat strengthened emphasis on some issues that were already addressed in the past which, however, may have become even more important under current conditions. Two examples may illustrate this point. First, biofuel support policies and their impacts on global consumption of agricultural commodities have become even more problematic in times of generally high prices on agricultural markets. Second, policies to support risk management have attracted rising attention in a more volatile market environment. It also appears to be the case that the important findings that the OECD's research on risk management has generated have not yet sufficiently found their way into actual policy making. Perhaps the case can be made that research and policy dialogue in this area is now as important, and therefore should receive as much attention, as the work on decoupling in the last decade or so.

New developments also raise new challenges for policy research. In this chapter, a number of issues are suggested that might benefit from OECD work.

Notes

1. Professor Emeritus, Department of Agricultural Economics and Rural Development, University of Göttingen.
2. The nature, determinants and policy implications of volatility on agricultural commodity markets are discussed more fully in Tangermann (2011) and the literature referenced there.
3. In recent editions of the *OECD-FAO Outlook*, average real prices over the projection period are compared to the average of the two year and ten year periods in the immediate past (see figures 1.15 in the 2014 *Outlook* and 1.9 in the 2013 *Outlook*). As these base periods include the peak prices of 2007/08 the step increase in the price level that began in 2007 is less visible in that comparison.
4. For a statistical analysis of the long-term movement of commodity prices, see Jacks (2013).
5. It would appear likely that in the medium to longer term the price ratios among many agricultural commodities, in particular between the different crops and between cereals and cereal-based livestock products, move in a less divergent way than implicit in projections represented in Figure 2.2, as substitution and complementarity relationships tend to bring about similar price trends.

6. The seven emerging economies included in the OECD's *Agricultural Policies: Monitoring and Evaluation* are Brazil, China, Indonesia, Kazakhstan, the Russian Federation, South Africa and Ukraine.

7. All results presented here were calculated from data in the OECD's PSE database.

8. Note that the OECD area does not include the six non-OECD member countries of the European Union, even though they are also covered by the EU's Common Agricultural Policy.

9. It should be noted that the producer NPC as defined by the OECD includes not only market price support but also payments per unit of current output (e.g. deficiency payments).

10. The increase of this indicator in New Zealand is irrelevant given that New Zealand's %PSE is below 1%.

11. In addition to the countries included above in the section on producer support, India is included here in the review of tariff levels.

12. It should, though, be noted that for many TRQs (accounting for around 40% of all TRQs between 2002 and 2008; more recent years may not be representative due to late notifications) no imports are notified, for various reasons.

13. This is the number of "physical" RTAs, each of which may include an agreement relating to goods, one on services and an accession to an RTA. If all these individual agreements are counted separately, 379 RTAs were in force mid-2014.

14. Australia, Brazil, Colombia, Iceland, Indonesia, Mexico, New Zealand, Panama, South Africa and Uruguay.

15. The source of the data used in this paragraph is (WTO, 2014d).

16. The most recent export subsidy notification for Turkey was 2000 and for Venezuela 1998.

17. Lists of rationales for imposing export restrictions are provided in Box 1 of Kim (2010) and Table 7 of Fliess and Mård (2012).

18. Liapis (2013) observes that "this may reflect the fact that more goods are classified as semi-processed rather than bulk".

19. Where the policy objective is a given degree (or increase) of self-sufficiency in food, quantities produced domestically or imported from abroad may be a relevant element. This policy orientation will be discussed in the next section.

20. The document also provides an overview of, and references to, all individual OECD studies on decoupling done over several years.

21. The surprisingly large production impact ratio of 2.16 found for payments based on output in one study has to do with the risk-reducing effect of the counter-cyclical component of this kind of payment in some countries, providing more risk protection than many forms of market price support.

22. At the time, sugar was not included in AGLINK.

23. In the second study, world prices for beef and veal (Mercosur market) rose by 2.4% at the end of the ten-year period studied, and for vegetable oils by nearly 2%. The butter price rose less and prices of cheese and skim milk powder more than in the first study.

24. It should be noted, again, that at the time sugar was not included in AGLINK.

25. The export impacts of payments based on output were also included in the analysis.

26. Other explanatory variables included in the regression analysis were exportable surplus and ending stocks.

27. See, for example, Headey and Fan (2008), Mitchell (2008), Wright (2009), Demeke, Pangrazio and Maetz (2009), Dawe and Slayton (2010), Headey (2011), Tananka and Hosoe (2011), Anderson (2012), Martin and Anderson (2012) or Anderson, Ivanic and Martin (2013).

28. In this citation, paragraph numbering and references to earlier sections of the report are omitted.

29. It must, though, not be forgotten that national trade policies to stabilise domestic markets have the tendency to destabilise international markets.

30. For a more comprehensive discussion of the interplay between national stockholding policies and trade measures, see Tangermann (2011).

31. For an overview of OECD work on multifunctionality up to 2006, see Abler (2008).

32. This view is obviously behind the notion, embedded in the preamble of the Agreement on Agriculture, that when making commitments under the Agreement all WTO members should have "regard to non-trade concerns, including food security and the need to protect the environment".

33. The most important findings of OECD work on risk management, as well as results of a number of country case studies, were published in OECD (2011).

34. Certain aspects related to societal concerns regarding food and agriculture were also dealt with in OECD (1999).

35. See for example the related document recently submitted to EU Ministers of Agriculture by the Italian Presidency of the European Union (2014).

36. One could debate the implications of resource constraints for "satisfactory" producer prices: where producers own the resources concerned (land, water), they benefit from rising rents.

37. The numbers suggested here are only illustrative, but their order of magnitude is derived from *Outlook* results regarding the rise in oil prices and the impact of oil prices on agricultural commodity prices (on the latter, see Figure 1.17 in OECD-FAO, 2012).

38. For a discussion of the "Indian problem", see Tangermann (2014) and the literature referenced there. Most of Sections 2 and 3 and a few other parts of the present chapter have been adopted in that paper.

References

Abler, D. (2008), "Multifunctionality in Agriculture: Evaluating the Degree of Jointness, Policy Implications", in OECD, *Multifunctionality in Agriculture: Evaluating the degree of jointness, policy implications*, OECD Publishing, Paris.
DOI: http://dx.doi.org/10.1787/9789264033627-2-en.

Anania, G. (2013), "Agricultural Export Restrictions and the WTO: What Options do Policy-Makers Have for Promoting Food Security?", *ICTSD Programme on Agricultural Trade and Sustainable Development, Issue Paper* No. 50. International Centre for Trade and Sustainable Development, Geneva.

Anderson, K. (2012), "Government trade restrictions and international price volatility", *Global Food Security*, Vol. 1, pp. 157-166.

Anderson, K., M. Ivanic and W. Martin (2013), "Food Price Spikes, Price Insulation, and Poverty", *NBER Working Paper* No. 19530, The World Bank, Development Research Group, Agriculture and Rural Development Group, Washington, DC.

Brink, L. (2015), "Current Domestic Policy Settings in the Context of Past and Potential International Agreements", in *Issues in Agricultural Trade Policy*, OECD, Paris.

Brooks, J. (ed.) (2012), *Agricultural Policies for Poverty Reduction*, OECD Publishing, Paris. DOI: http://dx.doi.org/10.1787/9789264112902-en.

Bureau, J. and S. Jean (2013), "The Impact of Regional Trade Agreements on Trade in Agricultural Products", *OECD Food, Agriculture and Fisheries Papers*, No. 65, OECD Publishing, Paris.
DOI: http://dx.doi.org/10.1787/5k3xznkz60vk-en.

Bureau, J. and S. Jean (2013b), *Do Yesterday's Disciplines Fit Today's Farm Trade? Challenges and Policy Options for the Bali Ministerial Conference*, Draft Issue Paper for the E15 Expert Group on Agriculture and Food Security, International Centre for Trade and Sustainable Development, Geneva.

Dawe, D. and T. Slayton (2010), "The World Rice Market Crisis of 2007-08", in D. Dawe (ed.), *The Rice Crisis – Markets, Policies and Food Security*, FAO and Earthscan, London, Washington, DC.

Demeke, M., G. Pangrazio and M. Maetz (2009), *Country Responses to the Food Security Crisis: Nature and Preliminary Implications of the Policies Pursued,* FAO Initiative on Soaring Food Prices, Food and Agriculture Organisation, Rome.

Deuss, A. (2015), "Review of the Performance and Impacts of Recent Stockholding Policies", in *Issues in Agricultural Trade Policy*, OECD, Paris.

Fliess, B. and T. Mård (2012), "Taking Stock of Measures Restricting the Export of Raw Materials: Analysis of OECD Inventory Data", *OECD Trade Policy Papers*, No. 140, OECD Publishing, Paris.
DOI: http://dx.doi.org/10.1787/5k91gdmdjbtc-en.

Fulponi, L., M. Shearer and J. Almeida (2011), "Regional Trade Agreements - Treatment of Agriculture", *OECD Food, Agriculture and Fisheries Papers*, No. 44, OECD Publishing, Paris.
DOI: http://dx.doi.org/10.1787/5kgg53fmnjxv-en.

Headey, D. (2011), Rethinking the global food crisis: The role of trade shocks. *Food Policy,* Vol. 36, pp. 136-146.

Headey, D. and S. Fan (2008), "Anatomy of a Crisis: The Causes and Consequences of Surging Food Prices", *Agricultural Economics*, Vol. 39, pp. 375-391.

Italian Presidency of the European Union (2014), *How Can EU Agriculture Contribute to the Food Security Challenge*. Background document for the informal Agrifish Council on 30.09.2014. Document 13364/14. Council of the European Union, Brussels.

Jacks, D.S. (2013), *From Boom to Bust: A Typology of Real Commodity Prices in the Long Run.* NBER Working Paper Series No. 18874. National Bureau of Economic Research, Cambridge MA.

Jones, D. and A. Kwiecinski (2010), "Policy Responses in Emerging Economies to International Agricultural Commodity Price Surges", *OECD Food, Agriculture and Fisheries Papers*, No. 34, OECD Publishing, Paris.
DOI: http://dx.doi.org/10.1787/5km6c61fv40w-en.

Josling, T., S. Tangermann and T. K. Warley (1996), *Agriculture in the GATT*, Houndmills, London, and Macmillan Press, New York.

Kim, J. (2010), "Recent Trends in Export Restrictions", *OECD Trade Policy Papers*, No. 101, OECD Publishing, Paris.
DOI: http://dx.doi.org/10.1787/5kmbjx63sl27-en.

Korinek, J., M. Melatos and M. Rau (2008), "A Review of Methods for Quantifying the Trade Effects of Standards in the Agri-Food Sector", *OECD Trade Policy Papers*, No. 79, OECD Publishing, Paris.
DOI: http://dx.doi.org/10.1787/235833787115.

Kubota, O. (2007), "Adjustment Options and Strategies in the Context of Agricultural Policy Reform and Trade Liberalisation", *OECD Food, Agriculture and Fisheries Papers*, No. 4, OECD Publishing, Paris.
DOI: http://dx.doi.org/10.1787/124462320780.

Liapis, P. (2013), "How Export Restrictive Measures Affect Trade of Agricultural Commodities", *OECD Food, Agriculture and Fisheries Papers*, No. 63, OECD Publishing, Paris.
DOI: http://dx.doi.org/10.1787/5k43mktw305f-en.

Martin, W. and K. Anderson (2012), "Export Restrictions and Price Insulation During Commodity Price Booms", *American Journal of Agricultural Economics,* Vol. 94 (2), pp. 422-427.

Mitchell, D. (2008), "A Note on Rising Food Prices", *Policy Research Working Paper* No. 4682. The World Bank, Washington, D.C.

OECD (2013a), *Agricultural Policy Monitoring and Evaluation 2013: OECD Countries and Emerging Economies*, OECD Publishing, Paris.
DOI: http://dx.doi.org/10.1787/agr_pol-2013-en.

OECD (2013b), *Policy Instruments to Support Green Growth in Agriculture*, OECD Green Growth Studies, OECD Publishing, Paris.
DOI: http://dx.doi.org/10.1787/9789264203525-en.

OECD (2013c), *Global Food Security: Challenges for the Food and Agricultural System*, OECD Publishing, Paris.
DOI: http://dx.doi.org/10.1787/9789264195363-en.

OECD (2011), *Managing Risk in Agriculture: Policy Assessment and Design*, OECD Publishing, Paris.
DOI: http://dx.doi.org/10.1787/9789264116146-en.

OECD (2010a), *An Assessment of International Commodity Agreements for Commodity Price Stabilisation*. Document TAD/CA/APM/WP(2010)36/FINAL, http://olisweb.oecd.org/vgn-ext-templating/TAD-CA-APM-WP(2010)36-FINAL-.ENG.pdf?docId=JT03302065&date=1305800918000&documentId=486364&organisationId=1&fileName=JT03302065.pdf .

OECD (2010b), *Policy Responses to Societal Concerns in Food and Agriculture*. Proceedings of an OECD Workshop. http://www.oecd.org/agriculture/agricultural-policies/46832852.pdf.

OECD (2008a), "Agricultural Policy Design and Implementation: A Synthesis", *OECD Food, Agriculture and Fisheries Papers*, No. 7, OECD Publishing, Paris.
DOI: http://dx.doi.org/10.1787/243786286663.

OECD (2008b), "A Cost-Benefit Framework for the Assessment of Non-Tariff Measures in Agro-Food Trade", *OECD Food, Agriculture and Fisheries Papers*, No. 21, OECD Publishing, Paris.
DOI: http://dx.doi.org/10.1787/220613725148.

OECD (2008), *Biofuel Support Policies: An Economic Assessment*, OECD Publishing, Paris.
DOI: http://dx.doi.org/10.1787/9789264050112-en.

OECD (2007a), *Agricultural Policy and Trade Reform: The Impact on World Commodity Markets*, OECD Publishing, Paris.
DOI: http://dx.doi.org/10.1787/9789264027886-en.

OECD (2007b), *Effective Targeting of Agricultural Policies: Best Practices for Policy Design and Implementation*, OECD Publishing, Paris.
DOI: http://dx.doi.org/10.1787/9789264038288-en.

OECD (2007c), "The Role of Compensation in Policy Reform", *OECD Food, Agriculture and Fisheries Papers*, No. 5, OECD Publishing, Paris.
DOI: http://dx.doi.org/10.1787/125487536033.

OECD (2006a), "Decoupling: Policy Implications", *OECD Papers*, Vol. 5/11.
DOI: http://dx.doi.org/10.1787/oecd_papers-v5-art38-en.

OECD (2006b), *Agricultural Policy and Trade Reform: Potential Effects at Global, National and Household Levels*, OECD Publishing, Paris.
DOI: http://dx.doi.org/10.1787/9789264025745-en.

OECD (2004), *A Review and Analysis of Export Competition Measures*. OECD internal document, 24 September.

OECD (2003a), *Farm Household Income: Issues and Policy Responses*, OECD Publishing, Paris.
DOI: http://dx.doi.org/10.1787/9789264099678-en.

OECD (2003b), *Multifunctionality: The Policy Implications*, OECD Publishing, Paris.
DOI: http://dx.doi.org/10.1787/9789264104532-en.

OECD (2002a), *Agriculture and Trade Liberalisation: Extending the Uruguay Round Agreement*, OECD Publishing, Paris.
DOI: http://dx.doi.org/10.1787/9789264196292-en.

OECD (2002b), *Measuring the Trade Effects of the SPS Agreement*. Document COM/AGR/TD/WP(2002)71/FINAL,
http://www.oecd.org/officialdocuments/publicdisplaydocumentpdf/?cote=COM/AGR/TD/WP(2002)71/FINAL&docLanguage=En.

OECD (2003), *The Impact of Regulations on Agro-Food Trade: The Technical Barriers to Trade (TBT) and Sanitary and Phytosanitary Measures (SPS) Agreements*, OECD Publishing, Paris.
DOI: http://dx.doi.org/10.1787/9789264105423-en.

OECD (2001), OECD (2001), *Market Effects of Crop Support Measures*, OECD Publishing, Paris. DOI: http://dx.doi.org/10.1787/9789264195011-en.

OECD (1999), *Food Safety and Quality: Trade Considerations*, OECD Publishing, Paris. DOI: http://dx.doi.org/10.1787/9789264174115-en.

OECD/FAO (2014), *OECD-FAO Agricultural Outlook 2014*, OECD Publishing, Paris. DOI: http://dx.doi.org/10.1787/agr_outlook-2014-en.

OECD/FAO (2012), *OECD-FAO Agricultural Outlook 2012*, OECD Publishing, Paris. DOI: http://dx.doi.org/10.1787/agr_outlook-2012-en.

Swinnen, J.F.M., and P. Squicciarini (2012), "Mixed Messages on Prices and Food Security", *Science*, Vol. 335, No. 6067, pp. 405 - 406.

Tanaka, T. and N. Hosoe (2011), "Does agricultural trade liberalization increase risks of supply-side uncertainty? Effects of productivity shocks and export restrictions on welfare and food supply in Japan", *Food Policy*, Vol. 36, pp. 368-377.

Tangermann, S. (2002), "Agriculture on the Way to Firm International Trading Rules", in Daniel L.M. Kennedy and James D. Southwick (eds.), *The Political Economy of International Trade Law. Essays in Honor of Robert E. Hudec,* Cambridge University Press, Cambridge.

Tangermann, S. (2005), "Is the Concept of the Producer Support Estimate in Need of Revision?", *OECD Food, Agriculture and Fisheries Papers*, No. 1, OECD Publishing, Paris. DOI: http://dx.doi.org/10.1787/845314770374.

Tangermann, S. (2011), *Policy Solutions to Agricultural Market Volatility: A Synthesis.* ICTSD Programme on Agricultural Trade and Sustainable Development, Issue Paper No. 33, International Centre for Trade and Sustainable Development, Geneva.

Tangermann, S. (2014), *Agriculture: Food Security and Trade Liberalization.* Paper prepared for the conference on "Challenges Facing the World Trade System" organized by J. Bhagwati, P. Krishna and A. Panagariya, Columbia University, New York, and Johns Hopkins University (SAIS), 29 September – 2 October, Washington, DC.

Thompson, W. and G. Tallard (2010), "Potential Market Effects of Selected Policy Options in Emerging Economies to Address Future Commodity Price Surges", *OECD Food, Agriculture and Fisheries Papers*, No. 35, OECD Publishing, Paris. DOI: http://dx.doi.org/10.1787/5km658j3r85b-en.

Tothova, M. (2009), "The Trade and Trade Policy Implications of Different Policy Responses to Societal Concerns", *OECD Food, Agriculture and Fisheries Papers*, No. 20, OECD Publishing, Paris. DOI: http://dx.doi.org/10.1787/221782147025.

van Tongeren, F., et al. (2010), "Case Studies of Costs and Benefits of Non-Tariff Measures: Cheese, Shrimp and Flowers", *OECD Food, Agriculture and Fisheries Papers*, No. 28, OECD Publishing, Paris. DOI: http://dx.doi.org/10.1787/5kmbt57jjhwl-en.

von Lampe, M. and H. Jeong (2013), "Design and Implementation of Food-Import Related Regulations: Experiences from Some Regional Trade Agreements", *OECD Food, Agriculture and Fisheries Papers*, No. 62, OECD Publishing, Paris. DOI: http://dx.doi.org/10.1787/5k44s9v9m86f-en.

Wright, B.D. (2009), "International Grains Reserves and Other Instruments to Address Volatility in Grain Markets", *World Bank Policy Research Working Paper* No. 5028, The World Bank, Washington, DC.

WTO (2014a), *Tariff Profiles, Summary Tables Download Facility*, WTO, Geneva. Available at http://stat.wto.org/TariffProfile/WSDBTariffPFReporter.aspx?Language=E.

WTO (2014b), *Trade Monitoring Database* WTO, Geneva. Available at http://tmdb.wto.org/.

WTO (2014c), Regional Trade Agreements, WTO, Geneva. http://www.wto.org/english/tratop_e/region_e/region_e.htm.

WTO (2014d), "Export Subsidies, Export Credits, Export Credit Guarantees or Insurance Programmes, International Food Aid and Agricultural Export State Trading Enterprises", Background Document by the Secretariat, Documents G/AG/W/125 and addenda 1, 2, 3 and 4, 21 May, WTO, Geneva.

WTO (2014e), "Annual Export Competition Review: Submission from the Cairns Group to the 74th Meeting of the Committee on Agriculture (COA) in June 2014", Document G/AG/W/129, 2 June, WTO, Geneva.

WTO (2013a), "Report (2013) of the Committee on Safeguards to the Council for Trade in Goods", Document G/L/1054, 29 October, WTO, Geneva.

WTO (2013b), "Tariff Quota Administration Methods and Fill Rates 2002-2011", Background Paper by the Secretariat, Document TN/AG/S/26/Rev.1, 28 March 2013, WTO, Geneva.

WTO (2013c), "Export Competition – Ministerial Declaration of 7 December 2013", Document WT/MIN(13)/40, 11 December, WTO, Geneva.

WTO (2011), *World Trade Report 2011: The WTO and preferential trade agreements: From co-existence to coherence*, WTO, Geneva.

WTO, ITC and UNCTAD (2013), *World Tariff Profiles 2013*. Geneva: WTO. Data available at http://stat.wto.org/TariffProfile/WSDBTariffPFHome.aspx?Language=E.

WTO, ITC and UNCTAD (2008), *World Tariff Profiles 2008*, WTO, Geneva.

Chapter 3

Current domestic policy settings in the context of past and potential international agreements

by
Lars Brink[1]

This chapter considers what is allowed or required under the rules and commitments of the Agreement on Agriculture (AoA) of the WTO and what could be allowed or required under the rules and commitments of an agreement corresponding to the draft modalities arrived at in 2008 under the Doha Development Agenda (DDA) of the WTO. The chapter also discusses some issues not addressed in the AoA or the draft modalities but which have come to the fore in the years since, such as at the 2013 WTO Ministerial conference. The purpose is to help to assess the pertinence of the draft modalities for the continued negotiations in agriculture.

3.1. Introduction

It is of interest to compare current or recent agriculture and trade policies of selected countries against actual or potential rules and commitments under the World Trade Organization (WTO). This chapter specifically considers what is allowed or required under the rules and commitments of the 1994 Agreement on Agriculture (AoA) of the WTO and what could be allowed or required under the rules and commitments of an agreement corresponding to the draft modalities arrived at in 2008 under the Doha Development Agenda (DDA) of the WTO (hereafter Rev.4).[2] It also discusses some issues not addressed in the AoA or the draft modalities but which have come to the fore in the years since, such as at the 2013 WTO Ministerial conference. The purpose is to help to assess the pertinence of the draft modalities for the continued negotiations in agriculture.

The chapter proceeds by reviewing each of the three "pillars" in the AoA and Rev.4: market access, export competition and domestic support. It summarises the major provisions under each pillar, and then reviews the status of the policy settings in each of several countries in comparison to what the rules and commitments of Rev.4 would require. This is followed by a discussion of several related issues, including that of acquiring food stocks at administered prices, which was prominent in the 2013 Ministerial conference and in subsequent WTO activities.

The chapter examines 20 countries, some in less depth than others.[3] The varying depth depends to some extent on the availability of data for a country. The 20 countries are Argentina, Brazil, Canada, China, the European Union (EU), India, Indonesia, Japan, Korea, Mexico, Nigeria, Norway, the Philippines, the Russian Federation, South Africa, Switzerland, Thailand, Turkey, the United States, and Viet Nam.[4] These countries accounted for 83% of gross production value in world agriculture in 2012 (calculated from FAO 2015). Some of the characteristics of these countries related to reviewing WTO rules and commitments are shown in **Table 2.1** (terms and abbreviations are explained later in this chapter).

In the AoA and the agriculture negotiations, a distinction is made between developed and developing countries. The WTO does not define which countries fall into which category. In agriculture, the following 13 countries are considered to be among the developing countries: Argentina, Brazil, China, India, Indonesia, Korea, Mexico, Nigeria, the Philippines, South Africa, Thailand, Turkey and Viet Nam. The following seven countries are considered to be among the developed countries: Canada, European Union, Japan, Norway, Russia, Switzerland, and the United States. The WTO recognises as least-developed countries (LDCs) those countries that have been designated as such by the United Nations. None of the 20 countries in this study is an LDC.

Many of the provisions in Rev.4 are worded in an unclear or ambiguous way. This is of course necessary in a negotiating document but opens the door to countries interpreting the provisions differently. Legal expertise would be required to convert Rev.4 provisions into a legally binding agreement. This missing step thus reduces to some extent the confidence attaching to any review of countries' positioning in relation to Rev.4 rules and commitments.

3.2. Background

Timeline towards the draft modalities and Bali

What is referred to here as policy is in reality a number of policy settings, such as the rules, constraints, or parameters imposed by governments under legislation, regulation, decree, administrative practice, etc. This may fall under the labels of a country's agricultural policy or trade policy or some other policy label. The policy settings of interest are those that are governed by the AoA and would be governed by a new agreement incorporating the specifics of the draft modalities. Some policy settings are as simple to compare to a commitment as an applied tariff relative to a bound tariff commitment. The complexity in this case comes from the large number of tariff lines. Other policy settings are not so directly governed by WTO commitments: in domestic support, the commitments operate on calculated applied support of a certain kind, and there are usually many policy settings working together to generate the support that is subject to a limit.

The Uruguay Round of trade negotiations resulted in a number of trade agreements and the establishment of the WTO in 1995. The AoA sets rules for trade and domestic policies in agriculture or for their effects. WTO members implemented their legally binding AoA commitments in market access, export competition and domestic support over the period 1995-2000 (for developed countries) and 1995-2004 (for developing countries). The 2000 or 2004 levels, respectively, have since remained as members' final bound commitments, inscribed in each member's WTO schedule of concessions and commitments. Members that have acceded to the WTO since 1995 have bound commitments from the year of accession, in some cases reaching their final bound level a few years after the year of their accession.

The AoA required negotiations to continue the process of agreeing "substantial progressive reductions in support and protection resulting in fundamental reform" in agriculture to begin in 1999 (WTO, 1995, Article 20). Those negotiations were then incorporated into the Doha Development Agenda (DDA) of wider trade negotiations, which was launched in 2001. By December 2008, the DDA had produced a set of so-called "draft modalities" in agriculture (WTO, 2008a). The WTO Secretariat explains that the draft modalities "contain formulas for cutting tariffs and trade-distorting subsidies and related provisions" and that they are the "chairperson's judgement of what members might be able to agree", based on what they had proposed and debated in the negotiations (WTO, 2008e).

The 2008 draft modalities are just that – only a draft and only modalities. They outline how a country is to arrive at its new commitments but they do not define the resulting commitments. This means that the draft modalities need to be interpreted in order to estimate what the corresponding commitments would be. The interpretation has to be made on the basis of only partial information and is both subjective and imperfect. Moreover, everything in the draft modalities "is conditional in the deepest sense" and "[c]ertain things are manifestly not yet agreed" (WTO, 2008a).

With the DDA negotiations having reached an impasse after 2008, Ministers agreed at the WTO Ministerial Conference in 2011 to advance the negotiations by focussing on certain issues on which Ministers agreed progress could be achieved. At the subsequent Ministerial Conference in December 2013 in Bali, Indonesia, Ministers adopted DDA decisions on four issues under the heading of agriculture: general services, public stockholding for food security purposes, tariff rate quota administration, and export competition. A decision by the WTO General Council in November 2014 laid down further precision and substance on the Bali decision on public stockholding.[5] These decisions, along with several other decisions outside of agriculture, are seen as the key to unlocking the DDA impasse.

Context for examining countries' positioning

With the passage of time, both since the entry into force of most WTO members' commitments in 2000 or 2004 and since the drafting of the 2008 draft modalities, international agricultural markets and countries' agricultural and trade policies have changed, in some cases significantly (OECD 2014a, 2014b). These developments motivate an examination of how countries are currently positioned in terms of their policy settings relative to the AoA commitments and to the commitments that would result if the provisions of the 2008 draft modalities were implemented. This examination also encompasses a discussion of the implications of the Bali decisions in agriculture.

Table 3.1. Attributes of studied countries

Country	OECD		WTO		Bound Total AMS	*de minimis* %	Export subsidy commitment	Number of TRQs	SSG as % of tariff lines	Mention in Rev.4
	In OECD	OECD M&E	Develop-ing	RAM or VRAM						
Argentina	-	-	Dg	-	BTAMS	10	-	-	-	-
Brazil	-	M&E	Dg	-	BTAMS	10	XS	2	-	-
Canada	OECD	M&E	-	-	BTAMS	5	XS	21	10%	6%, not 4%, as sensitive products
China (People's Republic of)	-	M&E	Dg	RAM	-	8.5	-	?	-	-
European Union	OECD	M&E	-	-	BTAMS	5	XS	87+	31%	85% (not 90%) as *ad val.* for tariff simplification
India	-	-	Dg	-	-	10	-	-	-	-
Indonesia	-	M&E	Dg	-	-	10	XS	2	1%	-
Japan	OECD	M&E	-	-	BTAMS	5	-	20	12%	8%, not 4%, as sensitive products
Korea	OECD	M&E	Dg	-	BTAMS	10	-	67	8%	-
Mexico	OECD	M&E	Dg	-	BTAMS	10	XS	11	29%	-
Nigeria	-	-	Dg	-	-	10	-	-	-	-
Norway	OECD	M&E	-	-	BTAMS	5	XS	232	49%	-
Philippines	-	-	Dg	-	-	10	-	14	13%	-
Russia	-	M&E	-	?	BTAMS	5	-	-	?	No mention in Rev.4. RAM? VRAM?
South Africa	-	M&E	Dg	-	BTAMS	10	XS	53	39%	-
Switzerland	OECD	M&E	-	-	BTAMS	5	XS	28	59%	Some tariffs above 100%
Thailand	-	-	Dg	-	BTAMS	10	-	23	11%	-
Turkey	OECD	M&E	Dg	-	-	10	XS	-	-	-
United States	OECD	M&E	-	-	BTAMS	5	XS	54	9%	PS AMS, PS blue
Viet Nam	-	M&E	Dg	VRAM	BTAMS	10	-	?	?	No reduction: OTDS, TAMS, *de minimis*, bound tariffs, in-quota tariffs

Notes: M&E: OECD monitoring and evaluation; Dg: developing; RAM: recently acceded member; VRAM: very recently acceded member; XS: export subsidy commitment; TRQ: tariff rate quota; SSG: special safeguard under AoA.

Source: Author's interpretation of relevant documents; TRQs: TN/AG/S/7; SSG: TN/AG/S/12.

The examination necessarily works with numerous hypothetical or artificial variables. Although information on countries' policy settings relates to situations several years prior to 2014, it is assumed that it adequately represents the situation in 2014. If agreement on the draft modalities of Rev.4 had been reached in 2014, time would be needed to translate the modalities of Rev.4 into a new agreement to replace or amend the AoA, which would probably allow a new or amended agreement to enter into force in 2016 at the earliest. Many of the new commitments specified in Rev.4 would then be phased in over several years before reaching their final bound levels. This examination nevertheless treats the final bound levels as if they were to apply in 2014.

3.3. Market access

Agreement on Agriculture

Under the AoA, countries replaced non-tariff border measures on imports with tariffs. Access opportunities are in some cases ensured by tariff rate quotas (TRQs): imports up to the given quota quantity can enter with a low or zero tariff rate and imports above the quota enter with a higher tariff rate. For many products where tariffs replaced non-tariff measures, a number of countries have the right to use a "special safeguard" in agriculture to impose an additional tariff if certain conditions are met regarding import volumes or prices. Some countries saw the ability to invoke the special safeguard as a necessary part of replacing non-tariff measures with tariffs.

Special rules for the imports of rice applied to Japan and Korea (and to Israel for sheepmeat and certain dairy products) for a certain period, and continue to apply for the Philippines. The rules include provisions for progressively increasing import quotas. Japan does not apply the special rules since 1999, Korea appears to have ceased application at the end of 2014, and the Philippines has negotiated a timeline to end on 30 June 2017 (WTO 2014h). The Philippines has increased the quota on rice imports and is reducing the in-quota tariff (WTO 2014g).[6] Its country-specific quotas are allocated to China, India, Thailand and Viet Nam, among others. The quotas available to Thailand and Viet Nam are several times larger than those of other suppliers. At the expiration of the special rules, the Philippines will apply ordinary customs duties to imports of rice.

Draft modalities

General

The Rev.4 provisions on market access concern tariffs and TRQs. Many countries would reduce bound tariffs, expand TRQs or introduce additional TRQs. Developing countries would generally be allowed lower or fewer tariff reductions and TRQ expansions. Different groups of products would be subject to provisions differing from the general ones, such as sensitive products, special products, commodities, tropical and diversification products, products subject to tariff escalation provisions, and products identified under long-standing preferences and preference erosion. Different groups of countries would enjoy different and usually less onerous treatment than the general rule, such as recently acceded countries, very recently acceded countries, small vulnerable economies and LDCs. The latter two groups are not represented in this report. Some countries are identified by name for particular treatment, while particular treatment is also provided for countries not identified by name but meeting certain characteristics. Rev.4 would apply specific procedures to certain issues, such as tariff simplification, and it would introduce rules that differ from those in the AoA and are available only to developing countries, such as a special safeguard mechanism.[7]

Altogether, it is impossible to specify the full effects of the Rev.4 market access provisions on individual countries' commitments. This is partly because of the complexity and overlapping nature of the market access provisions themselves, partly because of the menu of choices offered for some provisions, and partly because the outcome of the application of some provisions depends on data that is not publicly available. Countries are usually not forthcoming about the commitments they would take under rules that are still subject to negotiation and agreement. The following draws on a selection of publications that help shed light on some of the commitments individual countries may take under rules that are more or less similar to those of Rev.4.

Specifics on tariffs

The average of all the tariff cuts a developed country would make under Rev.4 is at least 54%. This would be achieved as the combined result of harmonising tariff cuts according to a tiered formula (where tariffs in a higher tier are cut by more than tariffs in a lower tier), treatment of sensitive products, cuts relating to tariff escalation and tropical products, and any additional cuts needed to reach the 54% target. The average of all the tariff cuts a developing country would make is no more than 36%. If the combined result of harmonising tariff cuts according to the tiered formula and the treatment of sensitive products implies an average cut of more than 36%, a developing country may apply lesser reductions proportionately across the tiers of the formula. Different rules apply to small vulnerable economies and to some other developing countries.

The harmonising tariff cuts under the tiered formula for developed countries range from 50% to 70%, depending on the level of the bound tariff being cut (**Table 3.2**). The top tier of tariffs, which face cuts by 70%, includes tariffs from 75% and up. The corresponding cuts for developing countries range from 33.3% to 46.9%. The top tier of tariffs to be cut by 46.9% includes tariffs from 130% and up (**Table 3.3**). A given bound tariff, such as 100%, will thus be placed in the highest tier for cuts by developed countries but only in the second highest tier for developing countries. Still gentler tariff cuts would be required from recently acceded developing countries, and very recently acceded countries would not be required to cut tariffs at all.

Table 3.2. Tariff cuts under harmonising tiered formula for developed countries

Paragraph in Rev.4	Thresholds for bound tariff	Tariff cut
Tier 61(a)	0-20%	50%
Tier 61(b)	20-50%	57%
Tier 61 (c)	50-75%	64%
Tier 61 (d)	More than 75%	70%

Source: Author's interpretation of WTO (2008a).

Table 3.3. Tariff cuts under harmonising tiered formula for developing countries

Paragraph in Rev.4	Thresholds for bound tariff	Tariff cut	
		Not recently acceded	Recently acceded (a)
Tier 63(a)	0-30%	33.3%	25.3% (b)
Tier 63(b)	30-80%	38%	30%
Tier 63 (c)	80-130%	42.7%	34.7%
Tier 63 (d)	More than 130%	46.9%	38.9%

Notes: (a) No cuts for very recently acceded countries (Viet Nam; Russia's status not identified).
(b) No cut if bound tariff is less than 10%.
Source: Author's interpretation of WTO (2008a).

Sensitive products and tariff rate quotas

Both developed and developing countries have the right to designate a number of tariff lines as sensitive products. The number corresponds to a given share of the country's tariff lines. The share is given as 4.00% for developed countries and 5.33% for developing countries. However, additional flexibility is allowed for Japan and Canada and for countries with bound tariffs structured by tariff line in a particular way, a group usually thought to comprise Norway, Switzerland and Iceland. More elaborate provisions are contemplated in a companion paper to Rev.4 (WTO 2008b). There may or may not be a requirement that sensitive products be only those for which TRQs already exist. The designation of sensitive products plays a role in determining the tariff cuts and the size of the TRQ expansion a country would undertake.

For sensitive products, Rev.4 indicates that tariff cuts may be smaller than according to the tiered formula but they must then be accompanied by increases in TRQs. Rev.4 specifies the relationship between tariff cuts and TRQ expansion, and the determination of the size of the TRQ expansion, which is determined in relation to a percentage of a country's domestic consumption. Detailed procedures are laid down regarding such things as the relationship between a product and the tariff lines associated with it, the measurement of domestic consumption of different products at particular levels of disaggregation, and the provision of necessary data for the 2003-05 period. The elaborate and data-intensive procedures seem designed to allow transparency for negotiators (but not necessarily the public) and to facilitate verification of the TRQ expansion that countries would undertake in their schedules. This may be an attempt to forestall a parallel to what, after the Uruguay Round, became known as "dirty tariffication".

The norm for TRQ expansion is that TRQs would be increased by at least 4% of domestic consumption if the tariff cut is smaller than the formula cut by a certain share. Deviating from the formula cut by less than that share is "rewarded" by having to increase the TRQ by less than 4% of consumption. Developing countries would, in similar circumstances, need to increase TRQs by a smaller extent than developed countries. Numerous other provisions allow for more or less flexibility in particular situations. For example, designation of a larger number of tariff lines (2 percentage points more) would be possible if accompanied by a larger TRQ expansion on those tariff lines. Moreover, Japan, Norway and Switzerland may be allowed a larger number of sensitive products than otherwise would be the case in exchange for a larger TRQ expansion or deeper or faster tariff cuts.[8] Also, developed countries with tariffs above 100%, or developing countries with tariffs above 150% after reduction would not be able to keep the tariffs at those levels unless the tariff was for a sensitive product and a particular TRQ expansion was undertaken.

Rev.4 specifies two alternative rules regarding the products that could be designated as sensitive and have a TRQ: either only those that had a TRQ before Rev.4, or any product. A companion paper to Rev.4 elaborates on this issue and outlines some constrained flexibility for the creation of new TRQs (WTO 2008c). Special rules would apply for Norway.

Developed countries would reduce certain bound in-quota tariff rates by 50% or to 10% (with some extra flexibility for Switzerland). Low in-quota rates would be cut to zero. Developing countries would reduce bound in-quota rates by 15%. The corresponding reduction for recently acceded countries would be 5%, and very recently acceded countries would not be required to reduce in-quota tariff rates at all.

Special products, tariff escalation, tariff simplification

Developing countries would be able to designate certain products as special products (which is different from the sensitive product designation). In the general case, up to 12% of the country's tariff lines could be so designated, based on 12 specific criteria for food security, livelihood security and rural development. The tariff cuts on these products would average 11%. A percentage of products would see no tariff cuts. Recently acceded countries could designate a slightly larger share of tariff lines as special products and would cut tariffs by slightly less. The 12 criteria for food security, livelihood and rural development include a wide variety of indicators, such as whether the product is a staple food in some way, or accounts for a large share of domestic consumption, production, employment, income, or expenditure, or it was notified as receiving certain kinds of domestic support by any WTO member and the product was exported by that member in any year between 1995 and 2001.[9]

Developed countries and perhaps some developing countries would cut tariffs by more than the formula cut on certain products identified in Rev.4 as being subject to tariff escalation treatment. Processed products with tariffs higher than the corresponding primary product would in many cases take the tariff cut of the tier above the tier where it belongs. Some moderating rules apply to this treatment. Moreover, this tariff escalation treatment does not apply to sensitive products. In cases where formula cuts and tariff escalation treatment do not eliminate tariff escalation, Rev.4 requires countries to engage with commodity-dependent producing countries to ensure satisfactory solutions.

Some countries express their tariffs on some products in other forms than *ad valorem*. Rev.4 requires the conversion of tariffs into *ad valorem* tariffs, subject to given methodological terms and conditions. Either all of a country's tariffs would be converted, or 90% of its tariffs would first be converted, followed by a review and a later decision on how to convert the remainder. The European Union would be able to retain 5% of tariffs as compound or mixed tariffs. Rev.4 foresees that some complex forms of bound tariffs (composition matrices) can be converted to specific tariffs. These tariff simplification provisions are thought to be aimed particularly at the European Union, which uses composition matrices for its tariffs on some products to a greater extent than most other countries. The method for converting tariffs to *ad valorem* tariffs depends on the use of import unit values from 1999-2001 and follows detailed procedures that were first circulated in 2005. The specificity of the procedures and the data are thought to be designed so as to ensure that all countries use the same data and procedures, which increases everyone's confidence in the results. A verification procedure is nevertheless built into the tariff simplification process. Even if a country does not convert all its non-*ad valorem* tariffs to *ad valorem* form, an *ad valorem* expression is needed in order to place the tariff in the appropriate tier for reduction.

Special agricultural safeguard, tropical products, preferences

Among the 20 countries in this study, 15 have commitments on a total of 668 tariff rate quotas in agriculture.[10] Most or perhaps all of the tariff lines with TRQs can apply the special agricultural safeguard (SSG) against imports. Rev.4 foresees first reducing the share of tariff lines eligible for the SSG to 1% of tariff lines for developed countries, and then eliminating the SSG. Developing countries would reduce the share to 2.5% of tariff lines but would not need to eliminate the SSG.

Rev.4 identifies numerous tropical and diversification products. Developed countries would undertake tariff cuts for these products under one of two alternative provisions, both of which occur over and above the tariff cuts resulting from the formula cuts. For products with tariffs below 25% (in one provision) or below 10% (in the other provision), the tariff would be reduced to zero. For products with the highest tariffs, the percentage cuts would be greater than those corresponding to the highest tariff tier in the tiered formula.

Rev.4 identifies about 54 products at the six-digit tariff line level under the heading "Long-standing preferences and preference erosion": it specifies that the tariff cuts for these products would be delayed by a certain number of years or would be implemented more slowly than otherwise would be the case.

Special safeguard mechanism

Rev.4 provides for a new "special safeguard mechanism" (SSM) to be available to developing countries only (the conditional nature of Rev.4 may apply particularly to its SSM provisions). It would use volume triggers for increases in a tariff by a given percentage or a given number of percentage points: the larger the import volume above a given threshold, the larger the allowed tariff increase. It would use price triggers for increases in the tariff by 85% of the difference between the trigger price and the import price. Some conditions and limitations would apply on the use of the SSM. A Rev.4 companion paper provides additional specificity on some aspects of SSM (WTO 2008d). Some of the issues discussed in the negotiations concern how long the SSM tariff could be applied and how it would relate to the pre-Rev.4 tariff binding. This latter issue is particularly relevant where all or some of a country's tariffs are not reduced under Rev.4: applying the SSM could raise the applied tariff above its pre-Rev.4 bound level.

Bali decision

At the conference in 2013, Ministers decided on an understanding on TRQ administration provisions in agriculture (WTO 2013e). In many cases, a country's imports under the TRQ regime for a product are consistently much below the quota quantity. Reasons for this include low supply of the product from exporters and a large domestic supply in the country applying the TRQ. It is also thought that the way the quota is administered can be a barrier to imports and result in this underfill.

Under the TRQ decision, in a situation of persistent underfill and where information-sharing and consultations have proven fruitless, the importing country would have to provide unencumbered access up to the quota limit through one of two prescribed methods (developing countries may also continue to use their existing method). In the process leading to this step, a fill rate threshold of 65% plays an important role. Several countries, including the United States, have opted out of applying the decision.

Market access situation

Changes in bindings

Countries' tariff bindings in recent years are, in most cases, the same as in 2000 (for developed countries) and in 2004 (for developing countries), the years by which the final bound commitment levels of the Uruguay Round were reached. In some situations, the bindings today (2014) are different from those in 2000 or 2004. This is the case where countries have renegotiated some of their bindings under the rules of the WTO, such as those relating to customs unions and free trade areas and to modification of schedules (Articles XXIV and XXVIII of the GATT of 1994). Other examples of tariff bindings changing over time are the following.

- The EU as a customs union has added member states since 2000, and some EU tariff or TRQ bindings in agriculture have likely been renegotiated in that context.
- The EU is reducing tariffs on some banana imports as part of the resolution of a WTO dispute.
- Japan and Korea abandoned quantitative import restrictions on rice only some years after the usual 1995 tariffication by other countries.
- Canada negotiated the introduction in 2009 of a TRQ regime for certain milk protein substances.
- India negotiated the introduction of TRQs for several product groups and products in agriculture.
- Countries that have acceded to the WTO since 2000 or 2004 often have tariff bindings that have been or are being phased down to their final bound level.
  - China, having acceded in 2001, completed its tariff reductions before 2014.
  - Viet Nam, having acceded in 2007, completed most of its tariff reductions by 2014.
  - Russian Federation, having acceded in 2012, implements some tariff reductions over several years.

For all these reasons, a country's recent profile of tariff bindings is in many cases not identical to the profile in 2000 or 2004, but overall the differences are likely only minor.

Table 3.4. Selected elements of tariff profiles in agriculture

Country	Tariffs in agriculture %				Share of agriculture tariff lines with TRQ	"Bound duty free" tariff lines in each of ten product groups		"Applied duty free" tariff lines in each of ten product groups	
	Average bound	Average applied	Diff. in points (bound less applied)	Trade-weighted average		Lowest share in any product group	Highest share in any product group	Lowest share in any product group	Highest share in any product group
Argentina	32.6	10.1	22.5	11.7	0.0%	0.7%	0.7%	6%	15%
Brazil	35.4	10.2	25.2	9.9	0.2%	0.4%	8%	2%	15%
Canada	16.8	15.9	0.9	13.9	9.5%	8%	90%	29%	100%
China (People's Republic of)	15.8	15.6	0.2	19.7	5.0%	2%	10%	2%	14%
EU27	13.5	13.2	0.3	8.4	11.3%	6%	100%	14%	100%
India	113.5	33.5	80.0	51.6	0.9%	0%	0%	1%	80%
Indonesia	47.0	7.5	39.5	4.3	1.0%	0%	0%	6%	20%
Japan	19.0	19.0	0	12.1	6.2%	7%	100%	6%	100%
Korea	56.0	52.7	3.3	91.8	13.5%	0.4%	9%	0.2%	100%
Mexico	45.1	19.7	25.4	31.3	6.9%	1%	2%	3%	100%
Nigeria	150.0	15.6	134.4	10.1	0.0%	0%	0%	0%	0%
Norway	135.2	51.3	83.9	36.2	30.6%	9%	100%	13%	100%
Philippines	35.1	9.9	25.4	10.7	9.2%	0%	0%	3%	3%
Russia	11.1	12.2	-1.1	14.7	3.2%	0.2%	100%	4%	100%
South Africa	40.4	8.4	32.0	9.2	36.0%	4%	55%	9%	88%
Switzerland	52.6	35.7	16.9	30.1	17.5%	3%	100%	11%	100%
Thailand	38.9	29.9	9.0	27.8	7.4%	2%	14%	1%	100%
Turkey	61.0	42.4	18.6	30.7	0.0%	0.2%	0.2%	1%	100%
United States	4.9	5.3	-0.4	4.1	4.5%	0.3%	59%	0.3%	61%
Viet Nam	19.1	16.2	2.9	7.7	1.1%	1%	24%	8%	44%

Source: WTO (2015)

Tariff profiles

While the bound tariffs are important in describing the market access conditions a country must offer under WTO rules, most countries apply lower tariffs on at least some tariff lines. Some countries apply tariffs below the bound tariffs on many products in agriculture. Keeping these circumstances in mind, the following picture of countries' bound and applied tariffs is developed on the basis of the WTO Tariff Profiles (WTO 2015). **Table 3.4** summarises the Tariff Profile data for the countries in this study. The applied tariffs are in most cases those of 2013. While a full-fledged analysis would review data on individual tariff lines, the present analysis in some situations looks at the average tariff in each of ten product groups in agriculture.

In implementing the tariff cuts under Rev.4, countries would reduce their bound tariffs over a number of years. Almost all countries in the study have at least some tariff lines on which they apply a lower tariff than the tariff bound in their WTO schedule. The extent of such "binding overhang" varies from country to country. Japan's profile shows no binding overhang. The US tariff profile shows very similar bound and applied rates in agriculture (it is not obvious why applied rates are higher than bound rates).[11] Among the countries with a positive difference, China and the European Union show only small differences (0.2 and 0.3 percentage points) between bound and applied tariffs in agriculture and Norway shows the largest difference (83.6 percentage points). The size of the difference matters. A country may see itself affected by a cut in a bound tariff because it would reduce its flexibility to raise the applied tariff in the future. A more direct effect arises when the cut in the bound tariff is large enough to force a reduction also in the applied tariff.[12] For a given percentage reduction in the bound tariff, this is obviously more likely to occur when the difference between the bound and the applied tariffs is small, as for China and the EU, and to some extent also for Canada and the United States.

The tariff profiles of all the countries in this study, except Argentina and Turkey, show the presence of TRQs in agriculture to a varying extent. In some situations a product with a TRQ also enjoys a high over-quota tariff, but this is not always the case. Depending on how countries select their sensitive and special products under Rev.4, TRQs would need to be expanded and in-quota tariffs reduced. The countries for which the rules about TRQs matter the most, because they have TRQs on a large share of their tariff lines, include South Africa (36% of tariff lines in agriculture), Norway (31%), Switzerland (18%), Korea (14%) and the European Union (11%).

Some countries with TRQs on only a small share of tariff lines may rely particularly on those TRQs for import protection in a given product sector and would thus be particularly affected by a TRQ expansion or a reduction of the in-quota tariff. This may be the case for Canada, which has during the DDA vigorously resisted a weakening of its import protection in certain sectors, such as dairy.

Extent of tariff reductions under the draft modalities

The effects of Rev.4 or Rev.4-like cuts on countries' applied tariff levels have been estimated in several studies. The benchmark work for this report is that of Laborde et al. (2011), which explicitly covers most, but not all, of the individual countries of interest here. The countries not mentioned are Argentina, the Philippines (possibly part of "Rest of Southeast Asia"), Korea (mentioned along with Chinese Taipei), and Norway and Switzerland (both as part of "Rest of Europe", which would include also Iceland), and Russia and Viet Nam (both have acceded to the WTO more recently than China). Laborde et al. (2011) apply Rev.4 reductions to countries' bound tariffs and assess the implications for the applied rates. The applied rates in that analysis are essentially those prevailing in 2004, adjusted with some important updates. **Table 5** shows some key results of the Laborde et al. (2011) study.

The Laborde et al. (2011) results indicate a differentiation among countries with regard to the consequences for applied tariffs under the Rev.4 commitment:

- Several countries would not reduce their average applied tariff at all: Brazil (average applied tariff of 4.8%), India (59.2%), Indonesia (7.6%), Mexico (3.9%) and South Africa (5.9%).

Several countries would reduce their average applied tariff only minimally, i.e. by 1 percentage point or less: China (from 7.8% to 7.5%), Korea (from 27.8% to 27.1%, as observed for Korea and Chinese Taipei together), Thailand (from 20.6% to 19.6%) and Turkey (from 13.6% to 13.2%).

- It is striking that the countries not reducing the average applied tariff or reducing it only minimally are not only countries with low average applied tariffs but also some with high average applied tariffs, such as India and Korea.

- Countries that would see reductions in their average applied tariff by more than 1 percentage point include Canada (from 10.7% to 8.6%), EU27 (from 15.9% to 10.2%), Japan (from 29.8% to 20.4%), Norway and/or Switzerland (from 37.4% to 28.2%), and the United States (from 4.8% to 3.0%).
  - In this group there is a pattern: the higher the pre-Rev.4 tariff, the larger the percentage point reduction, which is in line with the harmonising structure of the market access provisions of Rev.4.

Country-specific discussion for selected countries

The countries listed in **Table 3.5** may require some further discussion. Laborde et al. (2011) do not provide county-specific estimates for Argentina, Korea (aggregated with Chinese Taipei), the Philippines, Russian Federation or Viet Nam. Norway and Switzerland are aggregated.

Table 3.5. Tariff profiles before and after Rev.4 reductions

Country	Before Rev.4 reduction	After Rev.4 reduction	
	Average applied	Without flexibility	With flexibility
Argentina	No data	No data	No data
Brazil	4.8	4.7	4.8
Canada	10.7	5.1	8.6
China (People's Republic of)	7.8	5.3	7.5
EU27	15.9	6.6	10.2
India	59.2	54.6	59.2
Indonesia	7.6	7.0	7.6
Japan	29.8	14.0	20.4
Korea	27.8	18.5	27.1
Mexico	3.9	3.3	3.9
Nigeria	No data	No data	No data
Norway	37.4	19.5	28.2
Philippines	No data	No data	No data
Russia	No data	No data	No data
South Africa	5.9	5.3	5.9
Switzerland	37.4	19.5	28.2
Thailand	20.6	15.3	19.6
Turkey	13.6	10.9	13.2
United States	4.8	2.1	3.0
Viet Nam	No data	No data	No data

Notes: Analysis based mainly on 2004 data, with important updates. Flexibility refers to Rev.4 provisions other than reductions under the harmonising formula. "No data" refers to country not shown separately in source (Norway and Switzerland: see text).

Source: Laborde et al. (2011).

Argentina's tariff profile in terms of level and structure looks very much like that of Brazil, both with regard to bound tariffs and applied tariffs. It is thus tempting to suggest that Argentina's average bound tariff resulting from Rev.4 would, like Brazil's, be the same as the average applied tariff pre-Rev.4. However, the commodity specialisation, the agriculture trade pattern, and the trade and domestic policies of Argentina are very different from those of Brazil. For example, Argentina taxes several of its important export products. This calls for caution in making too much out of the similarity in tariff profiles, since the governments may choose to avail themselves differently of the flexibility in Rev.4.

Korea used the AoA provisions for delayed tariffication of import barriers for rice. After an extension in 2004, this waiver appears to have expired at the end of 2014. Access opportunities for imports of rice have increased considerably since 2005, reaching 8% of domestic consumption in 2014 (WTO, 2012a). Media reports that a 513% tariff replacing the quantitative restriction on rice imports from 1 January 2015 is contested by some countries (Korea Times, 2015).

Norway and Switzerland are aggregated (along with Iceland) by Laborde et al. (2011). There is some rationale for this, since both countries support their agriculture through import barriers and there are other similarities as well, such as the structure of agriculture. However, the WTO Tariff Profiles show that Norway has a higher average bound tariff and a higher average applied tariff, as well as a considerably larger share of tariff lines with TRQs. Norway has more than 1 100 tariff lines in agriculture. At most 67 tariff lines can therefore be designated as sensitive products if Norway uses the 6% ceiling allowed for some countries in paragraph 71 of Rev.4. In order to stay within its 67 tariff lines allotment, Norway may choose not to include cereals among its sensitive products.[13] It has not been possible to identify any studies on the changes in market access Switzerland might make in complying with Rev.4 commitments.

The Philippines applies tariffs in agriculture well below their bound levels. This by itself suggests that the Rev.4 reductions and new bindings would have little, if any, effect on the presently applied levels. However, the situation with regard to rice imports – the continued use of quantitative import restrictions instead of tariffs until 30 June 2017 – complicates the interpretation of tariff averages, as does the low binding coverage of only 67% of the tariff lines in agriculture.

The Russian Federation acceded to the WTO in 2012, reducing tariffs immediately on 60% of agricultural tariff lines (OECD 2013; Kiselev and Romashkin 2012). Some tariffs are being reduced to final bound levels by 2017. The average final bound rate in agriculture would be 10.8%, down from 13.2% before accession. Some products will have final bound tariffs of zero. TRQs are in effect for certain pork products until 2020, when a bound tariff will apply. TRQs also apply to imports of beef and poultry. Not having been party to the development of Rev.4 prior to its accession, Russia may or may not be identified as a recently acceded country. Although its accession is more recent than those of the countries explicitly identified in Rev.4 as very recently acceded, Russia is not so identified. If the Russia Federation were a recently acceded country, it would reduce final bound tariffs, starting one year after the tariff reaches its final bound level after accession. However, the reduction would apply only to tariffs above 10%, of which Russia has relatively few. In-quota tariffs of no more than 15% would not need to be reduced (the in-quota tariff for poultry is 25%). If it were a very recently acceded country, Russia would not reduce final bound tariffs in agriculture. Thus, depending on Russia's status under Rev.4 classifications, Rev.4 commitments on bound tariffs would have minimal or no effect on its applied tariffs.

Viet Nam acceded to the WTO in 2007. Named as a very recently acceded country in Rev.4, it need not undertake any reductions in final bound tariffs, including in-quota tariffs, in agriculture. Its applied tariffs would therefore not be affected by the Rev.4 commitments on bound tariffs.

Recent developments in tariff settings

The developments in international market prices for agricultural products in 2007 and later years prompted many countries to reduce their applied tariffs from their 2004 level, even setting some to zero.

This makes a difference for the interpretation of the Laborde et al. (2011) results, which were based essentially on 2004 levels. In general, the lowering of applied tariffs in 2007, 2008 and 2009 from their 2004 levels increased the margin between applied and bound tariffs, making it less likely that a Rev.4 reduction in a bound tariff would force a reduction also in the applied tariff. In other words, Rev.4 reductions in bound tariffs would be easier for countries to make when applied tariffs anyway were set at relatively low levels.

After the slump in early 2009, developments in international markets slowly brought prices of meat, dairy and cereals upwards, so that by 2012 and 2013 many prices were at, or close to, the levels seen in 2007 and 2008 (**Figure 3.1**). Still, if applied tariffs in agriculture in the intervening years of lower prices had been raised from their 2007 and 2008 levels, they had again by 2012 been set at levels that were somewhat lower than in 2007 (**Figure 3.2**).[14] This would, therefore, have been one more situation favourable to reducing bound tariffs while affecting applied tariffs only relatively little.

Figure 3.1. Commodity prices index 2006-2013

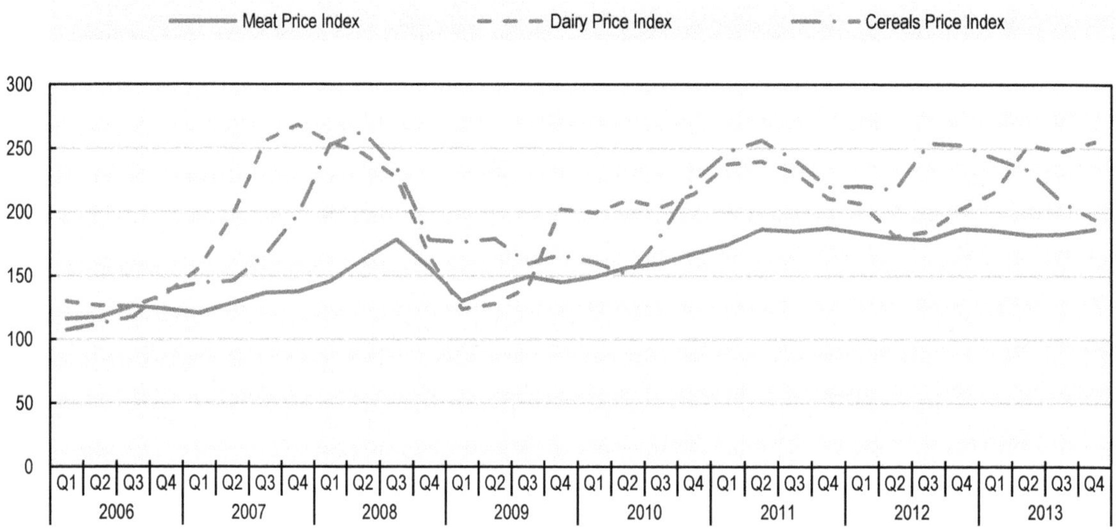

Source: OECD (2014a), http://dx.doi.org/10.1787/888933109099.

Figure 3.2. Change of average tariffs (MFN Applied) for agricultural products from 2007 to 2012

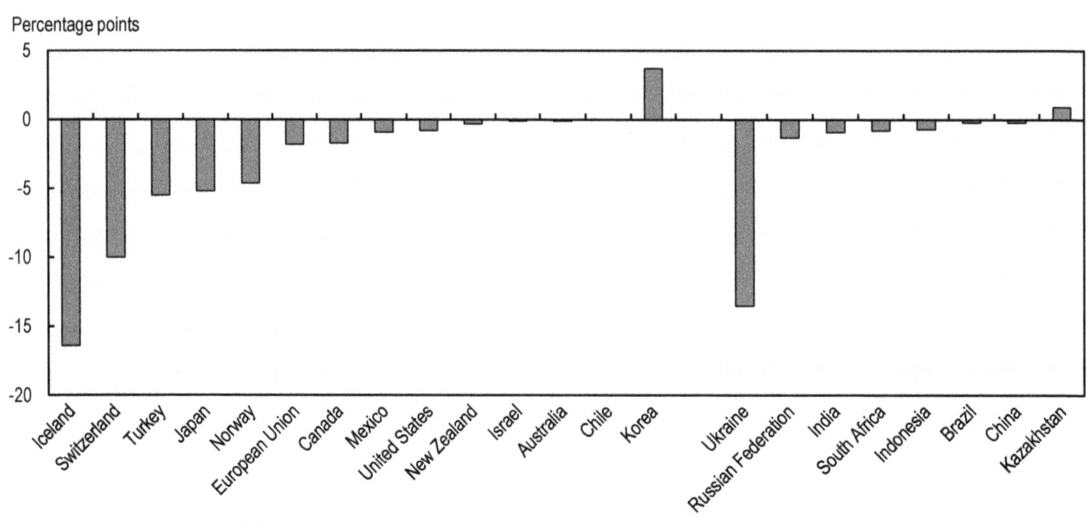

Source: Tangermann (2014).

In late 2013 and 2014, international prices of many agricultural commodities fell, occasioning some increases in agricultural tariffs again. By way of example and not as an inventory of countries' changes, in August 2013 the European Union resumed import duties on wheat and other cereals (import duties on maize, sorghum and rye had earlier been set to zero for 2010/2011, and in-quota import duties on feed wheat and barley had been suspended in 2011). Mexico in December 2013 increased the import tariff on white maize from zero to 20%. Turkey in 2013 increased duties on imports of some minor agricultural products while also reducing duties on some other such products. It is not yet clear if countries more generally have raised import tariffs in 2014, which would shrink the margin between bound and applied tariffs and make it more difficult to reduce bound tariffs as per Rev.4 without impinging on the applied tariff. In any case, as shown by Laborde et al. (2011), numerous countries could reduce bound levels as per Rev.4 without touching the level of the applied tariffs after recent increases in 2013 and 2014. The same reasoning would apply to changes in applied TRQs.

Market access digest

Tariff rates in agriculture have for most products and countries been bound at the same level since at least 2004, with some allowance for changes through renegotiation, accession and other developments. Since that time, world market prices for many agricultural products went through a peak period in 2007 and 2008, followed by further fluctuations into 2014. Most but not all countries apply tariffs at rates below the bound rates, and they in many cases adjust the applied rates in the opposite direction of the border price changes. Reducing bound tariffs according to Rev.4 rules would for most countries only reduce the margins between the bound rates and the rates applying in 2004 (Laborde et al., 2011).

It can be argued that, to the extent that applied rates actually have been changed, they had been lowered between 2004 and 2007 (or 2008). Data on the difference in agricultural tariffs between 2007 and 2012 indicate a slight additional lowering of applied tariffs, or at least not a general reversal of any 2004-07 reductions. As international prices of many agricultural products have fallen since 2012 and 2013, there could at present be a general tendency, if changes are to be made, towards increasing applied tariffs.

According to Laborde et al. (2011), the margins between bound tariffs and applied tariffs at the 2004 rates were large enough to allow bound rates after Rev.4 reductions to remain larger than the applied rates for several countries. For other countries, the Rev.4 reduction in the bound rates required reductions in the applied rates, although these reductions were quite small for several countries. This would suggest that, in general, the Rev.4 tariff reductions would not require large changes for most countries. However, this hypothetical reasoning would need to be anchored in actual analysis of countries' tariff settings in 2014. The same would apply to countries' TRQ settings. There are also cases where the reasoning based on tariff averages for a country masks the particular concerns a country faces in reducing tariffs for just a few products. To some extent, such situations have been addressed through the numerous special rules in Rev.4, but there may be situations where alternative solutions involving policy change might be considered.

The AMIS Market Monitor reports monthly on selected policy developments, including measures affecting imports and exports of wheat, corn, rice and soybeans (Market Monitor, 2013 and 2014). Between March 2013 and July 2014, the Market Monitor reported some lowering of an import barrier for one or more of these crops in Brazil, Indonesia, Korea, the Philippines and Russia. This took a variety of forms, including removal of a small import duty on grains, increasing import quotas and waiving tariffs, and applying temporary duty-free import quotas. However, over the same period there were numerous measures taken to impede imports, although the numbers, of course, say nothing about the significance or impacts of the measures taken. While it is thus difficult to identify a trend in either direction, the observations do suggest that many countries actively manage the level of applied import protection within their bound tariffs and TRQs.

3.4. Export competition

The declaration of Ministers on export competition at the Bali conference in 2013 stated that they are committed to enhancing transparency and improving monitoring in relation to all forms of export subsidies and to all export measures with equivalent effect. This would include holding annual discussions in the WTO Committee on Agriculture to examine developments in the field of export competition. The WTO Secretariat has accordingly compiled information from notifications and a 2014 questionnaire. The information covers export subsidies, export credits, export credit guarantees or insurance programmes, international food aid and agricultural exporting state trading enterprises (WTO, 2014a).

Export subsidies

Agreement on Agriculture

The schedules of 18 countries include reduction commitments on export subsidies (counting the EU28 schedule as one and counting none of its member states' schedules). In the set of countries in this report, the following do not have scheduled export subsidy commitments: Argentina, China, India, Japan, Korea, Philippines, Russia, Thailand and Viet Nam.

A country's export subsidy schedule shows ceiling commitment levels on budgetary outlays and quantities, disaggregated by a fairly standard set of commodity groups. Some countries' schedules show the set of tariff lines making up the commodity group. The commitment levels derive from countries' data on export subsidies in 1986-90, which they submitted in the Uruguay Round negotiations. The final bound outlay commitments and the final bound quantity commitments represent reductions from their average 1986-90 levels by certain percentages, which were smaller for developing countries. Developed countries reached their final bound commitment levels on export subsidisation (outlays and quantities) in 2000 and developing countries in 2004.

Draft modalities

Rev.4 foresees the gradual elimination of export subsidy commitments and other entitlements to provide export subsidies in agriculture. The phased elimination would see developed countries' commitments go to zero by 2013, with the phasing rules differing somewhat between those applying to outlay commitments and those applying to quantity commitments. Developing countries would phase out their outlay and quantity commitments by 2016. Certain other export subsidy provisions for developing countries face an end date of 2021.[15]

Bali declaration

In their declaration on export competition at the 2013 Ministerial conference in Bali, Ministers expressed regret that it had not been possible by then to achieve the elimination of export subsidies that was envisaged in 2005 (WTO, 2013f). The Bali declaration did not establish a new timetable for the elimination of export subsidies, but is clear about achieving it as soon as possible. In the meantime, Ministers undertook to the maximum extent possible to keep the level of export subsidies significantly below their commitment levels. Ministers recognised that the use of export subsidies has decreased.

Export subsidies: Situation

Countries are required to notify their use of export subsidies to the Committee on Agriculture. Countries with export subsidy commitments submit Table ES:1 notifications, indicating the budgetary outlays and the quantities subsidised. Countries without export subsidy commitments need to indicate annually that they have not provided export subsidies. Some countries without export subsidy commitments need, however, to submit Supporting Table ES:2 notifications. This notification reports the export subsidies the country has provided with reference to Article 9.4 of the AoA. The article allows developing countries, under certain conditions, to provide subsidies to reduce the costs of marketing exports of agricultural products and internal transport and freight charges to export shipments. This article is available to any developing country, whether it has export subsidy commitments or not. Article 9.4 treatment applies only in the "implementation period", which the AoA defines as "the six-year period commencing in the year 1995", i.e. ending in 2000. Some developing countries take the view, however, that Article 9.4 still applies and continue to provide the export subsidies in question.[16] Therefore, it cannot be taken for granted that developing countries without export subsidy commitments always notify nil export subsidies.

Among the countries in this report, the following developed countries have export subsidy commitments: Canada, the European Union, Norway, Switzerland, and the United States (**Table 3.6**). The developing countries with export subsidy commitments are Brazil, Indonesia, Mexico, South Africa and Turkey. In other words, 10 of the 20 countries studied have export subsidy commitments, with an even split between developed and developing countries. Among the 32 countries that acceded to the WTO between 1995 and 2014, only Bulgaria and Panama have export subsidy commitments. Of note is that China, the Russian Federation and Viet Nam do not have export subsidy commitments.

There is wide variation among countries in how current their export subsidy notifications are (**Table 3.6** reports on notifications from 2008 onwards, not the full time series). Some have notified up through 2013, while others lag behind by many years. Turkey's latest notification is for the year 2000. Most of the countries without export subsidy commitments have reported that they did not provide any export subsidies from 2008. This is the case for Argentina, China, Japan, Philippines, Russia, Thailand and Viet Nam. Also, Brazil, Indonesia and South Africa, which do have export subsidy commitments, have reported that they did not provide such subsidies. On the other hand, India and Korea, which do not have export subsidy commitments, reported export subsidies in some years from 2008 onwards. In doing so, they invoke Article 9.4. Mexico also refers Article 9.4 in reporting export subsidies in excess of its commitments.

While the absence of notifications for recent years for some countries weakens what can be said generally about the whole group of countries, a couple of patterns in **Table 3.6** stand out. One is that countries that do not provide export subsidies, whether they have export subsidy commitments or not, maintain that stance for several years.[17] Likewise, countries invoking Article 9.4 (Supporting Table ES:2 notifications) do so for several years.

Only a handful of products have been selected here, mainly corresponding to products that are important in world trade.[18] The products are actually groups of products, defined by each country at the tariff line level in the data underlying its scheduled commitments. There is some variation across countries in what they call the products entitled to export subsidies. **Table 3.7** gives an impressionistic overview of how countries' export subsidies relate to their commitment levels.

Drawing on **Table 3.7**, the fact that a country has final bound export subsidy commitments at the 2000 or 2004 level for several or many products does not mean that export subsidies were provided for all those products in 2008 or later. Some important products already received nil export subsidies by 2008. This development, coupled with the observation about many subsidisation patterns being stable over time in recent years, would facilitate countries' phasing out of export subsidy commitments under Rev.4. This is reinforced by the fact that some countries have also reduced or eliminated export subsidies since 2008, such as the EU on butter and butter oil; Norway on butter; Switzerland on dairy products, cattle, fruit and potatoes; and the United States on butter and butter oil. In some cases, the elimination of export subsidies results from legislative change, such as the 2014 Agricultural Act in the United States, while in other cases it results from international prices being high enough to obviate the pressure on governments to subsidise exports.

Table 3.6. Export subsidy commitments and notifications

Country	Export subsidy commitment	Details in Table 2.7	Export subsidy notifications					
			2008	2009	2010	2011	2012	2013
Argentina	No		No XS	No XS	No XS	No XS	No XS	
Brazil	Yes		No XS	No XS	No XS	No XS	No XS	
Canada	Yes	Yes	ES:1	ES:1	ES:1	ES:1		
China (People's Republic of)	No		No XS	No XS	No XS	No XS	No XS	
European Union	Yes	Yes	ES:1	ES:1	ES:1	ES:1	ES:1	
India	No		ES:2	ES:2				
Indonesia	Yes		No XS	No XS	No XS	No XS		
Japan	No		No XS	No XS	No XS	No XS	No XS	No XS
Korea	No		ES:2					
Mexico	Yes	Yes	ES:2	ES:2	ES:2	ES:2	ES:2	
Nigeria	No		No XS	No XS	No XS	No XS		
Norway	Yes	Yes	ES:1	ES:1	ES:1	ES:1	ES:1	ES:1
Philippines	No		No XS	No XS	No XS			
Russia	No		n. app.	n. app.	n. app.	n. app.	No XS	No XS
South Africa	Yes		No XS	No XS	No XS			
Switzerland	Yes	Yes	ES:1	ES:1	ES:1	ES:1		
Thailand	No		No XS	No XS	No XS	No XS	No XS	No XS
Turkey	Yes		No notifications					
United States	Yes	Yes	ES:1	ES:1	ES:1	ES:1	ES:1	
Viet Nam	No		No XS	No XS	No XS	No XS	No XS	

Notes: Table 2.7 in this chapter; XS = export subsidies; n. app. = not applicable; ES:1 and ES:2 are notification formats.

Source: Author's interpretation of WTO (2005), Ag-IMS, and notifications (mid-January 2015).

Table 3.7. Export subsidy outlays and subsidised quantities as percentage of commitments

	Outlays						Quantity					
	2008	2009	2010	2011	2012	2013	2008	2009	2010	2011	2012	2013
Canada												
Wheat and wheat flour	0%	0%	0%	0%			0%	0%	0%	0%		
Coarse grains	0%	0%	0%	0%			0%	0%	0%	0%		
Butter	0%	21%	5%	0%			0%	20%	4%	0%		
Skim milk powder	100%	100%	100%	100%			20%	19%	25%	21%		
Other milk products	99%	100%	100%	100%			22%	19%	23%	23%		
European Union												
Wheat and wheat flour	0%	0%	0%	0%	0%		0%	0%	0%	0%	0%	
Coarse grains	0%	0%	0%	0%	0%		0%	0%	0%	0%	0%	
Sugar	0%	0%	0%	0%	0%		0%	0%	0%	0%	0%	
Butter and butter oil	6%	4%	0%	0%	0%		0%	0%	0%	0%	0%	
Beef meat	2%	2%	5%	2%	0%		0%	0%	0%	0%	0%	
India ES:2												
Sugar	*54.1*	*87.6*		*USD million*			*45 546*	*3 411 654*	*tonnes*			
Plants and flowers	*0.9*	*0.4*					*650*	*340*				
Processed fruits and vegetables	*5.0*	*2.1*					*17 600*	*7 460*				
Animal products	*0.6*	*6.7*					*10 100*	*61 350*				
Fresh fruit and vegetables	*2.4*	*4.2*					*19 800*	*34 200*				
Korea ES:2												
Grain and processed food	*0.1*		*KRW billion*				*2*	*'000 tonnes*				
Livestock	*1.3*						*14*					
Vegetables	*11.0*						*46*					
Kimchi	*3.0*						*24*					
Fruits	*10.9*						*38*					

Table 3.7. Export subsidy outlays and subsidised quantities as percentage of commitments *(cont.)*

	Outlays						Quantity					
	2008	2009	2010	2011	2012	2013	2008	2009	2010	2011	2012	2013
Mexico ES:2												
Maize	4%	0%	0%	0%	0%		5%	0%	0%	0%	0%	
Beans	0%	0%	0%	0%	0%		0%	0%	0%	0%	0%	
Wheat	92%	149%	174%	123%	8%		60%	200%	123%	68%	7%	
Sorghum	0%	0%	0%	0%	0%		0%	0%	0%	0%	0%	
Sugar	0%	0%	0%	0%	0%		0%	0%	0%	0%	0%	
Norway												
Bovine meat	0%	0%	0%	0%	0%	0%	0%	0%	0%	0%	0%	0%
Swine meat	3%	35%	83%	52%	70%	97%	4%	40%	82%	53%	72%	100%
Butter	44%	76%	23%	1%	0%	0%	54%	57%	38%	7%	0%	0%
Cheese	59%	55%	57%	57%	52%	54%	81%	76%	76%	79%	75%	1%
Fruit and vegetables	0%	0%	0%	0%	0%	0%	0%	0%	0%	0%	0%	0%
Switzerland												
Dairy products	2%	1%	0%	0%			29%	9%	0%			
Cattle	25%	31%	0%	0%			42%	55%	0%			
Fruit	96%	99%	0%	0%			74%	69%	0%			
Potatoes	43%	38%	0%	0%			49%	76%	0%			
Processed products	65%	81%	67%	66%			No notif.	No notif.	No notif.			
United States												
Wheat	0%	0%	0%	0%	0%		0%	0%	0%	0%	0%	
Coarse grains	0%	0%	0%	0%	0%		9%	74%	0%	0%	0%	
Butter and butter oil	37%	7%	0%	0%	0%		29%	25%	0%	0%	0%	
Skimmed milk powder	9%	0%	0%	0%	0%		0%	0%	0%	0%	0%	
Bovine meat	0%	0%	0%	0%	0%		0%	0%	0%	0%	0%	

Notes: EU quantities of butter and butter oil and beef meat rounded to 0%; EU quantities of sugar are export licenses issued without subsidies. Switzerland: only five products are reported; "Processed products" has no quantity commitment level; no quantities notified. India and Korea: commitment levels are nil; no percentage calculated for outlays and quantities reported in ES:2 notifications.

Source: Author's calculations from notified data.

Summary of export subsidy situation

The picture across countries and products is varied. There seems to be a general tendency towards less use of export subsidies judging from this incomplete sample, but there are particular situations of ongoing or increasing subsidisation for some products in some countries. Part of the tendency towards less subsidisation is obviously the result of higher world prices, which reduce the pressure to subsidise exports or to reduce the outlays involved. However, some of the tendency is the result of countries' policy changes in the direction of reducing or eliminating export subsidies. For example, Switzerland eliminated export subsidies on basic agricultural goods in 2009 (WTO, 2013b: 3.2.5, para. 3.65) and suspended or abolished export subsidies on some products in 2012 (WTO (2013b), 4.1.3, para. 4.12). Successive reforms in the European Union, historically the largest user of export subsidies, have also reduced the use of export subsidies.[19] Indeed, the European Union indicated in responding to the WTO questionnaire in 2014 that the Common Agricultural Policy adopted in 2013 provides that export subsidies cannot be used other than as an exceptional measure (WTO, 2014a: 27).[20] In contrast, media speculated in August 2014 that the European Union might consider reintroducing export subsidies as part of its approach to dealing with trade difficulties with Russia (Agra Europe, 2014).

On the other hand, the sustained or increased use of export subsidies for some products in a few countries identifies situations where countries would need to undertake policy reform in order to meet the Rev.4 obligation to eventually eliminate all export subsidies. With the 2013 deadline having passed, a new deadline would need to be identified for the elimination by developed countries. Developing countries with export subsidy commitments might have a later deadline (three years later in Rev.4). Developing countries invoking Article 9.4 might enjoy a further reprieve before having to eliminate export subsidies to reduce the costs of marketing agricultural exports and of internal transport and freight charges to export shipments (five further years later in Rev.4, i.e. eight years after the deadline for developed countries). Thus, if an agreement with updated Rev.4 provisions were to take effect in 2014, the respective deadlines would be 2019 (for developed countries), 2022 (for developing countries with export subsidy commitments) and 2027 (developing countries invoking Article 9.4).

Assessment

Export subsidisation in agriculture is no longer as prevalent as it was at the time of negotiating the AoA in the 1990s, starting the DDA in 2001, or even drafting Rev.4 in 2008. While export subsidies were not eliminated by 2013 as had been envisioned, their use was much reduced. Indeed, in some of the intervening years, countries favoured export restrictions over export subsidies. Not using export subsidies is different, however, from committing not to use them. A country with export subsidy commitments in agriculture would seek to obtain something in return for giving up that right to subsidise exports in the future.[21] At the same time, the continued use of export subsidies remains a crucial element of some countries' support for certain products, as exemplified by Canada's complete use of its export subsidisation entitlements on dairy products. Nevertheless, the generally much reduced export subsidisation in recent years would seem to facilitate the taking of commitments to eliminate export subsidies over time, including those under Article 9.4.

Reaching such commitments could be most feasible in a context where adequate balances could be found among different negotiating interests. This relatively sanguine view needs to be tempered with the recognition that there are situations where the elimination of export subsidies in a particular sector would be predicated on several other policy changes also being made in the sector by the country concerned. The challenge would be to ensure that the need to address such situations did not become an obstacle to agreeing to eliminate export subsidies and committing to do so.

Export financing support

Agreement on Agriculture

The AoA addresses export credits, export credit guarantees or insurance programmes under the heading "Prevention of circumvention of export subsidy commitments". It does not, however, lay down rules for export financing support but expresses members' undertaking to work towards the development of internationally agreed disciplines to govern the programmes (Article 10.2). This effectively leaves the discipline on such programmes to the rules of the Agreement on Subsidies and Countervailing Measures. One effort towards developing internationally agreed disciplines is reported in OECD (no date), an effort resulting in the issue having been passed on to the WTO for consideration in the DDA.

Draft modalities

Rev.4 refers to export credits, export credit guarantees or insurance programmes as export financing support. It presents a set of provisions as a possible new article to replace AoA Article 10.2. In 1998, a few years after the entry into force of the AoA, the United States provided 88% of the subsidies accounted for under export credit in agriculture, the EU 7%, Canada 4% and Australia 1% (OECD 2001a). The credits of the United States had the highest subsidy component. It is therefore to be expected that the Rev.4 annex on export financing support particularly addresses the offensive interests of many countries with regard to such support being provided by the United States and the corresponding defensive interests of the United States.

Rev.4 identifies the forms of export financing support and the kinds of institutions providing it. The two elements of the discipline are maximum repayment terms and self-financing. The maximum repayment term allowed is 180 days (some countries' programmes have had repayment terms measured in years). Insurance or guarantee-type programmes must be self-financing, which means that the premiums charged over a rolling four-year period (six years for developing countries) must be large enough to cover the operating costs and losses of the programme in that period. Rev.4 indicates both 2010 and 2013 as possible start dates for these provisions but, with both of these years now in the past, Rev.4's alternative starting dates for the maximum repayment terms might apply: the first day of implementing the new agreement for developed countries, four years later for developing countries. Longer repayment terms would apply for credits to least-developed countries and net food-importing developing countries for the acquisition of basic foodstuffs.

Export financing support: situation

Five export credit guarantee programmes operated under the United States 2002 Farm Act: GSM-102, GSM-103, the Supplier Credit Guarantee Program, the Facilities Financing Guarantee Program and the Facility Guarantee Program (this paragraph draws on OECD (2011) and Schnepf (2014a)). GSM-102 accounted for about 90% of the value of exports covered under these programmes. As an outcome of the Brazil-driven WTO dispute *United States – Upland Cotton* and for other reasons, the United States suspended GSM-103 and the Supplier Credit Guarantee Program in 2006. The 2008 Farm Act eliminated GSM-103 and the Supplier Credit Guarantee Program and removed the cap on the fee charged on GSM-102 transactions. In addition, the credit subsidy under GSM-102 was capped. Some conditional changes to GSM-102 were also specified in the 2010 framework of Brazil and the United States for a mutually agreed solution to the cotton dispute (WTO 2010a). The 2014 Agricultural Act further modified GSM-102 by lowering the maximum repayment term from 36 to 24 months and gave the US Department of Agriculture additional flexibility to negotiate with Brazil on GSM-102. On 30 September 2014, Brazil and the United States concluded a memorandum of understanding which, among other things, sets the maximum repayment term under GSM-102 at 18 months (US Trade Representative 2014).

The United States has thus carried out several changes in its export financing support programmes. These changes mainly go in the direction of making US programmes more compatible with the provisions of Rev.4 but do not make them fully compatible.

As regards other countries, Argentina, China, Norway, and Thailand indicate they do not provide export financing programmes (WTO 2014a, page 23). **Table 3.8** summarises some elements of the information countries provided in response to the WTO questionnaire in 2014 (Brazil, Canada,

European Union, Japan, Switzerland, Turkey, United States and Viet Nam) (WTO 2014c). Table 2.8 and the questionnaire answers demonstrate that it is difficult to elicit information that is comparable across countries. That said, Table 2.8 does confirm that the United States operates the largest risk cover programme among the few countries that indicated the amount of agricultural exports covered by their export financing programmes. There is also a wide variation across countries in the premium rates their programmes charge and the maximum length of the repayment term.

Assessment

Because of the size of its export credit guarantee programme (GSM-102) and the programme's role in an earlier dispute, the United States is the focus of the provisions in Rev.4 concerning export financing support. A series of changes have been made to the programme over several years, including those to be made under a September 2014 understanding (US Trade Representative 2014). This should work in the direction of facilitating agreement on the provisions of Rev.4 concerning export financing support.

Exporting agricultural state trading enterprises

Agreement on Agriculture

The AoA does not address agricultural state trading enterprises (STEs), either as importers or exporters. However, Article XVII of the GATT 1994 sets out disciplines concerning the activities of state trading enterprises. The Uruguay Round established an understanding on the interpretation of that article, which requires countries to notify their STEs in accordance with this definition of STEs: "Governmental and non-governmental enterprises, including marketing boards, which have been granted exclusive or special rights or privileges, including statutory or constitutional powers, in the exercise of which they influence through their purchases or sales the level or direction of imports or exports."

Draft modalities

Rev.4 would require agricultural exporting STEs to comply with the provisions of its Annex K, which would be in a new article. The disciplines on the practices of agricultural exporting STEs would include the elimination of all forms of export subsidies, including those related to food aid and export credits, various forms of government financing and underwriting, and the use of agricultural export monopoly powers by STEs. This latter practice would be eliminated by 2013, although under some conditions the STE would be exempt from elimination of this practice if world exports of the product made up only a very small share of world agricultural trade in 2003-05. The exemption is specified in a footnote and the text to which it attaches may itself be subject to interpretation (e.g. "in parallel" *vs.* "by 2013"). Developing countries would be allowed to keep the export monopoly powers of agricultural exporting STEs under a range of conditions. Members with an agricultural exporting STE would have to notify the Committee on Agriculture of many aspects of the nature and operations of the STE.

Exporting agricultural state trading enterprises: situation

The WTO Secretariat's questionnaire on agricultural exporting STEs in early 2104 yielded responses from six of the countries included in this report: Brazil, Canada, China, India, Indonesia and Viet Nam (WTO 2014e). **Table 3.9** summarises some elements of the questionnaire responses. While Brazil and Indonesia have STEs that they classify as agricultural exporting STEs, these enterprises no longer export. Canada's agricultural exporting STE no longer has the exclusive monopoly powers on exports of wheat, durum wheat and barley from western Canada for which it has been known for several decades. One of Viet Nam's STEs in the rice trade seems to have relinquished its exclusive rights to one important market, the Philippines, in 2012. Only half of Viet Nam's rice exports are channelled through its STEs. India maintains numerous agricultural exporting STEs, most of which are concerned with onions. While important for domestic needs, onion is not large in world agricultural trade. India's sugar STE has the right to export sugar to the European Union and the United States under preferential tariffs.

Table 3.8. Export financing support: Selected data

Country	Program category	Premium rates or fees	Maximum repayment term	Value of agriculture exports covered
Brazil	One export credit programme	LIBOR	No data	2013: USD 15 million
Canada	Two risk cover programmes One direct financing support programme	No data No data	180 days 90-360 days	2007-08: CAD 152 mill. 2008-09: CAD 96 mill. 2009-10: CAD 91 mill. 2010-11: CAD 145 mill. 2011-12: CAD 134 mill. 2012-13: CAD 53 mill.
European Union	No export credit, export credit guarantees, or insurance programmes at EU level; only member states. Risk cover, credit insurance, direct financing support (15 programmes)	0.64% - 6.5%	Up to ten years	More than EUR 500 mill.
Japan	Three risk cover programmes	No data	Two years	2008: JPY 10 billion 2009: JPY 9 billion 2010: JPY 9 billion 2011: JPY 13 billion 2012: JPY 11 billion 2013: JPY 7 billion (partial)
Switzerland	One risk cover programme	No data	180 days	Negligible
Turkey	One export credit insurance programme	0.37%	360 days	No yearly data
United States	One risk cover programme	USD 1.34 per USD 100 of guarantee coverage	24 months	2008: USD 3 billion 2009: USD 5 billion 2010: USD 3 billion 2011: USD 4 billion 2012: USD 4 billion 2013: USD 3 billion
Viet Nam	Export credit	No data	No data	No data

Source: Author's interpretation of WTO (2014c) (G/AG/W/125/Add.2).

In comparison to the STEs mentioned in these five countries, it appears China's agricultural exporting STEs remain important actors with exclusive exporting rights in the country's trade in rice, maize, cotton, and tobacco. However, as the composition of China's grain trade has changed over time, especially since 2008, the role of China's STEs in exporting rice and maize has likely declined (Figure 3.3). Prior to 2008, China was a consistent and in many years significant net exporter of maize, and in some years also a net exporter of rice. From 2008 China has been a rapidly growing net importer of an aggregate of major grains, including distillers' dried grain with solubles. The net imports of maize and rice have in some recent years been of magnitudes similar to the net exports before 2008.

Figure 3.3. China's net grain imports, 2000-13

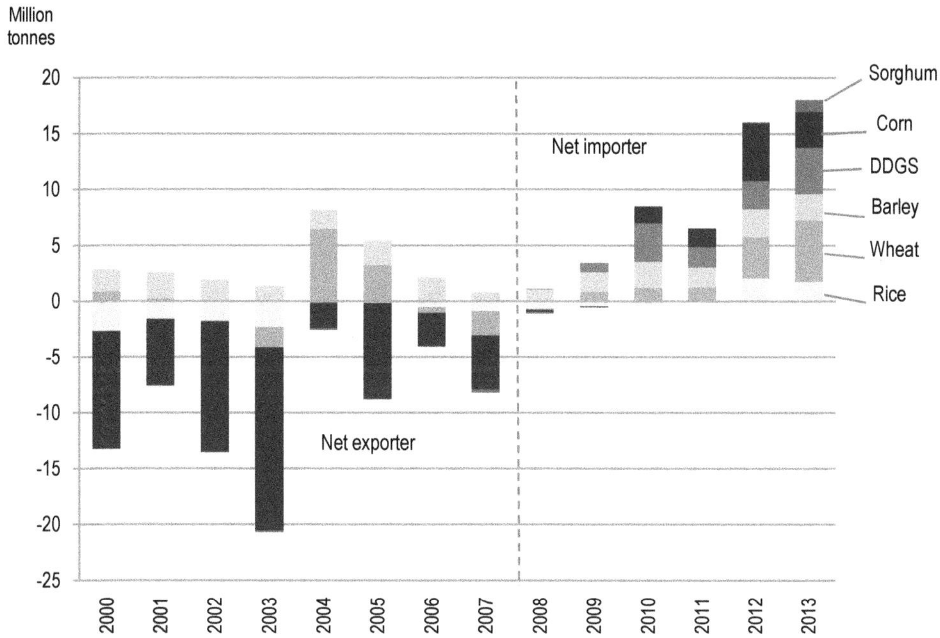

Source: Hansen and Gale (2014).

Assessment

The role of exporting STEs in several countries has shrunk over a number of years. Some such enterprises have ceased to export and some have given up the special rights or powers with which they had been endowed. These developments would seem to facilitate reaching agreement on the provisions in Rev.4 on submitting agricultural exporting STEs, especially those of developed countries, to additional disciplines. The anticipated entry into force of one of those disciplines by 2013 would obviously require updating.

International food aid

Agreement on Agriculture

The AoA addresses international food aid under the heading "Prevention of circumvention of export subsidy commitments". It requires countries to ensure that their food aid is not tied to commercial exports to the recipient countries, that food aid transactions are carried out in accordance with the official principles of the Food and Agriculture Organization of the United Nations (FAO), and that food aid is to the extent possible provided in fully grant form or on terms that are at least as concessional as those of the Food Aid Convention (Article 10.4).[22] The notification requirements of the Committee on Agriculture require notification within given timeframes of the quantity of food aid provided.

Table 3.9. Features of agricultural exporting state trading enterprises (STEs) of six countries

Country	Number of STEs	Name or description	Exporting practices	Government financing or underwriting	Export monopoly powers
Brazil	One	CONAB	Does not export		None
Canada	One	Canadian Wheat Board	Currently markets wheat, durum wheat, barley, canola and peas	In transition until 2017. Receives government borrowing guarantees; producer payment levels guaranteed by government	No longer in place
China (People's Republic of)	Several	Six (including COFCO) and 19 for tobacco	Rice, maize, cotton, tobacco		Exclusive right to trade
India	12 for onions, 1 for gum karaya, 1 for preferential quota sugar	Onion STEs mainly identified by state	Onion is domestically sensitive product, which motivates STEs		Exclusive right to export may be granted; export rights for raw sugar and white sugar to US and EU
Indonesia	One	BULOG	No exports of rice since 1997	Funding from state budget; commercial credit guaranteed by government	Government mandate to import, export, distribute rice
Viet Nam	Two for rice, also for coffee, tea, vegetables and fruit	For rice, identified by north and south	Half of country's rice exports exported by the two STEs		Exclusive right until 2012 for one STE to sell to Philippines; exclusive supplier for government-to-government contracts

Source: Author's interpretation of WTO (2014e) (G/AG/W/125/Add.4).

Draft modalities

Rev.4 requires international food aid to comply with the provisions of a possible new article to replace Article 10.4 of the AoA. The new article would reaffirm countries' commitment to maintain an adequate level of international food aid while making clear that the objective of the rules is to prevent commercial displacement. The disciplines applicable to all food aid transactions include that food aid be needs-driven, be in fully grant form, not be tied to commercial exports, not be linked to market development objectives, and that products must not, in most situations, be exported. Countries would commit to moving "increasingly towards more untied cash-based food aid".

Rev.4 includes disciplines for food aid transactions in emergency situations to ensure that the provision of food aid in such situations is not unintentionally impeded. They include rules for recognising an emergency and they prohibit monetisation, except for certain purposes in least-developed countries. The rules for non-emergency situations refer to assessing need, targeting food insecure groups and preventing or minimising commercial displacement. Monetisation would be prohibited except in certain situations. International food aid would need to be notified annually.

International food aid: situation

Several countries indicated in response to the WTO questionnaire in 2014 that they do not provide food aid, including Argentina and Norway (WTO 2014a: 24). No information was provided by Korea, Mexico, India, Indonesia, Philippines, or Turkey. The Cairns Group reviewed the information on food aid presented in WTO (2014d) (a precursor to WTO (2014i)) and prepared a partial summary of selected elements in table form (WTO 2014f). That table is reproduced below as **Table 3.10.**

The Cairns Group considered that, among the 14 countries reporting details on current food aid programmes (some of which are among the 20 countries featured in this report), the programmes of just over half already appear to be broadly consistent with the food aid annex (Annex L) in Rev.4. At least six members (Australia, Canada, the European Union, New Zealand, Switzerland and the United States) provide untied cash-based food aid (Annex L, paragraph 4). In the sample, the majority of food aid provided is cash based. Where countries provide in-kind food aid, most of the countries in the sample (Brazil, China, Japan, South Africa, Thailand and the United States) have provided aid to the World Food Programme or in response to emergency situations (Annex L, paragraphs 3 and 6). Three countries (China, Japan and the United States) explicitly permit monetisation of food aid in circumstances that are not emergency situations or where the beneficiary is not a least-developed country (Annex L, paragraph 8).

The Cairns Group stops short of analysing countries' compliance with the provisions of both the AoA and Rev.4, referring to the incompleteness of the available information. The group highlights the need for more information on the practice of monetisation, including the circumstances in which it is permitted, and what if any disciplines a country imposes on its use. The group also highlights the need for more information on the circumstances surrounding the provision of in-kind food aid, including information on occasions when it is not provided to an international organisation such as the World Food Programme in response to an emergency, and whether or not any conditions are put on such aid.

Among the five main programmes distributing US international food aid, the so-called Section 416(b) has been inactive since 2007 (Schnepf 2014b). The other four programmes were re-authorised by the Agricultural Act of 2014, which places greater emphasis on improving the nutritional quality of food aid products and on ensuring that sales of food aid commodities do not disrupt local markets. The act also modified some of the ceilings and floors on US food aid programme activities and created a small new local and regional purchase programme. While the new law thus made some modest changes to existing US food aid programmes, the US Administration had actually proposed some more sweeping reforms, such as eliminating monetisation, providing greater flexibility to procure commodities in local or regional markets overseas, and reducing the volume of commodities subject to US cargo preferences (at least 50% of government-impelled agricultural cargoes, which include food aid commodities, must be carried on US-flagged vessels, down from 75% prior to 2012).

Table 3.10. Overview of countries' food aid programmes

Country	Is aid provided on a cash basis?	Is aid provided "in-kind" i.e. actual commodities?	If aid is provided "in kind" is it provided to the WFP, a relevant international organisation or in response to an emergency?	Is the aid provided in fully grant form?	Is monetisation of the aid provided prohibited?
Australia	Yes. AUD 570 million in FY 2012/13	No	N/A	Yes	Yes
Brazil	No	Yes. USD 8 842 million of rice and USD 209 331 of beans	Yes to the WFP	Yes	Yes
Canada	Yes. 360 265 tonnes of commodities purchased	No	No	Yes	Yes
China (People's Republic of)	No	Yes. RMB 533 million of food aid	In part – a portion of aid was provided to the WFP	Yes	No
European Union	Yes. 405 000 tonnes equivalent of cash-based aid provided, one-quarter in wheat purchases	No	N/A	Yes	Yes
Japan	Unclear	Yes. JPY 10 billion	In part – a portion of aid provided through WFP	Yes	No
Russia	Yes. USD 50 million	No	N/A	Not specified	Not specified
South Africa	No	Yes. 100 tonnes of maize 2002	Yes. Response to emergency	Not specified	Not specified
Switzerland	Yes. 25 000 tonnes worth of cash grain equivalent	Yes. 3 144 tonnes of SMP and 96 tonnes of cheese	No	Yes	Yes
Thailand	No	Yes 500 tonnes	Yes. Response to emergency	Yes	Yes
United States	Yes. USD 577 million	Yes. USD 694 million worth of commodities	A portion to the WFP and a portion in response to emergency situations	Yes	No
Viet Nam	No	Yes. 14 000 tonnes of rice	Not specified	Not specified	Not specified

Notes: The information is based only on submissions made to the export competition questionnaire and the information compiled in WTO (2014d). The value or volume of aid is taken from the last available year in WTO (2014d). WFP: World Food Program.
Source: Adapted from WTO (2014f), a Cairns Group submission.

Assessment

The food aid programmes of the United States continue to attract international attention with regard to concerns about how they affect local markets in recipient countries and the market opportunities of commercial exporters. The changes in the rules for food aid expressed in Rev.4 are far from revolutionary, and the same can be said about the changes to US food aid programme, in the 2014 Farm Act. That nevertheless leaves a gap between the reform ambitions of Rev.4 and the modest changes introduced into the US food aid programme in 2014. In other words, the steps taken in US food aid policy – the programmes that matter the most internationally because of their size – may fall short of meeting the requirements of Rev.4. To confirm or refute such a hypothesis would require a comprehensive examination of US programmes in relation to the rules of Rev.4. That said, the food aid programmes of other countries might also need to be examined to assess their compatibility with the rules of Rev.4.

Export competition digest

Rules and commitments on export competition fall into the four categories of export subsidies, export financing support, agricultural exporting state trading enterprises (STEs), and international food aid. In Bali in 2013, Ministers recognised that the use of export subsidies had declined and expressed their desire to achieve the elimination of export subsidies as soon as possible. The much reduced use of export subsidies would seem to make it possible for countries also to commit not to use them in the future. Some phase-in periods and delayed application as indicated in Rev.4 might be part of such commitments. In the few situations where a country relies particularly on export subsidies in supporting a product sector, such commitments might be facilitated if part of a larger package of reforms. With regard to export financing support, changes have been made in a major US programme over several years and further changes may emerge. This should help to reach agreement on the provisions at issue in Rev.4. On agricultural exporting STEs, the reduction in their roles over recent years would seem to make it easier to reach agreement on the Rev.4 rules for their future activities. Also on international food aid, there have been some changes in US policy in the direction of aligning more with the rules of Rev.4. Those steps may fall short of what would be needed for an agreement. Analysis of international food aid programmes in terms of their compatibility with the rules of Rev.4 would be needed for a more solid assessment of the potential for reaching agreement on the Rev.4 provisions at issue.

3.5. Domestic support

Agreement on Agriculture

Exempt and non-exempt support

The AoA domestic support pillar concerns measures that do not operate at the border, such as producer payments and the use of administered prices, and imposes limits on some of the support provided through such measures. The criteria in the domestic support pillar allow countries to classify some of their domestic support measures under three major headings and to exempt the support under these measures from being counted towards the limits. The three headings are those of Annex 2 (often called the green box), Article 6.5 (often called the blue box), and Article 6.2 (often called the development box).[23] A set of criteria is specified under each of the three headings. Annex 2 measures must meet (a) the fundamental requirement that they have no, or at most minimal, trade-distorting effects or effects on production, (b) two basic criteria, essentially that the support be provided through publicly funded programmes and that the support not have the effect of providing price support to producers, and (c) sets of policy-specific criteria and conditions set out in Annex 2. Article 6.5 measures are direct payments under production-limiting programmes if the payments meet certain specified criteria relating to the fixity or size of the parameters on which payments are based. Article 6.2 measures are investment subsidies generally available to agriculture in developing countries, input subsidies generally available to low-income or resource-poor producers in developing countries, and support to producers in developing countries to encourage diversification from growing illicit narcotic crops.

AMSs, de minimis, and Total AMS

Support through measures that are not exempted under any of the three sets of criteria is measured through a number of Aggregate Measurements of Support (AMSs). Each AMS is subject to a level – either a threshold or a limit – calculated as a certain percentage of the value of production (VOP) in a year, with VOPs being measured for individual products for product-specific AMSs and for agriculture as a whole for the non-product-specific AMS.[24] The percentages, called *de minimis* percentages, are specified as 5% for developed countries and 10% for developing countries (Article 6.4). China uses 8.5% per its Protocol of Accession to the WTO.

For many countries the *de minimis* levels, which vary with values of production from year to year, are upper limits on the amounts of non-exempt support that can be provided. This is the case for the 99 countries that do not have a Bound Total AMS inscribed in their schedule (out of 131 schedules prior to the accession of Seychelles). Out of these, 95 are developing countries (including China). A total of 32 countries have a Bound Total AMS, of which 15 are developed countries and 17 developing countries. Countries with a Bound Total AMS are obliged to keep their applied AMS support, measured through a Current Total AMS, at no more than the Bound Total AMS level. The Current Total AMS in a year is the sum of all AMSs except those that are no larger than their *de minimis* levels. The *de minimis* levels for these countries are thus thresholds, not limits.

In the set of 20 countries in this report (7 developed and 13 developing), 14 have a Bound Total AMS (7 developed and 7 developing) (**Table 3.11**). The five developing countries without a Bound Total AMS are China, India, Indonesia, Nigeria, the Philippines, and Turkey. The levels of Bound Total AMS among the 14 countries range from USD 75 million (Argentina) to around USD 100 000 million (EU28), converted at 2008 exchange rates.

Draft modalities

Bound Total AMS and de minimis

Rev.4 would reduce the Bound Total AMS of 11 or 12 of the 14 countries with a Bound Total AMS in this report (**Table 3.11**). Argentina would not reduce its Bound Total AMS because it is less than USD 100 million. Viet Nam would not reduce its Bound Total AMS because it is named as a "very recently acceded member" in Rev.4. The treatment of Russia's Bound Total AMS is uncertain, since Russia is implementing reductions in 2012 to 2018 under its WTO accession commitments and it is not clear what, if any, reductions Russia would face after that.

The reduction percentages for Bound Total AMS would range from 30% for Brazil, Korea, Mexico, South Africa, and Thailand (developing countries) to 70% for the European Union and Japan (**Table 3.11**). The differences across countries in their present levels of Bound Total AMS are large when expressed in a common currency. Therefore the percentage reductions, large as they may seem for some countries, do not much change the rank ordering of the 14 countries in terms of their final Bound Total AMS after implementing the Rev.4 reductions.

Rev.4 would reduce the *de minimis* percentages of at least 12 of the 20 countries (**Table 3.12**). India, Indonesia, Nigeria, the Philippines, and Turkey would not reduce their 10% figure (developing countries without Bound Total AMS). China's accession documents refer to its 8.5% *de minimis* exemption in the context of Article 6.4, which may mean that China would not reduce that *de minimis* percentage. Viet Nam, as a very recently acceded country, would not reduce that percentage either. The developing countries with a Bound Total AMS – Argentina, Brazil, Korea, Mexico, South Africa and Thailand – would reduce the percentage from 10.0% to 6.7%. Canada, the European Union, Japan, Norway, Switzerland and the United States would reduce from 5.0% to 2.5%. Again, the treatment of Russia is unclear – as a developed country it would reduce from 5.0% to 2.5%, but if it were to be treated as a very recently acceded country, it would maintain its 5% figure. The reduction in any country's *de minimis* percentage means that, *ceteris paribus*, more AMSs may be counted in Current Total AMS. This occurs if some AMSs are between the 2.5% and 5.0% levels, or between the 6.7% and

10.0% levels for developing countries, and has implications for countries' ability to comply with their reduced Bound Total AMS under Rev.4.

Product-specific AMSs

Rev.4 would introduce upper limits or caps on the product-specific AMSs. For developed countries these caps would generally be based on their average applied AMS support during the period 1995-2000. However, many special rules would apply. The United States would have caps totalling the average product-specific AMS support provided in 1995-2000 but the caps would be distributed among products in proportion to the average product-specific AMSs in 1995-2004, not those of 1995-2000. The effect is to generate a larger cap for a few US crops, such as rice and cotton, making the caps on other products correspondingly smaller.

For developing countries the caps would be set in accordance with a variety of rules designed to give considerable flexibility to those countries that did not have large product-specific AMSs in a base period. A choice among three methods is offered. Method 1 makes the caps equal to the average product-specific AMSs in 1995-2000 or 1995-2004. Method 2 makes the caps equal to 20% of the products' average values of production in 1995-2000 or 1995-2004 (depending on the interpretation of Rev.4, China might under this method use 17%). Method 3 makes the caps equal to 20% of the annual Bound Total AMS in the "relevant" year of the period when Rev.4 commitments are implemented. Developed countries and developing countries using Method 1 would have access to further provisions for setting the caps if they had no or only small product-specific AMSs in the years on which their caps otherwise would be based.

The caps on product-specific AMSs are thus established from a menu of choices using country-specific data at a disaggregated level. This makes it impossible to generalise about the resulting patterns of caps or to establish with confidence the caps any particular country would choose. The extant analysis usually assumes that countries consider larger caps for themselves as more desirable than lower caps. Some analysis assumes that a developing country without a Bound Total AMS would not be subject to limits on product-specific AMSs, other than the yearly *de minimis* limits under Articles 6.4 as applied under Article 7.2(b). Other readings of Rev.4 could find that after these *de minimis* limits grow larger than the product-specific limits established under paragraphs 27(a) or 27(b) of Rev.4, these latter, smaller, limits would be the effective limits.

Few studies calculate the caps that would apply to a country's product-specific AMSs under Rev.4, and even fewer put the projected product-specific AMSs in the context of such caps. It is easy to calculate the average 1995-2000 or 1995-2004 product-specific AMSs. It is somewhat more complicated or at least laborious to determine the caps for products that had no or low product-specific AMSs in those periods. The patterns of product-specific AMSs differ greatly across countries. For example, Brazil, Canada and Korea notify AMSs for numerous products but most are small enough to be *de minimis* in all years. The opposite is true for the European Union, Norway and Switzerland for which AMSs in 1995-2000 are small enough to be *de minimis* are very rare. Korea, Mexico and Thailand notify AMSs that switch irregularly from non-zero to zero and back, making the choice between the 1995-2000 period and the 1995-2004 period important. Some developing countries have not notified for the full 1995-2004 period (Turkey), making it impossible to calculate the relevant average. The situation for recently acceded countries (Russia, Viet Nam) is unclear, since they have no notified time series of product-specific AMSs from 1995 onwards. Also, since developing countries can choose among different methods, it could be premature to choose any particular method for analytical purposes. Envisaging the pattern of limits on product-specific AMSs is thus complicated by several factors.[25] No attempt is therefore made here to establish the caps on product-specific AMSs that would result from applying the provisions of Rev.4.[26]

Table 3.11. Bound Total AMS before and after any Rev.4 reduction

Country	Level corresponding to 2008 Bound Total AMS in USD million	Currency of base data or of Bound Total AMS		Bound Total AMS in 2014	Rev.4 reduction		Bound Total AMS after any reduction
		Currency	Units		Reduction by	Paragraph/ sentence	
Argentina	75	ARS of 1992	Million	75	0%	16/3	75
Brazil	912	USD	Million	912	30%	16/1	638
Canada	4 031	CAD	Million	4 301	45%	13(c)	2 366
China (People's Republic of)	-	CNY	-	-	-	-	-
EU (a)	98 763	EUR	Million	67 160	70%	13(a)	20 148
India	-	INR	Million	-	-	-	-
Indonesia	-	IDR	Billion	-	-	-	-
Japan	39 616	JPY	Billion	3 973	70%	14/1	1 192
Korea	1 352	KRW	Billion	1 490	30%	16/1	1 043
Mexico	8 332	MXP of 1991	Million	25 161	30%	16/1	17 613
Nigeria (b)	-	No data	-	-	-	-	-
Norway	2 030	NOK	Million	11 449	52.5%	14/2	5 438
Philippines	-	PHP	-	-	-	-	-
Russia (c)	4 400	USD	Billion	9	51.1%	Not available	4.4
South Africa	244	ZAR	Million	2 015	30%	16/1	1 411
Switzerland	3 930	CHF	Million	4 257	52.5%	14/2	2 022
Thailand	571	THB	Million	19 028	30%	16/1	13 320
Turkey	-	TRY	-	-	-	-	-
United States	19 103	USD	Million	19 103	60%	13(b)	7 641
Viet Nam	243	VND	Billion	3 962	0%	19/1	3 962

Notes: (a) Bound Total AMS is for EU15 as given in source. Report G/AG/R/53 of 4 February 2009 gives EU27 Bound Total AMS as EUR 72 244 million. (b) Nigeria's G/AG/AGST/NGA shows no currency. (c) Russia reduces Bound Total AMS to USD 4.4 billion by 2018 under accession commitments (reduction percentage not specified). Not identified as RAM (recently acceded) or VRAM (very recently acceded) in Rev.4.

Source: WTO (2009); author's calculations.

Table 3.12. *De minimis* percentages

Country	*De minimis* percentage before Rev.4	Rev.4 reduction		*De minimis* percentage after any reduction
		Reduction by	Paragraph in Rev.4	
Argentina	10%	33.3%	31	6.7%
Brazil	10%	33.3%	31	6.7%
Canada	5%	50%	30	2.5%
China (People's Republic of)	8.5%	0%	See notes	8.5%
European Union	5%	50%	30	2.5%
India	10%	0%	32	10%
Indonesia	10%	0%	32	10%
Japan	5%	50%	30	2.5%
Korea	10%	33.3%	31	6.7%
Mexico	10%	33.3%	31	6.7%
Nigeria	10%	0%	32	10%
Norway	5%	50%	30	2.5%
Philippines	10%	0%	32	10%
Russia	5%		See notes	
South Africa	10%	33.3%	31	6.7%
Switzerland	5%	50%	30	2.5%
Thailand	10%	33.3%	31	6.7%
Turkey	10%	0%	32	10%
United States	5%	50%	30	2.5%
Viet Nam	10%	0%	33	10%

Notes: China: paragraph 31 refers to Article 6.4, which mentions 5.0% and 10.0% only, not 8.5%; assume China (developing country without BTAMS) does not reduce *de minimis* percentage; Rev.4 does not mention Russia.

Sources: *De minimis* percentage: AGST, notifications, accession documents; author's calculations.

Total blue box payments and product-specific blue box payments

Rev.4 would expand the set of direct payments that are excluded from Current Total AMS on grounds of meeting the blue box criteria: in addition, certain payments that do not require production would be excluded from Current Total AMS. However, Rev.4 would also impose a scheduled ceiling limit on total blue box support. For most developed countries, this would be a fixed limit equal to 2.5% of the average value of production in agriculture in 1995-2000. The corresponding limit for developing countries would be set at 5% of the value of production, which could be that of the 1995-2004 period if it is larger than in 1995-2000. Certain exceptional rules would apply to the blue box ceiling for particular countries that are not identified in Rev.4 (sometimes mentioned in common parlance as the Norway and Korea clauses). Recently acceded countries would establish their total blue box limit in similar ways as developing countries, using the 5% level. The total blue box limit for most countries would be a single fixed amount, although for at least one country (possibly Norway) that fixed level could be reached after two years of reduction. Estimates of the total blue box limits are shown in **Table 3.13**.

Rev.4 would also introduce limits on product-specific blue box payments. In the most basic case these limits are the average blue box payments a country made in 1995-2000 (1995-2004 for developing countries). Special rules would apply for the calculation of limits for the United States. Relatively few countries made blue box payments in that period: the European Union and some of its more recent member states, Iceland (1995 only), Japan, Norway and the United States (1995 only). Rev.4 has provisions for other countries to establish product-specific blue box limits, either as a sort of "trade-off" for scheduling lower limits on product-specific AMSs for the products concerned or as a share of the overall limit on blue box payments. The maximum share of that overall limit that could be devoted to product-specific blue box payments would be 2.5% for developed countries and 30.0% for developing countries.

A special rule allows a larger product-specific blue box limit than otherwise would be the case for a country that switches from AMS to blue box support for a product meeting certain criteria (this may be applicable to rice in Korea). The rules thus seem generally designed to facilitate a shift of support from the AMS type to types that meet the blue box criteria, particularly blue box support that is not product-specific.

Table 3.13. Total blue box limits

Country	Overall blue box limit based on years	Percentage of average value of production	Currency and units	Total blue box limit	Total blue box limit USD billion
Argentina	1995-2000	5%	USD million	1 015	1.0
Brazil	1995-2000	5%	USD million	2 601	2.6
Canada	1995-2000	2.5%	CAD million	761	0.5
China (People's Republic of)	1995-2004	5%	CNY billion	117	14.1
EU28	1995-2000	2.5%	EUR billion	6 912	7.8
India	1995-2004	5%	INR billion	230	5.1
Indonesia	1995-2004	5%	IDR billion	24 390	3.7
Japan	1995-2000	2.5%	JPY billion	252	2.2
Korea	1995-2004	5%	KRW billion	1 615	1.5
Mexico	1995-2000	5%	MXP 1991 billion	3 708	1.4
Nigeria	1995-2004	5%	No data	?	?
Norway	1995-2000	See notes	NOK billion	3.6	0.6
Philippines	1995-2004	5%	PHP billion	23 438	0.6
Russia				-	-
South Africa	1995-2004	5%	ZAR billion	2 539	0.4
Switzerland	1995-2000	2.5%	CHF billion	286	0.2
Thailand	1995-2004	5%	THB billion	27 575	0.8
Turkey	1995-2000	5%	TRY billion	2 166	2.2
United States	1995-2000	2.5%	USD billion	4 898	4.9
Viet Nam	1995-2004	5%	VND billion	6 254	0.5

Notes: Limits in USD billion are calculated from 1995-2000 or 1995-2004 values of production in local currency and USD in WTO (2010b) (also called S/21/Rev.5). Argentina may schedule Total blue box limit in ARS of 1992, like Bound Total AMS; USD value here results from values of production available only in USD. EU28 is based on sum of values of production of EU27 and Croatia. Norway: average 1995-2000 blue box payments reduced by 52.5% (para. 39 of Rev.4). Many amounts are rounded.

Source: Author's calculations.

Overall trade-distorting support

Rev.4 would introduce a bound ceiling limit on what could be called the Current Overall Trade-Distorting Support (OTDS). (Rev.4 does not use this term). Rev.4 specifies how countries are to calculate their Base OTDS, and it imposes reductions from this base for numerous countries. All or a large part of Base OTDS consists of a given share of the average value of production in 1995-2000 for developed countries and 1995-2000 or 1995-2004 for developing countries. Base OTDS for all countries without a Bound Total AMS, i.e. most countries, is calculated only as a given share (15% or 25%) of this historical value of production.

Base OTDS for nearly all countries with a Bound Total AMS is calculated as that share plus the limit on certain support, not the amount of applied support. Base OTDS for Norway and the European Union is calculated as the sum of average blue box support in 1995-2000, 10% of value of production, and the limit on certain support.

The Base OTDS would be reduced by different percentages for different countries, or not at all for some. **Table 3.14** indicates the estimated Base OTDS levels, the percentage reductions and the resulting Bound OTDS. As developing countries without a Bound Total AMS, the following countries in this report would not reduce their Base OTDS: China, India, Indonesia, the Philippines, Turkey and Viet Nam. It appears that their scheduled Bound OTDS would equal their Base OTDS (Rev.4 may be open to alternative interpretations on this point). Other countries would schedule Base, Annual and Final Bound OTDS entitlements.

Under Rev.4 commitments, each country would "ensure that the sum of the applied levels of trade-distorting support under each OTDS component does not exceed" the Bound OTDS levels (WTO 2008a, para. 11). In other words, Current OTDS must not exceed Bound OTDS, similar to the existing obligation that Current Total AMS must not exceed Bound Total AMS. This can be open to interpretation, since Rev.4 does not identify what is trade-distorting support. The Base OTDS is not calculated from levels of applied support, as outlined above, which opens the door to several interpretations of what constitutes the applied levels of trade-distorting support. For example, only the green box provisions include a requirement that exempt measures have no, or at most minimal, trade-distorting effects. No such requirement applies to blue box and Article 6.2 measures, which means that these measures can have large trade-distorting effects.

Other provisions in Rev.4 may also be open to interpretation. For example, it would allow recently acceded countries, without identifying them, to provide AMS support in excess of their OTDS commitment levels, if the AMSs are *de minimis* AMSs. There is no time limit on this provision. As the agricultural values of production grow, the *de minimis* allowances also grow. When they eventually exceed the OTDS commitment level, that commitment level will become inoperative as a constraint on AMS support. Depending on the criteria for being a recently acceded country, this provision might be enjoyed by China, Viet Nam, Russia and others.

Bali decisions

At the conference in December 2013, Ministers took two decisions on domestic support. One concerns certain programmes that are not expressly mentioned in Annex 2 (Green Box) under the heading "General services". In particular, the decision means that many programmes relating to land reform and rural livelihood security explicitly could be considered as green box "General services" programmes, including land rehabilitation, soil conservation and resource management, drought management and flood control, rural employment programmes, issuance of property titles, and farmer settlement programmes. The other decision concerns issues under the green box heading "Public stockholding for food security purposes", specifically the condition for exempting expenditures when stocks are acquired at administered prices. This decision is discussed in more detail in Section 2.6 below.

Information from notifications

The effects of countries' domestic support policy settings are revealed in their notifications to the WTO Committee on Agriculture. The Committee requires yearly notifications from most countries (including all the countries in this study). In a yearly notification, a country shows how it classifies its domestic support measures with regard to the criteria of Annex 2, Article 6.2, and Article 6.5 of the AoA, i.e. the green, blue and development boxes. The country specifies the support provided it claims meet the criteria to be exempt from limits. It reports the non-exempt support measured in each of the product-specific AMSs and in the non-product-specific AMS. It shows the calculation of Current Total AMS, if any, by distinguishing between the AMSs that exceed the *de minimis* threshold and the AMSs that do not.

Table 3.14. Calculation of Base OTDS and Bound OTDS

Country	Elements entering Base OTDS			Currency	Units	Base OTDS	Rev.4 reduction		Bound OTDS after any reduction
	Share of historical VOP	Bound Total AMS	Historical blue box payments				Reduction	Paragraph	
Argentina	X	X		ARS of 1992	million	5 149	37%	7	3 261
Brazil	X	X		USD	billion	13.9	37%	7	8.8
Canada	X	X		CAD	million	8 870	55%	3(c)	3 991
China (People's Republic of)	X			CNY	billion	584.4	0%	6	584.4
EU28	X	X	X	EUR	billion	120.8	80%	3(a)	24.2
India	X			INR	billion	1 151	0%	6	1 151
Indonesia	X			IDR	billion	121 948	0%	6	121 948
Japan	X	X		JPY	billion	5 483	75%	4	1 371
Korea	X	X		KRW	billion	9 566	37%	7	6 058
Mexico	X	X		MXP of 1991	million	43 702	37%	7	27 676
Nigeria	X			NGN	-	-	0%	6&10	-
Norway	X	X	X	NOK	billion	21.1	55%	3(c)	9.5
Philippines	X			PHP	billion	117	0%	6	117
Russia	X	X		USD	billion	8.7	37%	9	5.5
South Africa	X	X		ZAR	million	14 708	37%	7	9 315
Switzerland	X	X		CHF	million	5 970	55%	3(c)	2 687
Thailand	X	X		THB	million	156 902	37%	7	99 366
Turkey	X			USD	million	10 380	0%	6	10 380
United States	X	X		USD	billion	48.5	70%	3(b)	14.5
Viet Nam	X	X		VND	billion	35 234	0%	9	35 234

Notes: Base OTDS calculated in currency of Bound Total AMS, if applicable, or WTO (2010b) (TN/AG/S/21/Rev.5). No data on value of production for Nigeria in WTO (2010b). Table shows Russia assumed as recently acceded country; if a very recently acceded country, no reduction from Base OTDS. Many amounts are rounded.

Source: Author's calculations. Historical VOP from WTO (2010b) (Russia VOP from OECD PSE database); BTAMS from WTO (2009) (Russia FBTAMS from schedule; blue box from notifications).

Countries differ in how they classify measures and calculate support in interpreting the AoA, and also in how transparent and comprehensive they make their notifications. Moreover, although the Committee requires notifications to be submitted within a few months after the end of the relevant year, most countries lag several years behind the agreed timetable for notifications. The notified information consequently needs to be complemented with other information to bring the picture more up to date. However, because of the particularities in how measures are classified and support is measured in notifications, there is rarely a one-to-one correspondence between information in, for example, OECD monitoring and evaluation reports and what countries show in their notifications.[27]

Table 3.15 gives a very brief synopsis of how countries' applied domestic support in recent years relates to commitments on Bound Total AMS and to the *de minimis* rules under the AoA and Rev.4. The applied domestic support is the result of the particular policy settings used in the notified year. In concept, this is similar to an applied tariff, but the concepts differ greatly in that the applied domestic support is the combined outcome of many policy settings.

AMSs, de minimis, *Current Total AMS and Bound Total AMS: situation*

The 19 countries in **Table 3.15** have reported that they are in compliance with the existing rules and commitments under the AoA.[28] Most of these countries would have no problem fitting their recently applied AMS support within the confines resulting from Rev.4. Since Rev.4 in many cases does not further constrain their AMS support, it follows that their applied AMS support also meets their Rev.4 limits. This is the case for **India, Indonesia, the Philippines, Turkey and Viet Nam.**[29] These countries have no Bound Total AMS to be reduced and their *de minimis* percentage is not reduced. A question may be raised with regard to Turkey, both because its latest notification is only for 2001, and because its reporting of a product-specific AMS (sugar beets) is several times larger than its *de minimis* limit, which does not seem to comply with what the Agreement requires.[30]

Other countries are also found in a situation where recently applied AMS support seems to fit within the rules of Rev.4, although this assessment is, to some extent, also based on judgment.

- **Argentina's** increases in support appear to have been modest enough that, if the support were to be classified as AMS support, the resulting AMSs would remain *de minimis* even under the reduced Rev.4 *de minimis* percentage. Bound Total AMS would not be reduced under Rev.4.
- For **Brazil,** even though the non-product-specific AMS is a large item among its AMSs, its 2011/12 level remains below the reduced *de minimis* threshold of 6.7% and Current Total AMS is much below the reduced Bound Total AMS of Rev.4.
- Likewise, the **European Union** reports only few, if any, AMSs in the critical interval between the current 5.0% and the reduced level of 2.5% under Rev.4. The European Union also reports a Current Total AMS in 2011/2012 that falls far short of the Bound Total AMS, even under Rev.4. This pattern of EU support seems easily accommodated under Rev.4.
- **Japan** is in a situation similar to that of the European Union, with a 2012 Current Total AMS much below both the present Bound Total AMS and the considerably reduced Bound Total AMS of Rev.4.
- **Korea** also shows a Current Total AMS, albeit from as long ago as 2008, of 2% or 3% of the Bound Total AMS of the Agreement and as reduced under Rev.4. With the *de minimis* AMSs well below the reduced 6.7% thresholds under Rev.4, Korea would appear to be able to fit more AMS support into its *de minimis* AMSs, which could include reported increases in some kinds of support since 2008.
- **Mexico's** situation, although informed by a notification from 2007 only, appears to be very similar to that of Korea. In addition, Mexico has the advantage of having a Bound Total AMS in

an inflation-proofed (indexed) currency, which allows for growing nominal non-*de minimis* AMS support over time.

- **Nigeria** has notified nil domestic support of any kind for all years through 2011.
- **South Africa** reported nil AMS support in 2010 and earlier years, i.e. there were no AMSs, either *de minimis* or not. This makes for obvious compliance with both the Agreement and Rev.4.

A few countries appear to face problems if domestic support under recent policy settings were to be confronted with the rules and commitments of Rev.4.

- **Canada** has no problem staying below the present Bound Total AMS and also that of Rev.4 as long as the *de minimis* percentage is not reduced. However, any cut, but particularly the cut under Rev.4 from 5.0% to 2.5%, would make the 2011 non-product-specific AMS exceed its *de minimis* threshold. Including the large non-product-specific AMS, along with several smaller product-specific AMSs, makes Current Total AMS exceed the Rev.4 Bound Total AMS.
- **Norway's** Current Total AMS in 2013 was relatively close to its Bound Total AMS but amounts to 182% of its Bound Total AMS under Rev.4. Moreover, a couple of AMSs were in the critical interval between 2.5% and 5.0% of value of production, thereby exceeding the *de minimis* thresholds under Rev.4 and would further add to Current Total AMS under Rev.4. While output-based support may have decreased since 2013 measured in economic terms, most of Norway's AMS support is concentrated in a few products benefitting from applied administered prices. Although administered prices have been abandoned for several products, most recently for sheep and eggs in 2014, it is uncertain whether this reduces AMS support enough to bring Current Total AMS below the reduced Bound Total AMS of Rev.4 (Norway is discussed in more detail below).
- **Switzerland** does not exempt any AMSs from Current Total AMS on *de minimis* grounds. Thus, the Rev.4 reduction in the *de minimis* percentage does not affect Switzerland. The reduction in Bound Total AMS is, however, of great consequence: the 2012 Current Total AMS exceeds the reduced Bound Total AMS of Rev.4. The margin of excess is quite modest at 9% but is nevertheless a signal that the present policy support pattern would need adjustment under Rev.4.
- **Thailand** reports a Current Total AMS for 2008 that is 1% or less of its Bound Total AMS and of the reduced Bound Total AMS under Rev.4. This is, however, precarious because it depends on the rice AMS being *de minimis*. The 2008 rice AMS would not be *de minimis* under the reduced 6.7% of Rev.4. In fact, a 2008 rice AMS that is not *de minimis* would by itself be more than double the reduced Bound Total AMS of Rev.4. Depending on how Thailand manages its policy support for rice, it would be a challenge to comply with the Rev.4 rules and commitments.
- The 2012 Current Total AMS of the **United States** was well below its Bound Total AMS (USD 19.1 billion) and also below its Bound Total AMS under Rev.4 (USD 7.6 billion).[31] However, in a policy change more clearly demarcated than in many other countries, the applied policy support to be notified for 2014-18 will be governed by many other settings than those of 2012. Large crop payments can be made under the 2014 Agricultural Act in case of low prices or revenues, and there is also a potential for dairy payments in some years.[32] Payments under the two major new crop programmes in 2014 could sum to more than USD 7.4 billion under a particular set of assumptions regarding prices, yields, and programme participation (Zulauf and Orden, 2014).

Table 3.15. Assessment of Rev.4 reductions in Bound Total AMS and *de minimis* percentage

Country	BTAMS: Rev.4 as % of AoA	*de minimis* percentage: AoA to Rev.4	Assessment
Argentina	No reduction	From 10.0% to 6.7%	• 2008-09 CTAMS was at almost 100% of AoA BTAMS and almost 100% of Rev.4 BTAMS. • Only tobacco AMS exceeded *de minimis* threshold. • BTAMS expressed in inflation-adjusted currency units, allowing nominal increase over time. • Recent increases in policy support to dairy, beef, poultry and wheat. • If this support is classified as AMSs, they may be modest enough to remain as *de minimis* AMSs under the Rev.4 percentage of 6.7%.
Brazil	70%	From 10.0% to 6.7%	• 2011/12 CTAMS was at 8% of AoA BTAMS and 12% of Rev.4 BTAMS, because several product-specific AMSs were *de minimis*. • Previous years saw levels around 24% and 35%, respectively, when more AMSs exceeded *de minimis*. • Non-product-specific AMS, mainly credit-related support, was the largest AMS but remained well below its 6.7% *de minimis* threshold also under Rev.4.
Canada	55%	From 5.0% to 2.5%	• 2011 CTAMS was at 12% of AoA BTAMS and 22% of Rev.4 BTAMS. • Many AMSs were much below *de minimis*. • Non-product-specific AMS was close to *de minimis* threshold in recent years and exceeded the Rev.4 *de minimis* threshold. • Including non-product-specific AMS and product-specific AMSs greater than the 2.5% *de minimis* thresholds makes CTAMS exceed Rev.4 BTAMS.
China (People's Republic of)	No Bound Total AMS	No reduction?	• All 2008 AMSs were *de minimis* at levels no more than 2.5%. • Increasing support in more recent years according to OECD indicators may register also as increasing AMS support. • If the *de minimis* percentage were to be reduced to less than 8.5% under Rev.4, likelihood of a recent year's AMS exceeding the corresponding limit seems low. • If the *de minimis* percentage were not reduced under Rev.4, the absence of a BTAMS means Rev.4 does not affect the ease or difficulty of AMS compliance.
European Union	30%	From 5% to 2.5%	• 2011/2012 CTAMS was at 10% of AoA BTAMS and 32% of Rev.4 BTAMS. • Many AMSs were very small. • Few if any 2011/2012 AMSs were between 2.5% and 5.0% – thus little effect of Rev.4 reduction of *de minimis* percentage.
India	No Bound Total AMS	No reduction	• Only three AMSs reported for 2010-2011, of which two were shown as negative. • Rice AMS was claimed as *de minimis* (no value of production). • Later years' rice AMS possibly larger than 2010-2011 as a result of increased administered prices. • Because of absence of a BTAMS and no reduction in *de minimis* limits, Rev.4 does not affect the ease or difficulty of AMS compliance.
Indonesia	No Bound Total AMS	No reduction	• Nil AMS support reported for 2011 and earlier years. • According to the OECD, the dominant part of producer support is price support, which rose considerably in 2012 as minimum purchase prices were raised. • Indonesia does not account for these or other support components in AMSs. • Because of absence of a BTAMS and no reduction in *de minimis* limits, Rev.4 does not affect the ease or difficulty of AMS compliance.

Table 3.15. Assessment of Rev.4 reductions in Bound Total AMS and *de minimis* percentage (*cont.*)

Country	BTAMS: Rev.4 as % of AoA	*de minimis* percentage: AoA to Rev.4	Assessment
Japan	30%	From 5.0% to 2.5%	• 2012 CTAMS was at 15% of BTAMS and 51% of Rev.4 BTAMS. • De minimis AMSs were well below the 2.5% threshold of Rev.4. • The OECD reports that payment support increased in 2013, while price support declined, although Japan does not account for price support in rice AMS.
Korea	70%	From 10.0% to 6.7%	• 2008 CTAMS was at 2% of AoA BTAMS and 3% of Rev.4 BTAMS. • De minimis AMSs were well below the 6.7% threshold of Rev.4. • OECD producer support increased between 2008 and 2013, but Korea does not account for price support in rice AMS.
Mexico	70%	From 10.0% to 6.7%	• 2007 CTAMS was at 2% of AoA BTAMS and 3% of Rev.4 BTAMS. • Very few AMSs between 6.7% and 10.0% thresholds – either much larger or much smaller. • BTAMS expressed in inflation-adjusted currency units, allowing nominal increase over time. • Share of commodity-based support (price support and some payments) in gross farm receipts increased from 2007 to 2013 according to the OECD, but little of such support is represented in AMSs.
Nigeria	No Bound Total AMS	No reduction	• Without any domestic support of any kind, no problem meeting nil commitment.
Norway	47.5%	From 5.0% to 2.5%	• 2013 CTAMS was at 86% of AoA BTAMS and 182% of Rev.4 BTAMS. • A couple of de minimis AMSs between 2.5% and 5.0% thresholds. • Output-based support has declined since 2011, as per the OECD. • Most AMS support concentrated in a few products, where application of administered price matters greatly for the size of AMS. Administered prices recently abandoned for several products.
Philippines	No Bound Total AMS	No reduction	• 2010 AMS support reported for rice and maize only. • De minimis AMSs were at 3% and 0% of value of production, well below 10% limits. • Because of absence of a BTAMS and no reduction in de minimis limits, Rev.4 does not affect the ease or difficulty of AMS compliance.
Russia	-	-	• 2012 CTAMS was at 64% of 2012 BTAMS and 132% of 2018 BTAMS after full accession reductions. • Status of recently acceded (RAM) or very recently acceded (VRAM) is not specified in Rev.4. • If RAM, reduce BTAMS by 30% after full accession reductions and reduce de minimis percentage from 5.0% to 4.2%. • If VRAM, Rev.4 does not affect the ease or difficulty of AMS compliance: no reduction in either BTAMS or de minimis limits.
South Africa	70%	From 10.0% to 6.7%	• 2010 CTAMS was nil. No AMS support was reported, i.e. no de minimis AMSs. • No domestic market interventions, according to the OECD. • Because no AMS support is reported, Rev.4 does not affect the ease or difficulty of AMS compliance.
Switzerland	47.5%	From 5.0% to 2.5%	• 2012 CTAMS was at 52% of AoA BTAMS and 109% of Rev.4 BTAMS. • None of the 16 product-specific AMSs was claimed as de minimis; no non-product-specific AMS reported. • Because there are no de minimis claims, the Rev.4 reduction of de minimis percentage does not affect the ease or difficulty of AMS compliance.

Table 3.15. Assessment of Rev.4 reductions in Bound Total AMS and *de minimis* percentage (*cont.*)

Country	BTAMS: Rev.4 as % of AoA	*de minimis* percentage: AoA to Rev.4	Assessment
Thailand	70%	From 10.0% to 6.7%	• 2008 CTAMS was 0% (rounded) of AoA BTAMS and 1% of Rev.4 BTAMS. • Three AMSs were de minimis, of which two were almost nil and rice AMS was close to the 10% threshold. • Rice AMS exceeded the threshold in earlier years. • The 2008 rice AMS (no calculation details reported) by itself was 156% of AoA BTAMS and 223% of Rev.4 BTAMS. As de minimis it did not enter the CTAMS.
Turkey	No Bound Total AMS	No reduction	• Latest notification is for 2001. One AMS was not de minimis but was nevertheless excluded from CTAMS (which must be nil). • The excluded AMS was several times larger than the 10% de minimis threshold. • Other AMSs were much below their de minimis thresholds. • The OECD reports recent output-based support larger than in 2001. • Because of absence of a BTAMS and no reduction in de minimis limits, Rev.4 does not affect the ease or difficulty of AMS compliance.
United States	40%	From 5.0% to 2.5%	• 2012 CTAMS was at 36% of AoA BTAMS and 90% of Rev.4 BTAMS. • As many as 72 AMSs in 2012, of which 14 were larger than their de minimis thresholds, many were only a fraction of a percentage point of value of production, and nine were between 2.5% and 5.0%. • Therefore only moderate effect of Rev.4 reduction of de minimis percentage. • The OECD reported lower output-based support in 2013 than in several earlier years but noted importance of 2014 Farm Act combined with prices and revenues for future levels of support.
Viet Nam	No reduction	No reduction	• 2008 CTAMS was nil. Several AMSs were reported (including rice), all of which were only a very small fraction of their de minimis thresholds. • Because there is no reduction in either BTAMS or de minimis limits, Rev.4 does not affect the ease or difficulty of AMS compliance.

Notes: The table draws on countries' latest domestic support notifications (mid-January 2015), resulting in different years of observation among countries. Countries' own methods of expressing split years are retained here. BTAMS = Bound Total AMS; CTAMS = Current Total AMS.

Sources: Calculated from notifications G/AG/N/*, where * stands for: ARG/31, BRA/32, CAN/98, CHN/21, EU/20, IND/10, IDN/34, JPN/191, KOR/43 and KOR/43/Corr.1, MEX/21, NGA/15, NOR/78, PHL/42, RUS/5, CHE/167, ZAF/77, THA/75, TUR/14, USA/100, VNM/4. References to the OECD are OECD (2013) and OECD (2014). Also WT/TPR/S/277/Rev.1 (Argentina). Columns "BTAMS: Rev.4 as % of AoA" and "*de minimis* percentage: AoA to Rev.4" derive from Tables 11 and 12.

- Evaluating potential support in the **United States** in 2014 against the Bound Total AMS of AoA or Rev.4 needs to account for the change, introduced in the 2012 notification, to reporting premium subsidies for insurance as product-specific support.[33] This leaves more room within the non-product-specific AMS (*de minimis* threshold of some USD 20 billion; varies by year) for payments under new programmes. While the premium subsidies make some product-specific AMSs large enough to be counted in Current Total AMS, premium subsidies that are part of *de minimis* AMSs are exempted from Current Total AMS. If the new crop payments are reported as non-product-specific support, they can be accommodated within a *de minimis* non-product-specific AMS as long as they, along with some other minor non-product-specific support, do not exceed some USD 20 billion. This would make Current Total AMS stay well below the Bound Total AMS of USD 19.1 billion. The Rev.4 *de minimis* threshold for non-product-specific AMS is around USD 10 billion (varies by year). Without premium subsidies in the non-product-specific AMS, large payments under the two major new crop programmes could thus be accommodated in this AMS while it remains *de minimis*. The Rev.4 Bound Total AMS of USD 7.6 billion would then be available for a number of non-*de minimis* AMSs, some including premium subsidies and product-specific crop payments. Reporting support under the new crop programmes as product-specific or as non-product-specific thus matters greatly for Current Total AMS, especially under the reduced *de minimis* percentage of 2.5% and the reduced Bound Total AMS under Rev.4.

- Exempting some support in the **United States** under the Rev.4 rules on blue box programmes may be contemplated: the rules allow the exemption of certain direct payments that do not require production.[34] However, the Rev.4 product-specific blue box caps may be more binding than the product-specific AMS caps for most commodities, and the total blue box cap may be more binding than the Bound Total AMS (Glauber and Westhoff, 2015). These authors also find that the limit on OTDS could pose a problem. However, they see some premium subsidies for crop insurance possibly being made green box compliant. Such a policy change would make it easier to meet the Rev.4 limit on OTDS. Altogether, it is impossible to predict with confidence what notification choices the United States is likely to make, whether under the AoA or Rev.4.

For two countries, both of which have acceded to the WTO after 1995, the interpretation of Rev.4 can make a large difference in determining if recent domestic support conforms to the rules and commitments of Rev.4.

- **China** may or may not be required to reduce its *de minimis* percentage from 8.5%. If there is no reduction for China, its AMSs could even find room to grow from 2008 as a result of increasing support of some types. All of its AMSs were less than 2.5% in 2008, which leaves a margin for growth up to 8.5% of value of production. If the *de minimis* percentage were to be reduced from 8.5% to some unknown level, there would likely still be room to increase AMS support to that level.

- **The Russian** Federation is not mentioned in the 2008 Rev.4 since it acceded only in 2012. Rev.4 recognises that there are "recently acceded members" (RAMs) without identifying them, and it identifies some members by name as "very recently acceded members" (VRAMs). On the one hand, Russia acceded more recently than the named VRAMs. On the other hand, Rev.4 does not identify Russia as a VRAM. As a RAM, Russia would need to reduce its Bound Total AMS by 30.0% and reduce its *de minimis* percentage from 5.0% to 4.2%. It is not clear on what timetable the Bound Total AMS reduction would be implemented, since Russia is in the process of reducing Bound Total AMS until 2018 under its WTO accession protocol. Russia's 2012 Current Total AMS was significantly larger than the hypothetical final Bound Total AMS resulting from carrying out the Rev.4 reduction after implementing the accession reduction. As a VRAM, Russia would face no reduction in either Bound Total AMS or *de minimis* percentage. Thus, the challenge would simply be to ensure compliance with the 2018 final Bound Total AMS.

Most of the 19 countries in this study would thus face little or no difficulty in complying with the Bound Total AMS and *de minimis* provisions of Rev.4. Those that could face a challenge in complying include Canada, Norway, Switzerland, Thailand and the United States, as well as possibly Russia and China, depending on the interpretation of Rev.4. For some, such as Switzerland, which has already significantly changed its policies, the challenge would be moderate.

Caps on product-specific AMSs

Commitments under Rev.4 would include limits on each product's AMS, although not on the non-product-specific AMS. Assessing the compliance of support under developed countries' recent policy settings would involve calculating average product-specific AMSs for 1995-2000, as well as the corresponding *de minimis* thresholds, and applying the decision rules of Rev.4 for choosing among the options. Blandford and Orden (2011) have calculated the US caps on product-specific AMSs based on notifications. The 2012 US notification reports AMSs for many more products than the total in earlier notifications. It is clear, however, that 2012 AMSs for several products exceed their Rev.4 caps. Depending on the evolution of prices and revenues, as well as the classification of policies and support, US policy settings applying from 2014 onwards could generate more product-specific AMSs that exceed their caps. In the European Union, Josling and Swinbank (2011) consider that the caps on product-specific AMSs could constrain some commodities especially those where administered prices are applied (nine products in 2011/12). The EU policy provisions in force from 2014 retain essentially the same administered prices as before. Godo and Takahashi (2011) consider that some of Japan's product-specific AMSs under the policy settings introduced in 2010 would exceed their caps. Subsequent changes may have alleviated that concern for some products, although the AMSs for beef and pork have increased over the last three notified years (2010-12).

Developing countries establish their caps on product-specific AMSs under Rev.4 according to one of three options, and the chosen option has to be applied to all products. This latter requirement makes it less likely that developing countries choose Option (a), where the cap is the product's average AMS in 1995-2000 or 1995-2004. Because developing countries generally did not provide large product-specific AMSs in the two periods mentioned, their caps would not be large or would be large only for one or a few products. Option (b) is likely to establish more generous caps, equal to 20% of the product's average value of production in 1995-2000 or 1995-2004 (it is not clear whether China would enjoy a rate of 20% or 17%). This is twice the size of the *de minimis* limits in the periods mentioned. Those developing countries that have a Bound Total AMS (a total of 17) can use Option (c) to establish each cap as 20% of the country's Bound Total AMS in each year after the Rev.4 commitments come into force.[35] Among the countries in this study, Option (c) is open to Argentina, Brazil, Korea, Mexico, South Africa, Thailand and Viet Nam. The developing countries with the largest Bound Total AMS and thus the largest caps on product-specific AMSs under Option (c) are Mexico, Korea and Brazil.

Further analysis would be needed to shed light on the pattern of caps on product-specific AMSs that would emerge under each of the three options and the tightness of the limits on product-specific AMSs. This would be particularly interesting with respect to rice. It enjoys large economic support in many countries, as shown in OECD support measurements. At the same time, rice AMS is reported only as *de minimis* or not reported at all by several of the 20 countries in this study (India, Indonesia, Japan, Korea, Nigeria, the Philippines, Thailand and Viet Nam). In some cases this has to do with the absence of an administered price, while in other cases this seems insufficient as an explanation. Yang and Blandford (2011) use Option (b) for China and Korea, without indicating whether 8.5% or 10% is used for China. They also calculate the cap on rice AMS for Japan on the basis of historical *de minimis* thresholds.

Regardless of which option a country chooses, the caps on product-specific AMSs would be established as fixed nominal amounts (possibly excepting Argentina and Mexico). As values of production grow and the *de minimis* thresholds or limits also grow, they will at some point exceed the caps fixed in nominal terms (values of production in Japan are shrinking, not growing). It is not clear what would then, for a country without a Bound Total AMS, be the operative limit on a product's AMS

– the smaller cap on the product's AMS or the larger *de minimis* limit. One possibility is that the scheduled cap on a product-specific AMS overrides the *de minimis* thresholds or limits under a Rev.4 agreement, which makes for progressively tighter limits on product-specific AMS even as values of production grow. Another possibility is that the *de minimis* thresholds or limits give entitlements to product-specific AMSs larger than their scheduled caps, which effectively makes the caps of a certain size inoperative.

Blue box payments

Rev.4 would establish a ceiling on the total amount of a country's blue box support, i.e. direct payments meeting certain criteria. The ceiling would in most cases correspond to a certain percentage of historical value of production, with 2.5% applying to developed countries and 5.0% to developing countries (**Table 2.13**). Special rules would apply to Norway, which provides a large share of its domestic support in the form of blue box payments. In recent years, blue box payments have been notified by the European Union, Japan, and Norway. While the notified blue box payments of the European Union and Japan are well below the Rev.4 ceiling, Norway reports blue box payments well above the Rev.4 ceiling. Norway's blue box payments have increased in size over several years.

Rev.4 would also impose caps on product-specific blue box payments. Several special rules govern the size of these product-specific entitlements, both for developed and developing countries. In general, the caps on blue box payments for the EU, Japan, and Norway would be established in relation to historical blue box payments, such as those reported in WTO (2010c). For the United States, these caps would be based on the ceiling on total blue box support, apportioned to individual crops.

The European Union notifies blue box payments in a somewhat aggregated form but may foresee establishing caps on a truly product-specific basis, according to its data in WTO (2010c). This study does not attempt to reconcile EU notified blue box payments with the product-specific limits that might be established on the basis of WTO (2010c). EU blue box payments in recent years have, as a result of policy change, been much lower than in the 1995-2000 period represented in WTO (2010c).

While the United States has not for many years claimed any payments as exempt on blue box grounds, the programmes introduced with the 2014 Farm Act raise the possibility of payments being claimed as blue box compliant under Rev.4. The payments under two of those programmes do not require production, which may meet the requirement of Rev.4 for "new blue box" programmes. Moreover, payments are made on 85% or 65% of a farm's base acres, which might meet one of the criteria in Rev.4. The payments may also meet the criterion about fixed and unchanging bases and yields. If so, the United States has leeway to manage its crop payments within the combined confines of Rev.4 on AMS support and blue box payments.

On the basis of WTO (2010c), Japan might establish a limit on product-specific blue box payments to rice at JPY 79 billion. The notified amount of such payments in 2012 was much larger, at JPY 155 billion. Norway also does not report blue box payments by individual products in its notifications, which makes it difficult to assess how recent blue box payments compare to what the caps might be if based on WTO (2010c). It should be noted, however, that even if Norway's total blue box payments have increased in recent years, they are still at a lower level than in the 1995-2000 period on which the product-specific caps would be based. Regarding rice-specific blue box limits, Yang and Blandford (2011) calculate a limit for Japan in the same way as does WTO (2010c).

A developing country can establish product-specific blue box limits without having provided blue box payments in the past. Several special rules also apply. Yang and Blandford (2011) calculate the rice-specific blue box limits for China and Korea on the basis of an interpretation of Rev.4's rules for shifting from AMS to blue box support. Cheng (2011) sets the limit at 10% of the total blue box limit, as provided for in Rev.4. None of the developing countries in this study has notified any blue box support.

Overall trade-distorting support

Rev.4 introduces a limit on "the sum of the applied levels of trade-distorting support under each OTDS component". The limit is established from a base level, which for some countries stays fixed and for some countries is reduced. The base level, referred to as Base OTDS, is for most countries established as a given percentage of the average historical values of production. For most of the 20 countries in this study, the Base OTDS also includes the Bound Total AMS, and for Norway and the European Union it includes, additionally, the average historical blue box payments (the given percentage of the average historical values of production is in this case smaller). **Table 3.14** above provides some details of the elements of Base OTDS and the subsequent Bound OTDS after any reduction.

The Current OTDS is calculated in **Table 3.16** on the basis of the latest notifications available. The year of calculation ranges from 2007 for Mexico to 2012 for Japan, Russia and Switzerland. No calculation is shown for Turkey since its latest notification occurred in 2001. The Current OTDS is calculated under two assumptions: Current OTDS(1) is the sum of Current Total AMS, all *de minimis* AMSs and all blue box payments; Current OTDS(2) is the sum of Current OTDS(1) and all Article 6.2 support, i.e. certain investment and input subsidies in developing countries. The rationale for including Article 6.2 support in the Current OTDS indicator is that such support does not need to be provided through measures that meet the fundamental green box requirement of having no, or at most minimal, trade-distorting effects or effects on production. As trade-distorting support, it is therefore included in "the sum of the applied levels of trade-distorting support under each OTDS component".[36] This argument is strengthened by analysis showing that certain input subsidies, based on variable input use without input constraints, distort production at least as much as economic market price support (OECD 2001b; van Tongeren 2008).

It is clear from **Table 3.16** that most countries have no problem fitting their recent OTDS support, whether OTDS(1) or OTDS(2), within the final Bound OTDS. For some countries, the Bound OTDS is large enough to leave a very large margin above Current OTDS (Argentina, China, Indonesia, Korea, Mexico, the Philippines, South Africa, Thailand and Viet Nam). The margin is smaller but still sizeable for Brazil, Canada, the European Union, Japan, and Switzerland. In the case of India, the large input subsidies claimed under Article 6.2 bring OTDS(2) above the Bound OTDS, while OTDS(1) is very much below. For Norway, the Current OTDS in 2013 is as much as 50% larger than the Bound OTDS. For the United States, Current OTDS in 2012 of USD 12.1 billion was well below its Bound OTDS of USD 14.5 billion. The change in US support policies in 2014 will generate support levels that vary in opposition to prices and revenues. The elimination of one large payment programme, claimed in the green box, is to a large extent offset by more generous support under programmes that do not qualify as green box compliant. This could, *ceteris paribus,* result in more support accounted for in Current OTDS and increase the likelihood of exceeding the Bound OTDS.[37]

The Rev.4 rules on OTDS allow all recently acceded countries to exceed their Bound OTDS if the excess consists of *de minimis* AMSs. Countries' *de minimis* limits generally increase over time, which means that once they are large enough, the OTDS commitment for recently acceded countries is inoperative as far as AMS support is concerned. Among the countries in this study, China is usually considered a recently acceded country, while the status of Viet Nam (named a very recently acceded country) and Russia (acceded more recently than Viet Nam but obviously not named) seems subject to clarification.

Assessment of Current Total AMS

Applying an administered price for a product requires the calculation of WTO market price support and including it in the product's AMS. Because AMS support is subject to limit, the rules effectively penalise the application of administered prices. Over the last decade many administered prices have been eliminated or reduced. This is the case in, at least, Japan, the European Union, Switzerland, Norway and the United States. As a result, these countries' AMSs have declined, *ceteris paribus*. These declines are independent of any changes in the domestic or international market prices, and independent of changes in payment support. At the same time, the generally higher market prices of many important agricultural products since 2007 have in many cases reduced the payments that are included in AMSs, i.e. payments under measures that are not exempt. This has had a particularly large effect on the amount of AMS support reported by the United States. These two general developments have had the effect for several countries of increasing the margin between Current Total AMS and Bound Total AMS and made it easier for them to comply with the reduced Bound Total AMS levels of Rev.4. This has been facilitated by the relative rarity of AMSs falling in the critical interval between 2.5% and 5.0% (6.7% and 10.0% for some developing countries), which means that the Rev.4 reduction of *de minimis* percentages would have little effect on the Current Total AMS.

However, these general tendencies are offset by particular situations arising for several individual countries. Canada runs a risk of its non-product-specific AMS exceeding the *de minimis* level of Rev.4 and in so doing raising the Current Total AMS above the Bound Total AMS of Rev.4. Norway would experience difficulty with the Rev.4 Bound Total AMS, both because there is little margin to start with and because a couple of product-specific AMSs do fall in the critical interval of *de minimis* percentages. Switzerland could also face difficulty with Bound Total AMS because the Rev.4 reduction is greater than the recent margin. Thailand would be in a situation where the AMS for rice not only would switch from being smaller than the *de minimis* threshold to being larger than the Rev.4 threshold, but it would also be large enough to make Current Total AMS exceed Bound Total AMS under Rev.4. The United States would seem able to fit support under its past programmes within the Rev.4 levels of Bound Total AMS and *de minimis* but faces the possibility that support under the new payment programmes from 2014 would be more difficult to fit under the AMS limits.

Nevertheless, it appears that most countries in this study are well placed to comply with Rev.4 commitments on Bound Total AMS. This could apply to Argentina, Brazil, the European Union, India, Indonesia, Korea, Nigeria, Mexico, the Philippines, South Africa, Turkey and Viet Nam. Although some issues in interpreting Rev.4 may affect the assessment for China and Russia, they could be similarly well placed.

Assessment of product-specific AMSs, blue box payments, OTDS

Regarding product-specific AMSs, there are several instances where analysis has shown a likelihood that a country would exceed one or more of the caps introduced under Rev.4. Such analysis for other countries might indicate additional instances where the caps would not accommodate recent product-specific AMSs. In general, an increase in the administered price translates directly into a larger product-specific AMS, and there are likely numerous instances of such increases in recent years. For example, China and Indonesia are reported to have continued to raise their policy prices in the years after their last notifications. However, the rules of Rev.4 with regard to the establishment of caps on product-specific AMSs would allow the caps to be quite large, with the consequence that they would not immediately be a constraint.

While all countries would establish a limit on total blue box payments, only the European Union, Japan and Norway have in recent years provided such payments. Among these, Norway's recent total blue box payments have been large enough to exceed the Rev.4 limit. Regarding limits on product-specific blue box payments, Japan's recent payments for rice have been larger than the possible Rev.4 limit. If the United States were to classify some of its payments under the 2014 Farm Act as blue box payments, it would need to ensure that such payments met the applicable limits under Rev.4, whether on total box or on a product-specific basis.

Table 3.16. Calculation of current OTDS

Country	Currency	Units	Bound OTDS after reduction	Calculated applied trade-distorting support "Current OTDS"		Notified support				Latest year notified
				With Article 62	Without Article 62	Current Total AMS	*de minimis* AMSs	Article 6.5 blue	Article 6.2	
Argentina	ARS of 1992	Million	3 261	82	82	74	7	-	-	2008/09
Brazil	USD	Billion	8.8	4	3	0	3	-	1	2011/12
Canada	CAD	Million	3 991	3 068	3 068	522	2 546	-	-	2011
China (People's Republic of)	CNY	Billion	584.4	96	96	-	96	-	-	2008
EU28	EUR	Billion	24.2	11	11	7	1	3	-	2011/12
India	INR	Billion	1 151	1 544	104	-	104	-	1 440	2010/11
Indonesia	IDR	Billion	121 948	16 440	-	-	-		16 440	2011
Japan	JPY	Billion	1 371	984	984	609	220	155	-	2012
Korea	KRW	Billion	6 058	726	721	33	688	-	5	2008
Mexico	MXP of 1991	Million	27 676	3 247	1 882	589	1 293	-	1 365	2007
Nigeria	NGN	-	-	-	-	-	-	-	-	2011
Norway	NOK	Billion	9.5	15	15	10	0	5	-	2013
Philippines	PHP	Billion	117	14	7	-	7	-	7	2010
Russia	USD	Billion	5.5	7	7	6	1	-	-	2012
South Africa	ZAR	Million	9 315	-	-	-	-	-	-	2008
Switzerland	CHF	Million	2 687	2 212	2 212	2 212	-	-	-	2012
Thailand	THB	Million	99 366	30 092	30 092	169	29 923	-	-	2008
Turkey	USD	Million	10 380			Latest data is for 2001		-		
United States	USD	Billion	14.5	12	12	7	5	-	-	2012
Viet Nam	VND	Billion	35 234	9 730	1 632	-	1 632	-	8 099	2008

Notes: Bound OTDS after reduction from Table 14. With and without Art. 6.2 refers to whether or not Article 6.2 support is included in applied trade-distorting support. Many amounts are rounded.

Source: Author's calculations.

On OTDS, the comparisons indicate that all the developing countries in the study have no problem complying with their OTDS commitments, with one proviso: if Article 6.2 support is included in Current OTDS, India would significantly exceed its Bound OTDS. Among the developed countries, there is also in most cases a comfortable margin between the Current OTDS and Bound OTDS. Norway stands out as facing a large overshoot. The United States could also find itself facing overshoot situations, with the size of the excess possibly varying from year to year.

Domestic support digest

The AoA limits AMS support, i.e. support provided under programmes that do not meet the criteria for green box, blue box or development box exemption. Some countries have limits on individual AMSs, defined by the *de minimis* percentage applied to the value of production. Other countries have a limit on Current Total AMS, where AMSs below the *de minimis* threshold are excluded from the calculation. Rev.4 would reduce the limit on Current Total AMS for some countries and it would also for some countries reduce the *de minimis* percentage. Rev.4 would introduce fixed limits on product-specific AMSs. It would also introduce a limit on total blue box payments and limits on product-specific blue box payments. In addition, it would introduce a limit on all trade-distorting support, effectively a limit on Current OTDS. It is not clear whether Current OTDS includes or excludes Article 6.2 support, such as certain input subsidies.

Altogether, Rev.4 would thus introduce limits on additional measurements of support and reduce the limits and thresholds under AoA. However, the reductions would not apply to all countries, and when they apply they would apply differently to different countries. Likewise, the establishment of new limits would apply different generosity to different countries. The outcome is a set of rules and commitments that varies greatly among countries.

The general increase in agricultural product prices over the last decade has helped some countries to make smaller payments. This, in combination with the elimination or reduction of administered prices in several countries, has facilitated the accommodation of their recent or present support levels within the limits of Rev.4. However, in some cases the continued increases in administered prices work the opposite way, although only in a few cases do the larger AMSs or Current Total AMS exceed the country's constraints under Rev.4. Maintaining an AMS at its historical level has, for some countries, the consequence under Rev.4 of the AMS switching from being exempt on *de minimis* grounds to having to be included in Current Total AMS and even pushing indicator above the reduced Bound Total AMS.

Most countries – possibly all except one in this study – would have a comfortable margin between applied trade-distorting support measured as OTDS and the new Bound OTDS under Rev.4. The same can be said about the new limits on total and on product-specific blue box payments.

3.6. Discussion

Country-specific situations

In this examination of countries' situations in relation to Rev.4 rules and commitments, Norway and the United States are frequently identified or thought to be identified in Rev.4 in connection with a particular provision, or as being in a situation where recent or current policy settings would generate discord with Rev.4 rules and commitments, particularly in domestic support. The United States also attracts attention because it is a large agricultural trader. Norway and the United States are therefore discussed here with somewhat more depth than elsewhere in the study.

The frequent mention of Norway is no accident: even the WTO trade policy review (TPR) of Norway notes this situation (WTO 2012b). It is highly unusual that a TPR discusses the positioning of a country with regard to agriculture and a possible DDA outcome. The relevant TPR paragraph is as follows:

"A new multilateral agreement in the WTO on further reductions in agricultural subsidies could have major implications for Norway. Based on the state of play of the negotiations in December 2008, the Norwegian Government estimated that Norway's new annual ceiling for amber box, blue box, and present *de minimis* support would be around NKr 9.5 billion, including a reduction in amber box support of just over 50% (to NKr 5 438 million), and a ceiling for blue box support of NKr 3.56 billion. Expanded TRQs in combination with zero in-quota import duties would also impose more serious challenges for Norway's market regulation system than current WTO commitments. According to the authorities, these parameters would be very close to what Norway would consider acceptable given its policy objectives for the agriculture and food sector. However, despite the leeway for unilateral action and possible future obligations, there are no signs yet that Norway has taken steps to prepare for a negotiated outcome in the WTO, or advance reforms." (WTO 2012b; footnote deleted)

While Norway, of course, would need to prepare for a negotiated outcome in the WTO only on its own timetable, the issues identified in the TPR would seem more challenging than in most other countries in this study. In this regard, Blandford et al. (2010) and Gaasland et al. (2011) explore some options for policy change in Norway to comply with Rev.4 rules and commitments.

The United States emerges as generally well positioned in relation to Rev.4 rules and commitments, except in export financing support, international food aid, and some parts of domestic support. In domestic support, the US Agricultural Act of 2014 maintains and even increases the potential for large payments to be made when prices or revenues drop. While confident estimates of payments under the new programmes are not yet available (in January 2015) for the 2014 marketing year, it appears unlikely that Rev.4 limits could be exceeded (Zulauf and Orden 2014).[38] This is particularly so in light of the change to reporting insurance premium subsidies as product-specific support. However, even though many crop prices are projected to remain near their 2014 levels for several years, simulated combinations of price and yield outcomes generate many payments large enough that Rev.4 limits would be exceeded, especially on OTDS (Glauber and Westhoff 2015). Those simulations also suggest that, if some of the new crop payments were classified as blue box support, they would in many cases exceed the relevant Rev.4 limits. While the new dairy margin insurance programme may make generous payments in some situations, it is not clear how support under this programme will be accounted for in AoA and Rev.4 terms. In any case, because of large historical dairy support, the product-specific dairy AMS limit would be large.

The US 2014 Agricultural Act, like earlier agricultural laws, includes provisions for adjusting payments if needed to stay below the Bound Total AMS of the AoA (a "circuit-breaker" clause). Such provisions might be introduced with regard to commitments in line with Rev.4 if an agreement was reached. Other countries' policy measures may have provisions similar to the US "circuit-breaker". Even if they do not, a country can in practice adjust its policy settings such that its support for a given year stays within the limits of the WTO, whether in the AoA or Rev.4. This means that situations identified as those where Rev.4 commitments might be exceeded must not be seen as predictions. They only serve as elements in assessing the broader picture of the position if the Rev.4 rules and commitments were implemented today.

Public stock acquisition and administered prices

Food security, green box expenditures and AMS

Support to producers in the form of domestic support and border protection is often motivated by a country's stated desire to improve its food security by means of raising its self-sufficiency ratio.[39] The OECD considers that the link between a higher self-sufficiency ratio and improved food security is weak and a number of measures unrelated to self-sufficiency ratios – such as poverty reduction and social security schemes – can help to improve a population's food security status. Self-sufficiency targets often push countries towards higher market price support and other policies directly stimulating higher farm production. Food security is also invoked in the WTO context, specifically in the major issue debated at the Bali Ministerial conference in 2013 and subsequently in the WTO Committee on Agriculture, now with a view to agreeing and adopting a permanent solution by 2015. This is because the issue relates to AoA rules under the heading "Public stockholding for food security purposes", a heading in Annex 2, i.e. the green box. However, as WTO (2014k) puts it, "Supplying cheap food to the poor is not an issue here: it's allowed without limit."

The issue is rather one of using administered prices in acquiring stocks that are then released at administered prices. A footnote in the green box paragraph allows a developing country to exempt its expenditures on accumulating and holding food stocks for food security purposes at administered prices from counting as AMS support, even if the acquisition at such a price has the effect of providing price support to producers, which contravenes a basic green box criterion. This exemption is, however, available only in specific circumstances and under given conditions. The circumstances include meeting rules on how the programme is operated, and that such things as transparency and conduct accord with published criteria and guidelines. Exempting expenditures from being counted in AMS is thus conditioned on a price gap being accounted for in AMS. This price gap is the difference between the acquisition price and the external reference price.

Penalty for acquiring at administered prices

The idea of not counting certain price support as AMS support has been introduced repeatedly in the DDA, most recently by the G33 group of certain developing countries and championed by India at the Bali conference (WTO 2014k). Part of the issue is that accounting for the price gap in line with the rules of the AoA imposes a penalty on using an administered price, even if that administered price is below the level of the current year's international market price. Specifically, the AoA gap is the difference between the applied administered price and a constant that is equal to the external reference price in 1986-88. This generates a penalty that differs in size from the price support calculated using economic methods, but the AoA calculation is nevertheless called market price support, like the economic measurement of support. Moreover, while the economic measurement multiplies the price gap by total production, the AoA penalty multiplies the gap between the administered price and the constant by the production eligible to receive the applied administered price, which some countries interpret to mean a quantity much smaller than total production.

In the case of India, administered prices for important crops such as rice and wheat have been close to current international prices for many years, sometimes even below those prices. There has thus been relatively little support, and in some years no economic support, to producers. The rules of the AoA would, under some readings, require India to calculate very large penalties for using administered prices (Brink, 2014a). India may deviate from those rules in several ways and notifies AMSs for rice and wheat and some other crops that remain below its *de minimis* limits of 10% of value of production. Nevertheless, even using India's own method for calculating the penalty, its AMS for rice in 2011 and 2012 came quite close to its *de minimis* limit (it declined slightly in 2013) (Brink, 2014a). If India were to increase its administered price for rice by more than a certain extent, it could find itself with a rice AMS in excess of its *de minimis* limit. This could happen even if India uses the measurement methods, questioned in the Committee on Agriculture, that generate a relatively small penalty.

Why penalise the use of administered prices?

The particular measurement methods for what the AoA calls market price support, harking back to the economics-based antecedent, were not adopted by accident. They resulted from some countries' desire to accept a legally binding commitment only on a variable over which the government has control. This was not the case for the observed domestic market price, or for the international market price or border price as a reference. The government does control the administered price – this is what in the understanding of many makes it an administered price – and it does control the production eligible to receive the administered price. The constant used to measure the size of the penalty – based on 1986-88 prices – is not under government control but remains fixed.

There may also have been a motivation to penalise the use of administered prices when negotiating the AoA. The provisions were primarily but not exclusively designed to rein in the large economic market price support that were provided in what is now the European Union. The domestic market prices, maintained with the help of administered prices, were for many products in the European Union and elsewhere much higher than their international prices. Making it more difficult to continue using administered prices, not just pursuing a reduction of them, may have been part of the aim of some countries.[40]

This leads to the question of what role administered prices might have as countries pursue "the long-term objective referred to in the Agreement to establish a fair and market-oriented trading system through a programme of fundamental reform encompassing strengthened rules and specific commitments on support and protection in order to correct and prevent restrictions and distortions in world agricultural markets" and provide for special and differential treatment for developing countries "so as to be operationally effective and to enable developing countries to effectively take account of their development needs, including food security and rural development", as expressed in the Ministerial declaration launching the DDA (WTO, 2001). Economic analysis may help to clarify the effects and consequences of using administered prices, their effectiveness in achieving stated objectives, and the alternative instruments that could be used to achieve those objectives.

Change policy or change the rules?

Agriculture Agreement as the driver of policy reform

How to address the issue of administered prices and the rules of the AoA has generated many ideas. Some acknowledge that the rules of the AoA are written the way they are to make it difficult to use administered prices. With the advent of the AoA and the establishment of the WTO, many analysts hailed the agreement and countries' commitments under it. There was now a legal framework in place to curb then-existing distorting policy practices and to make it more difficult to introduce new distorting policies. Government policies in agriculture would finally be subject to international rules and commitments, and the reductions that countries committed to making would, in many cases, drive policy reform. The DDA was perceived as making progress towards fewer distortions in agricultural trade. The internationally binding rules and reduction commitments would ensure that countries do not continue applying or put in place policies that would make them exceed their WTO commitments.

Seeing WTO rules and commitments as governing what countries can do in terms of policies that affect agricultural trade underpins the idea of switching from using administered prices to using market prices when a government acquires stocks. This idea is noted by Brink (2014a) and Tangermann (2014). Of course, in practice it is not simply a matter of switching from using one price to another, since many rules, regulations, institutions, practices and interests are involved in decades-old policy regimes. Nonetheless, the idea is that the internationally binding rules and commitments of the AoA prevail over the interest of a government to maintain policy settings with effects that conflict with the AoA. Under this view, there would be no need and no scope for amending the AoA so as to facilitate the continued use of administered prices. Economic analysis of the use of administered prices could lend support for or against this view.

It might be argued that developing countries or countries selected in some other way should not, for whatever reason, need to adjust their policies because of WTO rules and commitments. Such a view would need to be reconciled with the view that distorting support distorts, regardless of where it is provided.

Established policy as the driver of changing the rules

The alternative view is that the interest of some governments in continuing to use administered prices should motivate a revision of the AoA rules. Instead of international commitments shaping policy, desired policy would shape international commitments. Numerous ideas have been elaborated for how the AoA rules might be changed to accommodate the continued use of administered prices.

Some of these ideas are based on making the measurement of what is called market price support in the AoA more similar to economics-based market price support. Some of them include provisions to limit to some extent the use of administered prices or to limit the effects of using them. Ideas in this vein have been suggested or mentioned by, for example: Diaz-Bonilla (2014), Konandreas and Mermigkas (2014), Matthews (2014a, 2014b), and Montemayor (2014).

A third line of thought exists on the topic of administered prices: that they should not be penalised (Josling et al., 1996; Tangermann, 2014). It is based on the fact that a gap between the domestic price and the border price can only be maintained with the help of border measures. Since border measures are constrained by the market access and export subsidy disciplines of the AoA, there would be no need to subject domestic pricing to the separate domestic support discipline. It is not entirely clear whether Uruguay Round negotiators ignored this aspect of domestic pricing or they recognised it but chose to effectively subject such pricing to more than one discipline.

A fourth line of thought is that adopted by Ministers at Bali (WTO 2013d) and given more precision and substance by the WTO General Council in 2014. No change was introduced in the AoA rules regarding the exemption of expenditures from AMS when using administered prices to acquire stocks, conditioned on accounting for a price gap in the AMS. However, under the Bali decision, as clarified, when in a developing country a product's AMS exceeds its *de minimis* limit, and if that country satisfies the criteria of the green box and the rules of the AMS calculation, including the use of the 1986-88 reference price, other countries shall not, under certain conditions, challenge that violation through the WTO dispute settlement mechanism. This also applies when a developing country in the same circumstances exceeds its Bound Total AMS. The availability of this *carte blanche* is circumscribed and conditioned in several ways, so as to alleviate other countries' concerns about the negative effects they might face as a result of a country's use of administered prices to acquire stocks.

Economic analysis

Thus, in investigating the economics of administered prices, it could be useful to develop a better understanding of what constitutes an administered price, what desirable and undesirable consequences their use may entail, what unintended consequences may emerge, and what alternatives might exist to achieve the same objectives. If the preponderance of economic evidence shows that the benefits of using administered prices outweigh the costs, what are the alternatives in designing WTO rules to make them more usable?

Emerging issues

General

Since the time of drafting Rev.4 in 2008 and earlier years, several issues affecting agricultural trade have emerged or have gained importance. They may not have had much or any influence on the contents of Rev.4 but they may nevertheless influence how countries today evaluate their positions in relation to the rules and commitments of Rev.4. Among such issues are those discussed by Bureau and Jean (2013a, 2013b) and McMahon and Desta (2012). They include new macroeconomic conditions, biofuels, the environment, food security, right to food, development, plant intellectual property, genetically modified organisms, regional and bilateral trade agreements, sanitary and phytosanitary measures, technical barriers to trade, private standards, climate change, and multifunctionality. Such topics are not addressed at all in Rev.4, since it hews closely to the structure of the AoA.

Export prohibitions and restrictions

However, one emerging issue is addressed to some extent in Rev.4 and AoA: the increasing and decreasing use of export restrictions of different kinds in the years since Rev.4 was drafted. The AoA has an article entitled "Disciplines on export prohibitions and restrictions", but the provisions are generally considered weak. For example, there are no commitments not to use certain measures or to use them only to a certain extent. Countries that rely on imports of agricultural products may thus feel insecure about the reliability of import flows, which can motivate a desire to increase self-sufficiency, as mentioned above.

Rev.4 would to some extent strengthen the disciplines of AoA on export prohibitions and restrictions. Rev.4 would, for example, require the elimination of certain existing export prohibitions and restrictions in foodstuffs and would provide for the possibility of time limits applying to new prohibitions and restrictions. It is not clear whether any recent or current policy settings in this area would contravene the rules of Rev.4.

The use of various forms of export restrictions in agriculture has been the subject of keen analysis.[41] Anania (2013) reviews much of the analysis and discusses several options for strengthening the disciplines in the form of a WTO agreement. They range from options that are more modest than those of Rev.4 to options more ambitious in terms of their capacity to limit the ability of exporting countries to hold back or discourage exports of agricultural products.

Need for long-term perspective

Some policy settings are changed frequently, sometimes within the year. Others remain in place for several years, such as the five-, six-, or seven-year periods for which agricultural policies are authorised in some countries. Others are even longer lasting. Commitments under the AoA remain in place for even longer. The Uruguay Round started in 1986 and was concluded only in 1994. The AoA came into effect in 1995. The DDA started in 2001 (effectively in 2000 for agriculture) and was not yet concluded in 2014. Over time spans such as these, the world of agricultural trade changes considerably. That speaks for taking a very long-term perspective as the context when looking at current policy settings and crafting rules and commitments.

Diaz-Bonilla (2014, Table 2) illustrates the changing rank order of agricultural exporters since the 1990s. In the 1990s, only one developing country was in the top five net agricultural exporters; altogether three were in the top ten. By 2010-11 there were three developing countries among the top five exporters, and five in the top ten. The increasing share of developing countries in world trade of food and agriculture is similarly illustrated by Bureau (2013b, Figure 1).

In terms of domestic support to agriculture, the world is changing (Figure 3.4 and 3.5). The four largest developed-country agricultural producers (the European Union, United States, Japan and Russia) exhibit a declining or already low level of WTO support not qualifying for the green box since 1995 (Brink 2014b). Four of the largest developing-country agricultural producers (Brazil, China, India and Indonesia) show a rising trend in support not qualifying for the green box, which includes Article 6.2 support for some of them.[42] These trends, using WTO indicators, more or less match the tendencies revealed through the OECD's Producer Support Estimates, which account for more policy measures than just domestic support measures in the AoA sense.

Pictures of past trends such as those mentioned say nothing about future developments. It is still worth considering the long-term implications of the trends if they were to continue. Projecting the trends forward would show a world where major agricultural producing and trading countries are heavy users of support that does not meet the green box criteria. Many of the large producers and traders in the future may be countries enjoying the flexibility that the AoA and Rev.4 accord developing countries. This is not to say that all developing countries will take advantage of such flexibility and provide large amounts of support. It may mean that the interests of future low-support and future high-support developing countries diverge. Among the 20 countries in this study, there may be some in each group.

Figure 3.4. Non-green-box support in the EU, Japan, Russia and the United States

Per cent of value of production in agriculture

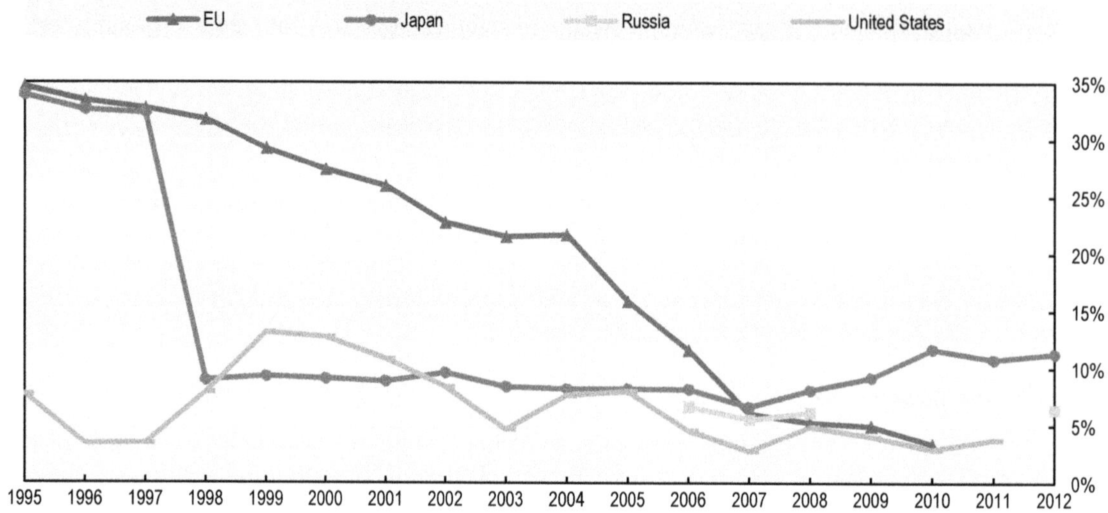

Source: Brink (2014b).

Figure 3.5. Non-green-box support in Brazil, China, India and Indonesia

Per cent of value of production in agriculture

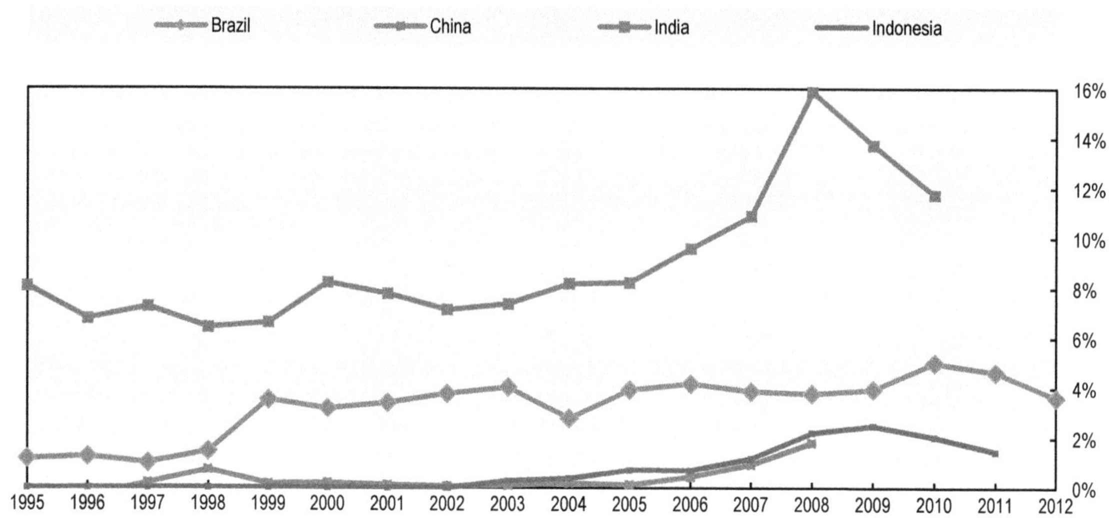

3.7. Conclusion

The examination of the policy settings of 12 developing and 7 developed countries finds that few countries would need to change their settings very much if at all in order to conform with the rules and commitments of an agreement corresponding to Rev.4, if implemented immediately and in full. This is the combined result of policy settings having already been changed since the drafting of Rev.4, the rules and commitments of Rev.4 being sufficiently generous and/or tailored to accommodate the situations of individual countries, and international prices of many agricultural products generally having increased since the time of drafting Rev.4. Some situations would arise where policy change would be needed to meet requirements in one of the three Rev.4 pillars, i.e. market access, export competition, and domestic support, or for a particular product or set of products. Overall the situation in 2014 thus looked more conducive even than in 2008 to achieving the "gain" of agreeing on Rev.4 rules and commitments while incurring relatively little "pain".

Rev.4 is written to include a plethora of provisions to accommodate the needs of particular countries or groups of countries. These provisions reduce the trade liberalising effect of the corresponding agreement as a whole but may serve to make agreement possible where otherwise it would not have been possible. At the most primary level these provisions distinguish between developed and developing countries, but they also go far beyond that important self-selection by countries. They are in some cases designed to harmonise the commitments by which various countries would need to abide. Most of these provisions are written in a sort of code, where identifying the country or countries benefitting from the provision requires analysis of data external to Rev.4. This is further complicated by provisions that offer a menu of choices, some with trade-offs between tighter and looser constraints, and some without such trade-offs.

A common perception is that the DDA in agriculture stalled in 2008 owing to the inability of India and the United States to agree on the rules for special safeguard mechanism (SSM). This would especially involve the question of whether, once SSM was triggered for a product, its applied tariff could exceed not only the Rev.4 bound tariff but also the pre-Rev.4 bound tariff. Under this narrative, if SSM had been agreed, countries would have entered into commitments in line with those resulting from Rev.4. A more nuanced narrative recognises the threshold nature of the SSM question but sees its resolution as a necessary – but not sufficient on its own – condition for countries to agree to enter into Rev.4 commitments on agriculture. Other issues in agriculture remained unresolved at that time, although progress was being made in negotiating their resolution. Developments in international markets and in countries' policy settings since 2008 have eliminated some but not all of the points on which further negotiations at that time were needed. Some new policy settings may even have made an agreement more difficult to reach. Agreeing on SSM could have facilitated, and could have provided an impetus towards, countries also resolving those outstanding issues, especially those concerning market access and those concerning developing countries. The resulting modalities, the subsequent legal text, and countries' eventual commitments would not have been identical to those envisaged under Rev.4 but would have resembled them.

In the intervening years since the drafting of Rev.4, numerous issues have arisen in the area of agricultural trade and policy writ large. They were generally not addressed in depth in the three pillars of the AoA, and consequently they did not garner much if any attention in Rev.4. They nevertheless affect the trading environment and hence they define the context for further multilateral negotiations. Increasing market access under bilateral and regional trade agreements is one important part of that context: countries have changed and are changing their border measures, although not on a multilateral basis. Market access is being improved for some countries into some countries. The context is also changing through the shifting roles of developing and developed countries in agricultural trade and changes in how and how much they support their producers, increasing attention to what is often called food security and in many cases involves trade policy moves to increase self-sufficiency ratios or contain domestic price rises, greater policy attention to the roles – positive and negative – of agriculture in climate change and environmental quality, and many more. Countries' desire or lack of desire to address such issues through agricultural trade policy may play a greater role in conditioning the WTO negotiating climate than will the extent to which commitments on market access, export competition and domestic support are now more easily entered into than in 2008.

Notes

1. Independent Advisor. The helpful comments of May Chow and Gregory MacDonald are gratefully acknowledged. This paper has been prepared for the OECD Trade and Agriculture Directorate. The views expressed are those of the author and do not necessarily reflect those of the OECD or OECD member country governments.
2. The draft modalities of interest here are those contained in the WTO document TN/AG/W/4/Rev.4 (WTO, 2008a). They are therefore referred to as Rev.4.
3. Contrary to WTO practice, this study refers to WTO members as countries. The scheduled commitments in agriculture of the 28 European Union (EU) member states are overridden by the scheduled commitments of the European Union, itself a WTO member. Switzerland and Liechtenstein, both WTO members, are subject to the commitments of the single schedule of Switzerland-Liechtenstein, here referred to as Switzerland.
4. China refers to the People's Republic of China, the EU to the European Union with the number of member states varying by the year of reference, Korea to the Republic of Korea, and Russia to the Russian Federation.
5. Section 6.2 of this chapter clarifies the reason for the name of this issue and why it is raised as an issue.
6. The quota volume, more than double the volume applying between 2005 and 2012, is fixed from 2014. The in-quota tariff rate of 40% in 2014 is reduced to 35% in 2015.
7. The special agricultural safeguard in the AoA is usually referred to as SSG, as entered in countries' schedules, while the mechanism in Rev.4 is called SSM.
8. These provisions for Japan, Norway and Switzerland are in square brackets, signifying perhaps an even greater tentativeness and difference of opinion than for the rest of the text. See also WTO (2008b).
9. This refers to domestic support classified as AMS or blue box support; see later section on domestic support.
10. Canada (21), China (10), EU (128), India (4), Indonesia (2), Japan (20), Korea (67), Mexico (11), Norway (232), Philippines (14), South Africa (53), Switzerland (26), Thailand (23), United States (54) and Viet Nam (3), drawing on WTO (2015). Russia also has TRQs. The WTO indicates that 37 members have a total of 1 374 TRQs, which likely includes those in the schedules of individual EU member states. http://www.wto.org/english/tratop_e/agric_e/ag_intro02_access_e.htm.
11. The negative difference between the average bound and the 2012 applied tariffs of Russia is likely due to the process of tariff reductions having been just initiated with Russia's WTO accession in 2012.
12. Laborde et al. (2011) point out that this so-called "pain" a country experiences in cutting tariffs is accompanied by the less easily observed "gain" it experiences because other countries cut their tariffs.
13. This hypothesis, based on personal communication with officials, differs from the 81 sensitive products, including grain, suggested by Blandford et al. (2010).
14. Not shown in Figure 2, Viet Nam's average tariff on agricultural products in 2013 was lower than in 2007 (WTO, 2013a).
15. The export subsidy provisions thus differ from market access and domestic support, where Rev.4 does not specify particular years for full implementation.

16. See, for example, questions and answers regarding Mexico (Ag-IMS ID 61066) and India (Ag-IMS ID 67055, 68044) and information regarding Korea (WTO (2012a), III(3)(iii), para. 128). Some countries suggest that the Ministerial declaration in Hong Kong in 2005 authorises the continued use of Article 9.4. The declaration says "Developing country Members will continue to benefit from the provisions of Article 9.4 of the Agreement on Agriculture for five years after the end-date for elimination of all forms of export subsidies." The interpretation of this sentence is unclear, especially in view of the fact that countries have not yet agreed on such an end date. It is also unclear what is the legal authority of a Ministerial declaration, relative to that of the AoA.

17. The ES:1 notifications for some countries with export subsidy commitments indicate nil export subsidies for individual products (Brazil, Indonesia, South Africa). Table 1 shows them as "No XS" in the same way as for those countries without export subsidy commitments, which simply state that they did not provide any export subsidies.

18. The Committee on Agriculture requires countries that are significant exporters of certain products or groups of products to submit annual notifications of their volume of exports of those products. The updating of which countries are significant exporters has proven contentious in the Committee. It is nevertheless not an issue in Rev.4 and is therefore not discussed further here.

19. The zeroes in **Table 3.7** for EU sugar in recent years mask export subsidies small enough to result in percentages rounding to zero.

20. The European Union clarifies "exceptional" as meaning "Which is only available to the extent and for the time necessary to address threats of market disturbance caused by significant price rises or falls on internal or external markets or other events and circumstances significantly disturbing or threatening to disturb the market." (WTO, 2014a: 27).

21. This is the mercantilistic view. An economics-based view would see the abolition of export subsidy entitlements as desirable in itself and would not see a trade-off as being necessary.

22. The Food Aid Convention expired in 2012 (http://www.foodaidconvention.org/en/Default.aspx). The Food Assistance Convention entered into force on 1 January 2013 (http://www.foodassistanceconvention.org/en/about_fac/about.aspx).

23. The "development box" also has other meanings, referring sometimes to special and differential treatment for developing countries more generally than just Article 6.2 of the AoA.

24. Support provided for an agricultural product in favour of the producers of the basic agricultural product is usually called a product-specific AMS. Support provided in favour of agricultural producers in general is usually called non-product-specific AMS.

25. These factors include the rule that a scheduled limit would not be less than the historical *de minimis* level, the question of what is the applicable limit when in the future a *de minimis* level becomes larger than the scheduled limit, and the issue of what limit (nil or *de minimis*) applies in the future to the AMS for a product without a scheduled limit. The motivation for introducing caps on product-specific AMSs is thought to be a desire to curb a country's room to provide a few large product-specific AMSs within the limit of its Bound Total AMS, not to prohibit any product-specific AMS at all. The possibility of exempting *de minimis* AMSs from Current Total AMS under the AoA and the continuation of *de minimis* exemptions under Rev.4 match this view. However, Rev.4 does not seem clear on whether any AMS support would be allowed on products for which no limit is scheduled.

26. Reference can be made to studies such as Jean et al. (2008), Nassar et al. (2008), Yamashita (2008), Tian (2009), Blandford and Josling (2011), Blandford and Orden (2011), Cheng (2011), Cororaton (2011), Gaasland et al. (2011), Godo and Takahashi (2011), Gopinath (2011), Josling and Swinbank (2011), and Nassar (2011).

27. See, for example, Josling and Mittenzwei (2013) for a fairly optimistic view of the correspondence between OECD data and WTO notifications for some countries and Brink (2015) for a less sanguine impression relating to a couple of other countries.

28. See, for example, Josling and Mittenzwei (2013) for a fairly optimistic view of the correspondence between OECD data and WTO notifications for some countries and Brink (2015) for a less sanguine impression relating to a couple of other countries.

29. Regarding India, it has been suggested that alternative readings of the AoA than India's would generate AMSs in excess of the *de minimis* limits (Brink, 2014a). This would be the case also under Rev.4, since the limits are the same.

30. Article 7.2(b) obligates a country without a Bound Total AMS, such as Turkey, to keep each AMS at a level not exceeding its *de minimis* limit.

31. Regarding the United States, the nature and levels of support, the limits under AoA and Rev.4 and the periodic changes in policy are of interest to many analysts, which motivates a more detailed discussion than for other countries. The situation of the United States is also addressed below in the "Discussion" section.

32. The United States changed its dairy policy in 2008 such that WTO market price support for dairy declined from USD 4.8 billion to USD 2.9 billion. The 2014 Farm Act abolished administered prices for dairy products, which eliminated WTO market price support for dairy. These reductions in Current Total AMS thus resulted from policy changes, in contrast to the reductions resulting from changes in reporting practice with respect to insurance programmes.

33. Recent US notifications show two significant changes in reporting practice unaccompanied by policy change. From the 2009 notification only premium subsidies to producers under crop and revenue insurance are reported as part of non-product-specific AMS. They amounted to USD 7.0 billion in 2012. The 2012 notification started to report the premium subsidies on crop and livestock insurance as part of each product's AMS (68 crops and 4 livestock products) instead of non-product-specific AMS.

34. Production is generally not required for payments under two of the new programmes in the 2014 Farm Act (Price Loss Coverage and Agriculture Risk Coverage – County), while production is required under Agriculture Risk Coverage – Individual (US Department of Agriculture, 2014c).

35. Rev.4 refers to the "implementation period" without defining it and possibly leaving it without an end date. In the AoA the implementation period is effectively defined as the period 1995-2000.

36. However, a precursor to Rev.4, the 2004 Framework Agreement, mentions "all trade-distorting domestic support, as measured by the Final Bound Total AMS plus permitted *de minimis* level and … Blue Box payments" (WTO, 2004). The reference to a *de minimis* level was dropped in arriving at the wording of Rev.4.

37. For Norway, Blandford et al. (2010) and Gaasland et al. (2011) explore policy options to address Current OTDS exceeding Bound OTDS, if it came to pass. For the United States, an amendment of the "circuit-breaker" clause in its Farm Act could help to alleviate such Rev.4 situations (the current clause essentially reduces payments in order to meet AoA limits.)

38. However, as Zulauf and Orden (2014) suggest, if Rev.4 rules and commitments had been in place for 2014, the 2014 Agricultural Act would not have had the same programme payment provisions as those actually enacted.

39. OECD (2013: 25) reports on such efforts as follows. "Several countries maintain specific targets for food self-sufficiency rates, motivated by concerns about food security for their consumers. China maintains a 95% self-sufficiency target for grains, while Indonesia has set self-sufficiency targets for rice, sugar, soybeans, maize and beef to be achieved by 2014. The new Basic Plan on Food, Agriculture and Rural Area in Japan envisages an increase in the self-sufficiency ratio of its calorie supply to 50% by 2020, compared to 41% in 2008. … A Doctrine on food security states minimum self-sufficiency targets of at least 85-90% for a range of agricultural products in Russia, including among others, grains, sugar, vegetable oil, meat and dairy products. … and increased agricultural output in order to ensure food security is among the general objectives for agricultural policy in both Brazil and Turkey."

40. It may be tempting to seek to make a distinction between the use of administered prices for the purpose of supporting prices by buying into intervention stocks and for the purpose of building stocks for food security purposes. However, stated purposes are not easy to adhere to strictly over time, and stated purposes are not necessarily the same as actual purposes (the term "mission creep" comes to mind). The OECD's policy monitoring addresses this problem by classifying policies according to their implementation criteria, not their purpose, objective, goal, etc. The complex criteria and conditions established for the treatment of acquisition at administered prices, both in footnote 5 of paragraph 3 of Annex 2 of AoA and in the Bali declaration on this topic, seem to be attempts to address the fundamental problem arising from classifying policy measures by their stated objectives.

41. Export restrictions may mean only quantitative export restrictions or quantitative export restrictions and export taxes. This distinction matters greatly for a country like Argentina, which taxes exports of many important agricultural products. In early 2014 its export taxes stood at 20% for corn and barley, 23% for wheat, and 5-10% for soybeans. Wheat and corn exports are administered through quotas and export authorisation. Export taxes on oilseeds and products were 5.0% (peanut oil), 23.5% (peanuts), 30.0% (sunflower seed meal and oil), 32.0% (sunflowerseed, soybean meal, soybean oil), and 35.0% (soybeans) (US Department of Agriculture 2014a, 2014b).

42. Among the world's ten largest agricultural producers, Nigeria has notified that no domestic support was provided up through 2011 and Turkey has not notified since 2001 (the OECD indicates economic support in Turkey at a level higher than the average among OECD countries).

References

Agra Europe (2014), Russian food import bans – how can the EU react? 11 August, https://www.agra-net.net/agra/agra-europe/policy-and-legislation/eu/russian-food-import-bans-how-can-the-eu-react-450258.htm (viewed 20 August 2014).

Anania, G. (2013), Agricultural export restrictions and the WTO – What options do policy-makers have for promoting food security? Issue Paper No. 50, International Centre for Trade and Sustainable Development.

Blandford, D., I. Gaasland, R. Garcia and E. Vårdal (2010), How effective are WTO disciplines on domestic support and market access for agriculture? *The World Economy* 33(11) pp. 1470-1485.

Blandford, D. and T. Josling (2011), "The WTO agricultural modalities proposals and their impact on domestic support in the EU and the United States" in W. Martin and A. Mattoo (eds) *Unfinished Business? The WTO's Doha Agenda*. Washington, DC: CEPR and the World Bank.

Blandford, D. and D. Orden (2011), "United States" in D. Orden, D. Blandford and T. Josling (eds) *WTO Disciplines on Agricultural Support – Seeking a Fair Basis for Trade*. Cambridge: Cambridge University Press.

Brink, L. (2014a), "Support to agriculture in India in 1995-2013 and the rules of the WTO", *Working Paper #14-01*, International Agricultural Trade Research Consortium, St. Paul, Minnesota.

Brink, L. (2014b), "Evolution of trade-distorting domestic support" in *Tackling Agriculture in the Post-Bali Context*, International Centre for Trade and Sustainable Development, Geneva.

Brink, L. (2015), "Farm support in Ukraine and Russia under the rules of the WTO" in *Transition to Agricultural Market Economies: The Future of Kazakhstan, Russia, and Ukraine*, (eds.) A. Schmitz and W. Meyers, CABI, Cambridge, USA and Wallingford, UK.

Bureau, J.-C. and S. Jean (2013a), "International agricultural trade and negotiations: Coping with a new landscape", *FOODSECURE Working Paper* No. 08, March.

Bureau, J.-C. and S. Jean (2013b), "Do yesterday's disciplines fit today's farm trade?" in *Strengthening the Multilateral Trading System*, Proposals and Analysis, Agriculture and Food Security Group, The E15 Initiative, International Centre for Trade and Sustainable Development and the International Food & Agricultural Trade Policy Council, http://e15initiative.org/wp-content/uploads/2014/03/AG_Proposals_Analysis.pdf.

Cheng, F. (2011), "China" in D. Orden, D. Blandford and T. Josling (eds), *WTO Disciplines on Agricultural Support – Seeking a Fair Basis for Trade*, Cambridge University Press, Cambridge.

Cororaton, C. (2011), "Philippines", in D. Orden, D. Blandford and T. Josling (eds), *WTO Disciplines on Agricultural Support – Seeking a Fair Basis for Trade*, Cambridge University Press, Cambridge.

Diaz-Bonilla, E. (2014), "On food security stocks, peace clauses, and permanent solutions after Bali", *Working Paper*, International Food Policy Research Institute, June, http://ebrary.ifpri.org/cdm/singleitem/collection/p15738coll2/id/128209/rec/3.

FAOSTAT (2015), Food and Agriculture Organization of the United Nations, http://faostat3.fao.org/home/E.

Gaasland, I., R. Garcia and E. Vårdal (2011), "Norway" in D. Orden, D. Blandford and T. Josling (eds), *WTO Disciplines on Agricultural Support – Seeking a Fair Basis for Trade*, Cambridge: Cambridge University Press.

Glauber, J. and P. Westhoff (2015), 50 shades of amber: The 2014 farm bill and the WTO, Invited paper presented at the session The 2014 Farm Bill: An Economic Post Mortem, Allied Social Science Associations (ASSA) Annual Meetings, Boston, Massachusetts, 4 January.

Godo, Y. and D. Takahashi (2011), "Japan", in D. Orden, D. Blandford and T. Josling (eds), *WTO Disciplines on Agricultural Support – Seeking a Fair Basis for Trade*, Cambridge University Press, Cambridge.

Gopinath, M. (2011) "India", in D. Orden, D. Blandford and T. Josling (eds) *WTO Disciplines on Agricultural Support – Seeking a Fair Basis for Trade*, Cambridge: Cambridge University Press.

Hansen, J. and F. Gale (2014), "China in the next decade: Rising meat demand and growing imports of feed", *Amber Waves*, Economic Research Service, U.S. Department of Agriculture, 7 April.

Jean, S., T. Josling and D. Laborde (2008), *Implications for Brazil of the May 2008 draft agricultural modalities*, International Centre for Trade and Sustainable Development, Geneva.

Josling, T., S. Tangermann, and T.K. Warley (1996), *Agriculture in the GATT*, Houndmills, Macmillan Press, London and New York.

Josling, T. and K. Mittenzwei (2013), "Transparency and timeliness: The monitoring of agricultural policies in the WTO using OECD data", *World Trade Review* 12, pp. 533–547. doi: 10.1017/S1474745612000535

Josling, T. and A. Swinbank (2011), "European Union", in D. Orden, D. Blandford and T. Josling (eds) *WTO Disciplines on Agricultural Support – Seeking a Fair Basis for Trade*, Cambridge University Press, Cambridge.

Kiselev, S. and R. Romashkin (2012), "Possible effects of Russia's WTO accession on agricultural trade and production", *Issue Paper* No. 40, International Centre for Trade and Sustainable Development, Geneva.

Konandreas, P. and G. Mermigkas (2014), "WTO domestic support disciplines: Options for alleviating constraints to stockholding in developing countries in the follow-up to Bali", *Research Working Paper* No. 45, FAO Commodity and Trade Policy, Food and Agriculture Organization, Rome.

Korea Times (2015), "U.S., China oppose Korea's 513% rice tariff", 6 January, http://www.koreatimes.co.kr/www/news/biz/2015/01/123_171178.html (viewed 9 January 2015).

Laborde, D., W. Martin and D. van der Mensbrugghe (2011), "Implications of the Doha market access proposals for developing countries", *Policy Research Working Paper* WPS5679, World Bank, Washington DC.

Market Monitor (2013 and 2014), "Policy developments, Agricultural Market Information System, various issues", http://www.amis-outlook.org/amis-monitoring/monthly-report/en/ (viewed 28 September 2014).

Matthews, A. (2011), "The impact of WTO agricultural trade rules on food security and development: an examination of proposed additional flexibilities for developing countries", *IIIS Discussion Paper* No. 371, Institute for International Integration Studies, August.

Matthews, A. (2014a), "Food security and WTO domestic support disciplines post-Bali", *Issue Paper* No. 53, International Centre for Trade and Sustainable Development, Geneva.

Matthews, A. (2014b), "Trade rules, food security and the multilateral trade negotiations", *European Review of Agricultural Economics*, Vol. 41(3) pp. 511-535.

McMahon, J. and M. Desta (eds.) (2012), *Research Handbook on the WTO Agriculture Agreement – New and Emerging Issues in International Agricultural Trade Law*, Edward Elgar Publishing, Inc., Cheltenham.

Montemayor, R. (2014), "Public stockholding for food security purposes: Scenarios and options for a permanent solution", *Issue Paper* 51, International Centre for Trade and Sustainable Development, June.

Nassar, A. (2011), "Brazil", in D. Orden, D. Blandford and T. Josling (eds), *WTO Disciplines on Agricultural Support – Seeking a Fair Basis for Trade*, Cambridge University Press, Cambridge.

Nassar, A., C. Cabral da Costa, and L. Chiodi (2008), Implications for Brazil of the July 2008 draft agricultural modalities, International Centre for Trade and Sustainable Development, Geneva.

OECD (2014a), *Agricultural Policy Monitoring and Evaluation 2014 – OECD Countries*, OECD Publishing, Paris.
DOI: http://dx.doi.org/10.1787/agr_pol-2014-en.

OECD-FAO (2014b), OECD/FAO (2014), *OECD-FAO Agricultural Outlook 2014*, OECD Publishing, Paris.
DOI: http://dx.doi.org/10.1787/agr_outlook-2014-en.

OECD (2013), *Agricultural Policy Monitoring and Evaluation 2013: OECD Countries and Emerging Economies*, OECD Publishing, Paris.
DOI: http://dx.doi.org/10.1787/agr_pol-2013-en.

OECD (2011), *Evaluation of Agricultural Policy Reforms in the United States*, OECD Publishing, Paris.
DOI: http://dx.doi.org/10.1787/9789264096721-en.

OECD (2008), *The Export Credits Arrangement 1978-2008: Achievements and Challenges*, Paris. http://www.oecd.org/tad/xcred/40594872.pdf.

OECD (2001a), *An analysis of officially supported export credits in agriculture*, OECD, Paris. http://www.oecd.org/trade/agricultural-trade/1911035.pdf

OECD (2001b), *Market Effects of Crop Support Measures*, OECD Publishing, Paris.
DOI: http://dx.doi.org/10.1787/9789264195011-en.

Orden, D., D. Blandford and T. Josling (eds) (2014), *WTO Disciplines on Agricultural Support – Seeking a Fair Basis for Trade*, Cambridge University Press, Cambridge.

Schnepf, R. (2014a), *Status of the WTO Brazil – U.S. cotton case*, CRS Report R43336, Congressional Research Service, 21 February, http://nationalaglawcenter.org/wp-content/uploads/assets/crs/R43336.pdf.

Schnepf, R. (2014b), "International food aid programmes: Background and issues", *CRS Report* R41072, Congressional Research Service, 23 June, http://nationalaglawcenter.org/wp-content/uploads/assets/crs/R41072.pdf.

Tangermann, S. (2015), "Are Past OECD Analyses of Agricultural Policy Reforms Relevant to Current Policy and Market Settings?", in *Issues in Agricultural Trade Policy*, OECD, Paris.

Tian, Z. (2009), *Implications for China of the December 2008 draft agricultural modalities*, International Centre for Trade and Sustainable Development, Geneva.

US Department of Agriculture (2014a), "Argentina – Grain and feed annual 2014", *GAIN Report,* Number (no number), Foreign Agricultural Service, Washington, DC.

US Department of Agriculture (2014b), "Argentina – Oilseeds and products annual 2014", *GAIN Report,* Number (no number), Foreign Agricultural Service, Washington, DC.

US Department of Agriculture (2014c), Agricultural Act of 2014 (2014 Farm Bill), Title I information about the Agriculture Risk Coverage (ARC) and Price Loss Coverage (PLC) programmes. Notice ARCPLC-4, Farm Service Agency, https://www.fsa.usda.gov/Internet/FSA_Notice/arcplc_4.pdf (viewed 17 September 2014).

US Trade Representative (2014), United States and Brazil reach agreement to end WTO cotton dispute, http://www.ustr.gov/sites/default/files/20141001201606893.pdf (viewed 1 October 2014).

van Tongeren, F. (2008), "Agricultural Policy Design and Implementation: A Synthesis", *OECD Food, Agriculture and Fisheries Papers*, No. 7, OECD Publishing, Paris.
DOI: http://dx.doi.org/10.1787/243786286663.

WTO (2015), Tariff profiles,
http://stat.wto.org/TariffProfile/WSDBTariffPFReporter.aspx?Language=E, January 2015

WTO (2014a), “Export subsidies, export credits, export credit guarantees or insurance programmes, international food aid and agricultural exporting state trading enterprises”, Background document by the Secretariat, G/AG/W/125, Committee on Agriculture, World Trade Organization, 21 May.

WTO (2014b), Export subsidies – Addendum. G/AG/W/125/Add.1, Committee on Agriculture, World Trade Organization, 21 May.

WTO (2014c), Export credits, export credit guarantees or insurance programmes – Addendum, G/AG/W/125/Add.2, Committee on Agriculture, World Trade Organization, 21 May.

WTO (2014d), Food aid – Addendum, G/AG/W/125/Add.3, Committee on Agriculture, World Trade Organization, 21 May.

WTO (2014e), State Trading Enterprises – Addendum, G/AG/W/125/Add.4, Committee on Agriculture, World Trade Organization, 21 May.

WTO (2014f), Annual export competition review, Submission from the Cairns Group to the 74th meeting of the Committee on Agriculture (COA) in June 2014. G/AG/W/129, Committee on Agriculture, World Trade Organization, 2 June.

WTO (2014g), Request for waiver relating to special treatment for rice of the Philippines, G/C/W/665/Rev.4, Council for Trade in Goods, 27 March.

WTO (2014h), Goods Council approves Philippine waiver request for rice, Council for Trade in Goods, http://www.wto.org/english/news_e/news14_e/good_24jun14_e.htm.

WTO (2014i), “Food aid – Revision”, G/AG/W/125/Add.3/Rev.1, Committee on Agriculture, World Trade Organization, 16 September.

WTO (2013a), “Viet Nam”, WT/TPR/S/287/Rev.1, Trade Policy Review, Report by the Secretariat, Trade Policy Review Body, 4 November.

WTO (2013b), “Switzerland and Liechtenstein”, WT/TPR/S/280/Rev.1, Trade Policy Review, Report by the Secretariat, Trade Policy Review Body, 16 August.

WTO (2013c), “General services”, WT/MIN(13)/37 and WT/L/912, Ministerial Conference, Ninth Session, Bali, 3-6 December.

WTO (2013d), “Public stockholding for food security purposes”, WT/MIN(13)/38 and WT/L/913, Ministerial Conference, Ninth Session, Bali, 3-6 December.

WTO (2013e), “Understanding on tariff rate quota administration provisions of agricultural products", as defined in Article 2 of the Agreement on Agriculture. WT/MIN(13)/39 and WT/L/914, Ministerial Conference, Ninth Session, Bali, 3-6 December.

WTO (2013f), “Export competition”, WT/MIN(13)/40 and WT/L/915, Ministerial Conference, Ninth Session, Bali, 3-6 December.

WTO (2012a), "Republic of Korea", WT/TPR/S/268/Rev.1, Trade Policy Review, Report by the Secretariat, Trade Policy Review Body, 8 November.

WTO (2012b), "Norway", WT/TPR/S/269/Rev.1, Trade Policy Review, Report by the Secretariat, Trade Policy Review Body, 13 November.

WTO (2010a), "Joint communication from Brazil and the United States", WT/DS267/45, 31 August.

WTO (2010b), "Total value of agricultural production", TN/AG/S/21/Rev.5, Committee on Agriculture, Special Session, 25 October.

WTO (2010c), "Supporting data to calculate product-specific blue box limits", TN/AG/S/25, Committee on Agriculture, Special Session, 9 November.

WTO (2009), "Total Aggregate Measurement of Support. Revision", TN/AG/S/13/Add.3/Rev.1, Committee on Agriculture, Special Session, 23 November.

WTO (2008a), "Revised draft modalities for agriculture", TN/AG/W/4/Rev.4, Committee on Agriculture, Special Session, 6 December.

WTO (2008b), "Revised draft modalities for agriculture – sensitive products: designation", TN/AG/W/5, Committee on Agriculture, Special Session, 6 December.

WTO (2008c), "Revised draft modalities for agriculture – sensitive products: tariff quota creation", TN/AG/W/6, Committee on Agriculture, Special Session, 6 December.

WTO (2008d), "Revised draft modalities for agriculture – special safeguard mechanism", TN/AG/W/7, Committee on Agriculture, Special Session, 6 December.

WTO (2008e), "Chairperson's texts 2008, Agriculture: negotiations", http://www.wto.org/english/tratop_e/agric_e/chair_texts08_e.htm.

WTO (2005), "Export subsidy commitments", TN/AG/S/8/Rev.1, Committee on Agriculture, Special Session, 2 February.

WTO (2004), "Decision adopted by the General Council on 1 August 2004", WT/L/579, 2 August.

WTO (2001), "Ministerial declaration", WT/MIN/(01)/DEC/1, Adopted on 14 November 2001, Ministerial Conference, Fourth Session, Doha, 20 November.

Yamashita, K. (2008), *Implications for Japan of the July 2008 draft agricultural modalities*, International Centre for Trade and Sustainable Development, Geneva.

Yang, M.-H. and D. Blandford (2011), "Asian rice policies and WTO commitments on domestic support under existing and proposed Doha Round provisions", presented at joint annual meeting of the Agricultural and Applied Economics Association and the Northeastern Agricultural and Resource Economics Association, Pittsburgh, Pennsylvania, 24-26 July, http://ageconsearch.umn.edu/bitstream/103665/2/Yang_and_Blandford.pdf (viewed 15 August 2014).

Zulauf, C. and D. Orden (2014), "The U.S. Agricultural Act of 2014: Overview and analysis", *IFPRI Discussion Paper* 01393, International Food Policy Research Institute, December.

Chapter 4

Review of the performance and impacts of recent stockholding policies

by
Annelies Deuss[1]

This chapter reviews the literature on the recent performance of stockholding policies that influence prices. The first section provides definitions of the different types of stock, according to their primary purpose, focusing especially on buffer stocks and social safety net stocks. The next section identifies which variables will be used to examine the performance of these two types of stocks and addresses some of the general issues that are known to influence their performance. Then, the effectiveness of buffer stocks and social safety net stocks is reviewed using recent country case experiences. The fourth section describes the distributional and fiscal impacts of these types of stocks, as well as their effect on the private sector and international spillovers. The last section concludes.

4.1. Introduction

The 2007-08 food price crisis led to a loss of confidence in the ability of international markets to guarantee a stable food supply. As a result, countries began to reconsider public stockholding policies as a way to address price volatility and food shortages. One of the policy responses during the crisis was to release stocks at subsidised prices[2] while many countries were actually stock-building mid-crisis. This renewed interest in keeping public stocks was furthered by the realisation that price spikes tend to coincide with low stock-to-use ratios (Wright, 2012). Even though international crop prices have mostly fallen back since 2011 and most export restrictive measures that partly caused the crisis are no longer in use, many developing countries keep building public stocks.

Past experiences with public stocks, however, show that the creation of domestic stocks is often very costly and can negatively affect other countries. This was for example the case with the intervention stocks that were created under the Common Agricultural Policy in the European Union (EU) during the 1980s-1990s. In an attempt to support farmers' incomes, boost agricultural production and stabilise markets, farmers received a fixed minimum price for their products. When the internal price fell below the intervention price, the intervention agencies in the member states bought up any surplus, thereby increasing demand and stabilising prices. However, starting in the 1980s, this policy led to overproduction and the creation of huge surpluses, which had to be stored or exported. Since the intervention price was set well above the world market price, export subsidies were given to compensate exporters for the gap between the internal price and world market price. These subsidised exports depressed international prices and hurt other exporting and importing countries which could not compete with the lower prices of EU products. By the 1990s, this policy had incurred huge costs for storage and export subsidies provoking a reconsideration of the policies and a long reform process that began in 1992. By the late 1990s, the intervention stocks had been drawn down.

Other countries besides the European Union that created public stocks experienced similar problems. In fact, many developed countries that implemented farm income support policies, accumulated stocks as a by-product of these policies. Maintaining these stocks put a financial strain on a country's budget and guaranteeing that prices remained stable required some degree of isolation from the market, often in the form of import tariffs to protect domestic producers from international competition. In cases where surpluses were generated, such as in the EU and United States, export subsidies were granted, which depressed international prices. As a result, these price support programmes with their accompanying stock creation started out as domestic measures, but eventually spilled over to international markets through the creation of trade barriers and their impact on world prices.

In current stockholding programmes stock accumulation is often no longer an outcome but an explicit purpose of the policy. The effects, however, can be similar to those of price support programmes as both programmes share the same objectives of stabilising prices and influencing the levels of prices. In the cases where stocks are created to improve the food security situation of the country, price levels can also be affected because of the distribution of food at subsidised prices.

The increasing prevalence of public stockholding policies calls for a better understanding of the programmes that are currently in place. It is important to analyse whether these programmes are able to reach their objectives and examine their impact. It is particularly of interest to evaluate those stockholding programmes that influence prices, directly or indirectly, as they can potentially also affect neighbouring countries.

The purpose of this chapter is to review the literature on the recent performance of stockholding policies that influence prices. The chapter is organised as follows. The first section provides definitions of the different types of stocks according to their primary purpose. This chapter will focus on buffer stocks and social safety net stocks, as these are the two types of stocks that influence prices. The next section identifies which variables will be used to examine the performance of these two types of stocks and addresses some of the general issues that are known to influence their performance. Then, the effectiveness of buffer stocks and social safety net stocks is reviewed using recent country case experiences. The next section describes the distributional and fiscal impacts of these types of stocks, as well as their effect on the private sector and international spillovers. The final section concludes.

4.2. Scope of the study

Terminology

Governments can decide to accumulate or release stocks for a variety of reasons. Public stocks can be acquired or sold to provide price incentives to farmers, stabilise prices in domestic markets, mitigate the effects of sudden price rises, or offer stable prices to consumers. Governments can also decide to build or distribute stocks in order to set up or replenish a strategic stockpile aimed at securing an adequate supply of food, distribute food to vulnerable household and people suffering from chronic food insecurity, respond to urgent food needs arising from emergency situations, or reduce the impacts of a fall in production.

The objective of this chapter is to analyse the performance of national public stockholding policies[3] that influence prices. In order to identify these policies, it is useful to classify stockholding programmes according to their primary purpose. This study distinguishes between the following three types of stocks[4]: buffer stocks, social safety net stocks and emergency stocks (Box 4.1). The two types of stocks that will be evaluated in this chapter are buffer stocks and social safety net stocks as these influence prices, either directly or indirectly. While buffer stocks have an explicit market price objective, social safety nets focus on the provision of cereals or food at subsidised prices. Emergency stocks will not be considered as they are only released to provide emergency relief and are not intended to influence domestic market prices.

Even though the above classification suggests a clear distinction between the different types of stocks, it is not straightforward to unequivocally identify those policies in practice. First of all, most stockholding programmes have multiple purposes and often one agency is tasked with completing several objectives. Second, the goals for holding public stocks can change over time. That is, a stock that was acquired with the purpose of stabilising domestic prices can be used for food distribution programmes. Finally, there are no unanimously used definitions in the literature to classify the different types of public stocks. OECD (2010) and Tangermann (2011), for example distinguish between two types of stocks based on their purpose (emergency reserves and strategic stocks), whereas the World Bank (2012b) defines three types of stocks (buffer stocks, food safety net stocks and emergency stocks). Furthermore, some call stocks that aim to stabilise prices buffer stocks, while others refer to them as strategic reserves, stabilisation stocks, regulation or regulatory stocks, or intervention stocks[5]. In addition, some buffer stock schemes seek to influence the fundamental level of prices while others do not.

Box 4.1. Types of public food stocks

Buffer stocks are used to stabilise commodity prices. Buffer stocks aim to protect producers from price drops and/or consumers from price hikes.

Social safety net stocks function as working stocks for regular food distribution programmes. These stocks aim to provide social safety nets for the impoverished and the chronically food insecure.

Emergency stocks are kept to provide assistance during transitory food shortages and crises, which are caused by sudden supply shocks, such as natural disasters.

Stockholding policies and domestic policies

Not only is it complicated to distinguish between the different stockholding policies, it is also practically impossible to separate stockholding policies from other domestic policies. Any government programme that involves buying or releasing cereals leads to the creation of public stocks. As a result, it is not easy to distinguish between policies where stock creation was the purpose of the policy and those where stock creation was the outcome of a policy. This is particularly relevant when comparing buffer stock programmes with price support programmes.

To clarify how buffer stocks and price support programmes are linked, it is important to understand how buffer stocks are designed. The working principle of a buffer stock is that the government buys stock when the market price of the commodity falls below a certain level and releases stock when the market price is above a specific level. The government implements buffer stock schemes by setting a floor price and a ceiling price. The floor price indicates the trigger price at which the government will buy stock, while the ceiling price specifies when the government will start selling its stock. By setting a floor price and a ceiling price, the government creates a "price band", i.e. a range between which it wants to keep prices.

Even though buffer stocks schemes are defined as policies that stabilise prices by keeping prices between a price band, in practice, buffer stocks are mostly used to raise producer prices. In these situations, the distinction between price support programmes and buffer stock schemes becomes blurred, as both programmes support producers by offering them higher prices. In the case of buffer stocks, these prices are often referred to as "procurement prices" while they are called "support prices" in the case of price support programmes.

4.3. Performance of recent public stockholding policies that influence prices

Defining the variables of interest

To analyse the performance of buffer stock schemes and social safety net stocks, it is necessary to identify appropriate outcome variables. These outcome variables indicate how successful stockholding policies are at achieving their primary purposes (Table 4.1).

In the case of buffer stocks, the variable of interest differs according to the specific purpose (and design) of the buffer stock: whether the buffer stock aims to stabilise overall prices, or whether it aims to raise producer prices or lower consumer prices. In cases where buffer stock schemes only impose a floor price, the government intends to support producers by offering them a minimum price. The performance of these types of buffer stocks can be assessed by analysing farm incomes or producer prices. Buffer stocks with ceiling prices are designed to protect consumers from price hikes and their effectiveness can be evaluated by examining if consumer prices reached lower and more stable levels. The performance of buffer stocks with a price band can be assessed by measuring whether they reduced domestic market price volatility and/or successfully raised producer prices and/or reduced consumer prices.

The performance of social safety net stocks can be analysed by evaluating food security indicators. FAO (2014) identifies a set of indicators that capture various aspects of food insecurity, such as percentage of the population that is undernourished and prevalence of malnutrition. Consumer price levels and price stability are also indicators of food security. Note that these latter two outcome variables are also used to analyse the performance of buffer stocks. This is not surprising as consumer interests are addressed by both types of stockholding programmes. In the case of buffer stock programmes, there is an explicit objective to stabilise market prices, while social safety net stocks focus on the provision of cereals or food at subsidised prices.

Besides their performance, it is also important to analyse the distributional impacts of public stockholding policies, their influence on the fiscal situation of a country, as well as how they affect the private sector and neighbouring countries. Some of these impacts will be mentioned alongside the performance variables in the country case reviews. A more detailed evaluation will be presented in the next section, "Other impacts of recent public stockholding policies".

Table 4.1. Performance variables for the different stockholding programmes

Type of stock	Performance variables
Buffer stock programmes	Reduced price volatility Increased producer prices Decreased consumer prices
Social safety net stocks	Improvement in food security indicators Reduced price volatility Decreased consumer prices

Some initial considerations on the potential of stocks to achieve their primary purposes

The potential of buffer stocks and social safety net stocks to achieve their purposes is complicated by a set of factors that are intrinsically linked to their design. Before describing in detail recent country experiences with these types of stocks, it is useful to first address these general obstacles. Some of these factors relate to public stocks in general, while others are specific to buffer stock schemes and social safety net stocks.

When a government sets up a public stockholding policy, it first has to decide what it wants to achieve by implementing this programme. As mentioned in the terminology section, it is not uncommon for a stockholding scheme to have multiple purposes and for one agency to be in charge of several types of stocks. However, the successfulness of a stockholding programme decreases and its costs increase as the programme has more objectives. This problem is particularly acute when the objectives are contradictory in nature, e.g. when the programme intends to improve food security by offering lower consumer price while at the same time supporting producer prices. The multiplicity of objectives is identified as one of the main causes of failures of stockholding policies, and of buffer stocks in particular (Dorosh, 2009; World Bank, 2012b).

The government also has to make several decisions related to the design and overall working of the scheme. Each of these decisions is crucial as they all influence the overall performance and functionality of the programme. With regards to the design, the government has to decide upon the physical amount of stock to keep and how to finance the programme. In the case of buffer stocks, the government has to choose the levels of the floor and/or ceiling prices while for social safety net stocks it has to select the level of subsidised prices. Additionally, there are also some practical issues that have to be handled, such as setting up the rules and trigger mechanisms for replenishment and release, the composition of the stock, the location of warehouses and release stations, and the management of the stocks. Tangermann (2011), the World Bank (2012b) and OECD (2010) explain in detail the complexity of each of these design-related and practical decisions and provide some suggestions on how to tackle them.

Buffer stocks and price stabilisation

Buffer stocks can only stabilise prices up to a certain extent. That is, the nature of buffer stocks is such that the government is limited in the amount it can sell or buy. If a country is faced with a few consecutive years of low availability and high prices, then it will exhaust its buffer stock. Once the buffer stock is depleted, it loses its capability to lower prices. Conversely, if a country keeps on buying stock to raise producer prices or sets floor prices too high with respect to the market price, then the government will eventually run out of funds and be left with huge stockpiles. This was for example the case with the "rice pledging scheme" that was installed in Thailand (see also later in this chapter).

Buffer stocks struggle with a mismatch of objectives when they intend to increase prices for producers while also reducing prices for consumers. Not only is it very costly to achieve both objectives, it is also challenging to achieve them simultaneously. Programs that raise prices for producers, usually also raise them for consumers, and vice versa for schemes that aim to lower prices.

Even when buffer stocks succeed at stabilising prices, the question remains whether buffer stocks were more cost-effective than other policy options. In that sense, buffer stocks create opportunity costs as less funds are available for other programmes that could also have reduced price volatility, maybe even at a lower cost and more effectively. These other policy options include programmes that support private storage, trade, commodity markets, insurance mechanisms and safety net programmes.

Finally, past experiences with buffer stock schemes demonstrate that they have not been an effective instrument to stabilise prices. The collapse of the International Commodity Agreements was partly linked to their failure to stabilise price movements using buffer stocks. Developed countries have also found that they lead to unsustainable levels of price support and/or huge stockpiles that were dumped or sold at a loss.

Social safety net stocks and food security

The design of social safety net stocks focuses on the release of the stock. However, the acquisition of the stock can have an impact on food security. If the stock is acquired at above market prices and raises producer prices, then this usually also raises the price for consumers, which is in conflict with the stated food security objectives to keep consumer prices reasonable or low. Even if the stock is acquired at market prices, it is still possible that market prices rise as a result of the stockholding policy if the government decides to acquire a large amount of stock and/or keeps the stock in storage for a relatively long period.

Similarly as with buffer stocks, there is a limit to the potential of social safety net stocks to improve food security. Once a stock is depleted, it loses its capability to provide cereals or food for distribution programmes.

Review of country case studies

This section reviews country case studies of national public buffer stocks and social safety net stocks that were implemented in the last 15 years. The review focuses on those countries for which recent studies are available that evaluate the performance of these types of stocks using the outcome variables that were described above. Besides examining the performance of stocks, the review will also address potential distributional impacts of stockholding programmes. A more detailed evaluation of the distributional impacts, fiscal impacts, impacts on the private sector and international spillovers will be presented in the next section.

As mentioned above, price support programmes and buffer stock schemes can be easily confounded. Since it is not the purpose of the chapter to cover price support programmes, this review only considers those studies that clearly indicate that stock procurement or release was an explicit purpose of the policy.

Social safety net stocks often operate through various distribution channels, which each might have different working principles (e.g. distribution of food at subsidised prices versus food for work programmes) and targeting practises. It is beyond the scope of this chapter to evaluate each of these distribution channels. Instead, the review will mainly focus on those stockholding programmes that have a clear buffer stock component and then analyse any associated social safety net stocks.

At this point, a few remarks have to be made regarding the reviewed literature. First, none of the studies on buffer stocks control for any other factors that could have contributed to price volatility. In particular, the role of trade policies, actions of private traders, private stocks, the macroeconomic environment, and production levels in (de)stabilising prices are ignored in most of the studies and certainly are not accounted for in any empirical analysis. At best, a study will mention the confounding factors. This is not a criticism as it is indeed an extremely complex, if not impossible, task to disentangle the impact of trade policies, macroeconomic factors and domestic policies on price volatility.

Second, most studies on buffer stocks examine producer price increases rather than consumer price decreases. This is not surprising as buffer stocks are by nature more adapt at preventing price drops (guaranteeing a floor price) than curtailing price spikes (maintaining a ceiling price). This relates back to the point mentioned above regarding the natural limit of stocks: once stocks are depleted, the buffer stock can no longer prevent price rises. Buffer stock intervention is therefore more effective at limiting price fails than curtailing the incidence and magnitude of price spikes (Wright, 2012). Also, in practice, it is rare to encounter buffer stock programmes that operate using a price band; most buffer stock schemes only have a floor price.

Finally, buffer stocks are rarely used as a price stabilisation mechanism in Latin America and the Caribbean, South Africa, Europe and Central Asia. Accordingly, the review of buffer stock case studies will focus on experiences in African and Asian countries.

Experiences in Africa

Buffer stocks in eastern and southern Africa are generally run by grain trading enterprises (GTE). Often, these GTEs are also in charge of social safety net stocks. GTEs lost importance in the late 1980s and 1990s following economic reforms. However, they re-emerged in the early 2000s and are now again dominant players in African grain markets (Jayne, 2012).

Certain operational features of GTEs raise concerns about their potential to reach their objectives. First, these enterprises not only operate with the purpose of stabilising prices, but also have other objectives such as providing grains in cases of emergencies, distributing food aid, providing food assistance and managing international trade (FAO, 1997). As mentioned above, one of the main reasons why public stock systems often fail is because they aim to achieve too many objectives with one instrument. Second, GTEs generally do not follow established intervention rules for purchasing and releasing stocks and rarely commit to floor and ceiling prices (Poulton et al., 2006). This lack of transparency and predictability is detrimental to the well-functioning of the scheme as it diminishes the confidence of consumers and private traders in buffer stocks (Jayne, 2012).

Table 4.2. Grain trading enterprises in Africa that deal with buffer stocks

Country	Name of grain trading enterprise
Kenya	National Cereals and Produce Board (NCPB)
Zambia	Food Reserve Agency (FRA)
Malawi	Agricultural Development and Marketing Corporation (ADMARC)
Ethiopia	Ethiopian Grain Trade Enterprise (EGTE)
Tanzania	National Food Reserve Agency (NFRA)

Kenya's National Cereals and Produce Board (NCPB) and **Zambia**'s Food Reserve Agency (FRA) both aim to stabilise prices by procuring and selling cereals at administered prices. In addition, they also hold stock for food security and famine relief. Case studies suggest that their stockholding programmes were able to reduce aggregate price volatility over time. Jayne et al. (2008) estimate that Kenya's NCPB stabilised maize market prices between 1989 and 2004. Mason and Myers (2013) show that Zambia's FRA stabilised maize market prices between 1996 and 2008. However, maize price volatility in Kenya and Zambia between 2005 and 2011 was higher than in South Africa, which is the international reference price for Eastern and Southern Africa and does not have buffer stocks. In particular, the World Bank (2012b) estimates that price volatility[6] between January 2005 and May 2011 reached 12% in Kenya and 14% in Zambia, while it was only 9% in South Africa.

The buffer stock policies in Kenya and Zambia are reported to have led to higher producer prices. In Kenya, average price levels increased around 20% between 1995 and 2004 (Jayne et al., 2008), while mean maize producer prices in Zambia rose by 17% between 1996 and 2008 (Mason and Myers, 2013). However, the food security impacts of the stocks are not unanimously positive. While consumers in Kenya benefited from relatively lower prices during times that market prices could have been high, consumer prices in Zambia rose even more than producer prices, namely 19% during 1996-2008. As a result, the price support policy of FRA negatively affected net buyers of maize in Zambia and is unlikely to have any positive welfare effects on poor households. Moreover, the benefits of higher prices in both programmes tend to be captured by the more affluent and food secure farmers. In Kenya, surveys indicate that the price support policy of NCPB led to a transfer of income from poor rural households and urban consumers to large maize-selling farms.

Malawi's Agricultural Development and Marketing Corporation (ADMARC) is responsible for the marketing of all agricultural products and management of food security reserves, besides stabilising prices through buffer stocks. During the 2001-03 food crises and the 2007-08 price spikes, Malawi's buffer stock schemes were not effective at reducing maize price volatility. The main reasons for this were lack of clear guidelines, mismanagement and exclusion of the private sector (Jayne and Tschirley, 2009; Minot and Rashid, 2013).

Buffer stocks in **Ethiopia** are operated by the Ethiopian Grain Trade Enterprise (EGTE). EGTE was established in 1992 with mandates to stabilise producer and consumer prices, earn foreign exchange through exporting grains to the world market, and maintain a strategic food reserve for disaster response and emergency food security operations. EGTE proved unsuccessful at stabilising prices and withdrew from its price stabilisation activities by the early 2000s, except for two *ad hoc* interventions during 2003 when cereal prices collapsed and during the price spike of 2007-08. Rashid and Negassa (2011) examine cereal price variability during the past three decades and show that price volatility was lower during the 1990s, when EGTE operated its buffer stock, compared to the 2000s, when EGTE had withdrawn from cereal price stabilisation. The authors argue that the higher price volatility in the 2000s cannot be attributed to the absence of EGTE. The same authors indicate that the high price variability was caused by production shocks in 2002-03 and by unpredictable market behaviour during 2006-08, when domestic prices were higher than import parity prices.

Starting in 2007, EGTE's market intervention increased through subsidised sales of wheat. Dorosh and Ahmed (2009) demonstrate that government imports and sales in 2008-09 effectively lowered market wheat prices. However, the authors also note that market prices were still high relative to import parity prices and that similar results could have been obtained through trade if the government had not inhibited private sector imports. Furthermore, domestic grain prices remained high well into 2009, even though international grain prices had already dropped by that time (Minot and Rashid, 2013). Finally, AFD (2014) points out that as a result of the sale of government stock less wheat was available for emergency and food security interventions as these stocks are not separated from buffer stocks in Ethiopia.

Tanzania's Strategic Grain Reserve (SGR) was established in 1991 with the objectives to stabilise staple grain prices, advise the government on food security policy, and supply food for emergency assistance. Since the volumes of purchases and sales accounted for only 4% of market surplus, the SGR did not have any significant impact on grain prices (Minot, 2010). Following the 2007-08 food price crisis, SGR was merged with other departments to form the National Food Reserve Agency (NFRA), which now covers an even larger set of objectives. The new agency most probably will not have much effect on grain prices since it holds 5% as a core strategic grain reserve.

Experiences in Asia

Similar to the grain trading enterprises in Africa, most of the agencies in Asia that manage stocks have multiple mandates, which complicates the functioning of these agencies. The buffer stock schemes in Asia are considered to be relatively more successful at stabilising prices than those in Africa for two reasons. First, most buffer stocks in Asia consist of rice. Since rice production in Asia is irrigated, it is less variable than maize production in Africa. Second, the gap between import and export parity prices in Asia is smaller than in Africa (World Bank, 2012b).

Table 4.3. Agencies in Asia that manage buffer stocks

Country	Name of agency managing buffer stocks
Philippines	National Food Authority (NFA)
Indonesia	Badan Urusan Logistik (BULOG)
India	Food Corporation of India (FCI)
China (People's Republic of)	China Grain Reserve Corporation (SINOGRAIN)
Thailand	Rice pledging scheme
Malaysia	PadiBeras National Berhad (BERNAS)

The **Philippines** National Food Authority (NFA) is tasked to stabilise rice prices by keeping farm prices high and retail prices reasonable for consumers. In addition, the NFA also has the mandate to guarantee stable rice supply during emergencies and calamities by releasing rice from its stocks. Intal et al. (2012) show that the NFA was ineffective at influencing producer prices because it only procured a relative small share of regional output. On the other hand, the NFA was able to stabilise domestic prices of rice compared to the international markets in the 1990s and 2000s. However, the reason for NFA's success in ensuring price stability is not a result of its buffer stocks scheme but is attributed to its dominant role in importing rice in the country. The NFA imports 35% of the import allocation of rice at duty-free rates while 65% is imported by the private sector (Tobias et al., 2012).

Even though consumer prices were more stable in the Philippines, they did not lead to lower volatility of producer prices. Indeed, the World Bank (2012b) demonstrates that the volatility of retail and wholesale rice prices was 3% between 1990 and 2011, while the volatility of farm (paddy) prices was 11.6%. Moreover, these lower consumer prices are only enjoyed by a small portion of the population. World Bank (2007) shows that only 10 to 12 per cent of the poorest population bought rice at subsided prices in 2007/08, with the remainder of rice bought at prices above world market level.

Buffer stocks in **Indonesia** are managed by Badan Urusan Logistik (BULOG). BULOG was created in 1967 with a rice price stabilisation policy that was implemented using a price band. Starting from 2005, the focus shifted from a price-band policy to setting a floor or procurement price while selling subsidised rice to the poor via the Raskin programme. Evaluating the performance of buffer stocks on price stabilisation in Indonesia in the past decade is complicated by Indonesia's trade policy. Until the early 2000s, Indonesia was one of the world's largest rice importers. To boost domestic production, it implemented an import ban in 2004, which resulted in a surge of domestic prices. By isolating itself from the international market, Indonesia's rice prices were shielded from the global food price hikes in 2007-08 (Figure 4.1).

Figure 4.1. Indonesian and Thai wholesale rice price, January 2000 - September 2011

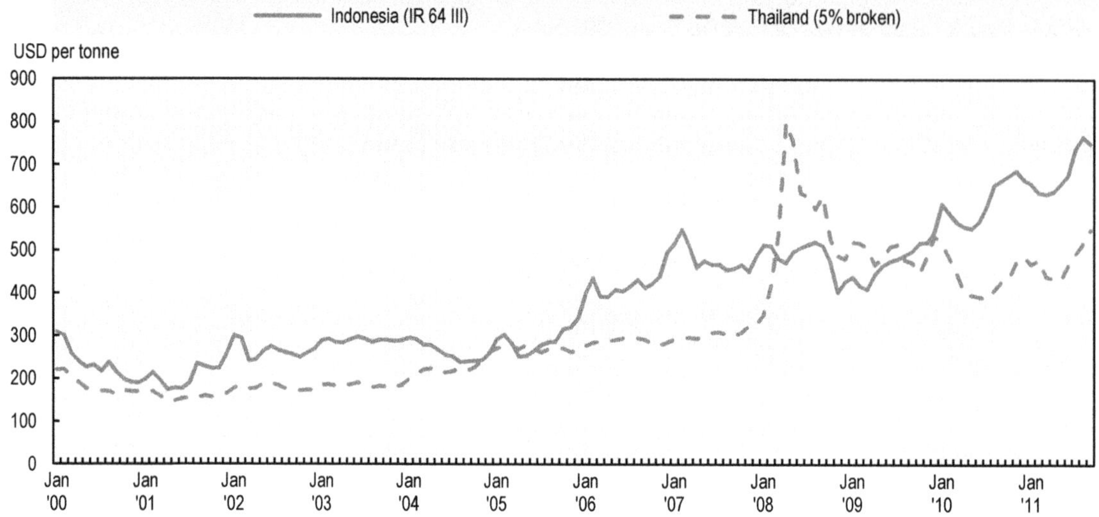

Source: OECD (2012) and FAO-GIEWS (2014).

Indonesia's rice price moved to a higher level since 2005, but it is unclear how much can be attributed to the buffer stock programme (high procurement prices) and how much to its trade policy (import ban). As was the case in Kenya and Zambia, most of the gains of the higher procurement prices were captured by the more affluent farmers (McCulloch and Timmer, 2008).

Social safety net stock activities in Indonesia are co-ordinated through Raskin. Raskin is reported to have good coverage, which is likely due to the fact that it distributes subsided rice to almost twice the number of beneficiaries as planned. However, as a result of this wide targeting, 70% of the subsidised rice reaches beneficiaries who are not poor and it is estimated that one in six of the 20% richest households receive Raskin rice. This inefficient targeting comes at the expense of poor households, which receive considerably less rice than their intended monthly quota (World Bank, 2012a).

The Government of **India** implements its price stabilisation and food security policies through the Food Corporation of India (FCI). In particular, the FCI's objectives are: i) to provide farmers remunerative prices, ii) to make food grains available at reasonable prices, particularly to vulnerable section of the society, iii) to maintain buffer stocks as measure of Food Security, and iv) to intervene in market for price stabilisation. McCreary (2012) examines the performance of the FCI with regards to the objectives that relate to price stabilisation, namely i), ii) and iv). His conclusions seem to indicate a success-story. The author reports that the FCI has been successful at providing remunerative prices for wheat and rice and that the FCI reduced price volatility of wheat and rice during the period 2006-12. The author also shows that consumer prices were more stable with than without the FCI reserve policy.

There are, however, some factors that urge us to be cautious about these results. First, the study ignores the impact of trade policies on prices. Between 2007 and 2011, India imposed export bans on rice and wheat. These bans not only protected India from the spikes in international prices in 2007-08 but also contributed to price hikes in India's trading partners and are considered to have increased world price volatility. Second, FCI's storage policy does not seem to follow the standard rules. That is, FCI did not release stocks when prices were high; instead, it kept accumulating stock and its releases did not keep up with accumulation (Gouel, 2013).

In addition, there are doubts regarding the programme's contribution to food security as it can decrease net availability of food grains and can even lead to an increase in market prices. Saini and Kozicka (2014) show that between 2000 and 2012, production of wheat and rice rose by 29%. However, net availability of food grains over that same period decreased by almost 1%. This gap between production and net availability is directly linked to the rising levels of government stocks rather than to India's exports. Indeed, during the years in which India imposed its export bans, this gap even increased by 64%.

The programme's influence on market prices is related to the sharp rise in the quantity of grains that are procured and that are kept in stock. The level of stocks more than tripled between July 2006 and July 2014 (Figure 3.2). In July 2014, the level of public stocks was 65.3 million tonnes, which was more than double the norm established by the government. Since 2008, stocks have been consistently above the mandated norms. If the FCI continues to procure large amounts of food grains but does not release grain when needed, less grain will be available in the open market, which will in turn put upward pressure on market prices. As a result, the stockholding programme could in fact increase food insecurity.

Figure 4.2. Stocks of wheat and rice in India: actual stock levels *vis-à-vis* mandated norms (million tonnes)

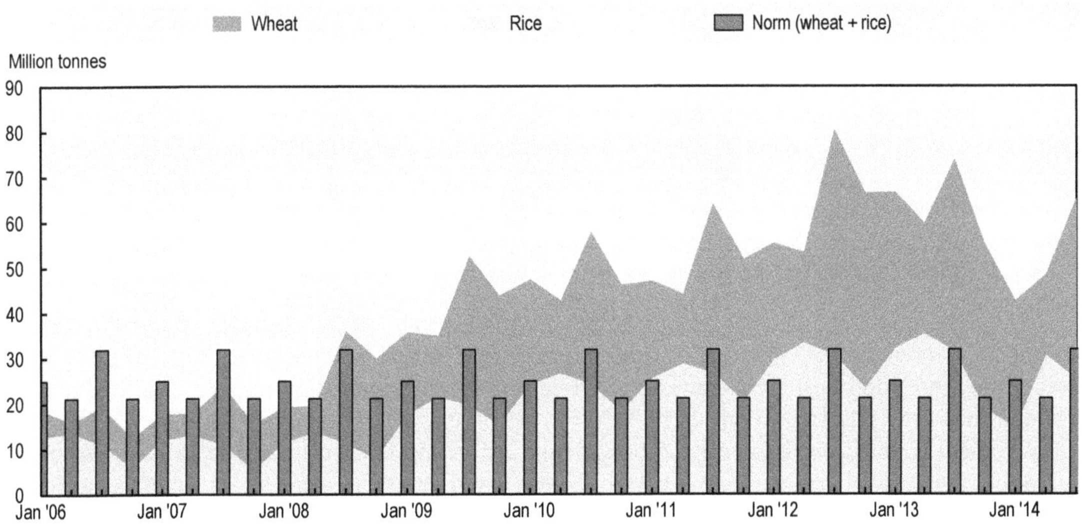

Source: FCI (2014).

In 2013, the National Food Security Act (NFSA) was passed, which aims to provide food security to 67% of the population by distributing a fixed amount of subsidised grain each month. The large coverage of this act will inevitably intensify the requirements for food grain procurement, storage and distribution. Consequently, the act will amplify the impacts of India's buffer stock programme on the welfare of its population, the fiscal budget, and the private sector. Given the size of India's stocks compared to the world's total utilisation, there will also be considerable potential impacts on the world market. In July 2012, for example, India's stocks of rice and wheat accounted for more than 6 and 7% of the world's total rice and wheat utilisation (Saini and Kozicka, 2014). Releasing even part of these stocks on the world market could significantly influence world prices.

China's buffer stock policy is implemented by the China Grain Reserve Corporation (SINOGRAIN), which was established in 2000. Besides managing grain and oilseed reserve stocks, SINOGRAIN is also responsible for the procurement of grains and oilseeds, stock maintenance, interprovincial shipments and international trade of grain. The government stocks consist mainly of rice, wheat, and maize (OECD, 2009). The exact size of government state reserves is a state secret, which complicates any analysis of the impact of stockholding policies on prices and volatility.

Even though the mandate of SINOGRAIN is to purchase commodities when prices are low and release them when prices are high, it seems that SINOGRAIN is not releasing grain and oilseed reserves adequately or with a timing that is consistent with this objective, even when consumer prices are high.

Carter et al. (2012) note that SINOGRAIN might function more as a price support scheme than a true buffer stock scheme. The current price support schemes are implemented in two forms: a "minimum purchasing price" programme and a "temporary stocking purchase" programme. Under the "minimum purchasing price" programme, a guaranteed minimum price has been applied to rice (since 2004) and to wheat (since 2006) in some targeted regions. The "temporary stocking purchase" programme was implemented in 2008 and offers price supports for maize, soybean, rapeseed and cotton in designated regions. Both programmes offer fixed prices that are based on the market situation.

The support prices are raised every year, leading to a steady growth in prices for all commodities covered in the price support programmes. Farmers do not seem to fully benefit from these higher prices, though, while traders and marketing agencies are indirectly taking advantage of these programmes. Xu, Xi and Zhang (2010) report that farmers overwhelmingly prefer to sell grain below the minimum price to traders instead of selling it at the minimum price to SINOGRAIN because farmers want to avoid the cost and inconvenience of transporting and marketing their grains. The traders then sell the corn to state-owned depots at the minimum price.

China's buffer stock policy is cited as one of the reasons why China experienced stable domestic food prices during the 2007-08 food price crisis. Trade insulation, however, most probably played an even bigger role in shielding China from international price volatility. This becomes apparent when analysing price volatility of wheat, rice and soybean during the food price hike (Figure 3 and Figure 4). China holds buffer stocks for all three crops, but almost does not trade rice and wheat, while it imports most of its soybeans for domestic consumption. Rice and wheat prices displayed much less volatility in Chinese markets compared to the international market during the last decade, and certainly during the 2007-08 price hike. The prices of soybean however, followed the US soybean price surge (Gale, 2013).

In 2011, **Thailand** reinstated a rice pledging programme in which it bought rice from domestic producers at a premium to the world market price and stored any surplus. The purpose of the programme was to help boost the incomes of the rice farmers. The intervention price Thailand paid was rather high, namely THB 15 000 (around USD 460) per tonne, 40-50% higher than the market prices. The government counted on financing the programme by selling rice on the global markets at an even higher price. Since Thailand was the world's largest exporter at the time and several countries had imposed export bans in response to the price crisis, the government expected that by stockpiling rice, it would decrease the global supply of market and consequently cause a rise in world prices.

Figure 4.3. China wheat price support and market price, 2004-14

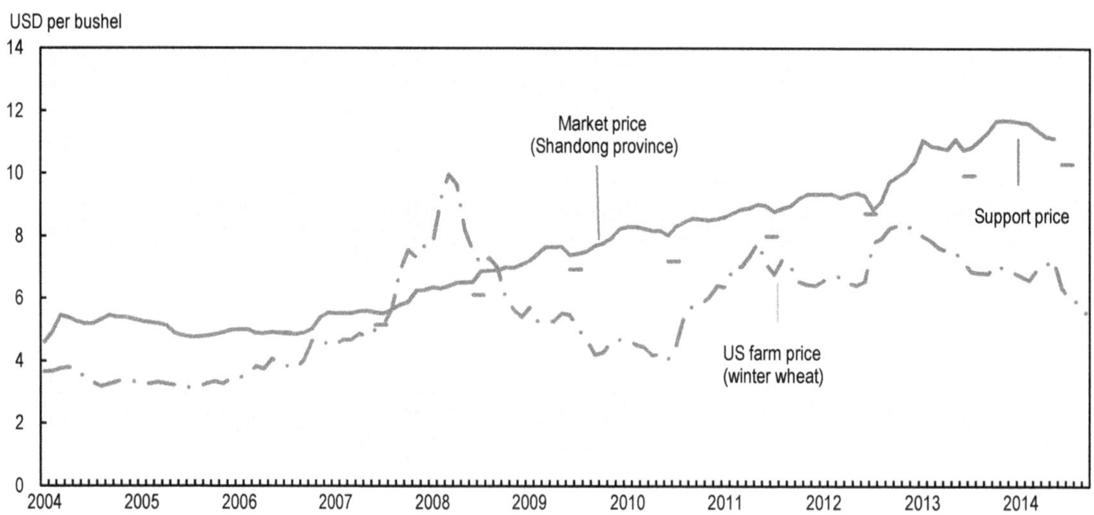

Source: USDA, Economic Research Service analysis of data from China National Grain and Oils Information Center, China National Development and Reform Commission, and USDA, National Agricultural Statistics Service.

Figure 4.4. China soybean price support and market price, 2004-14

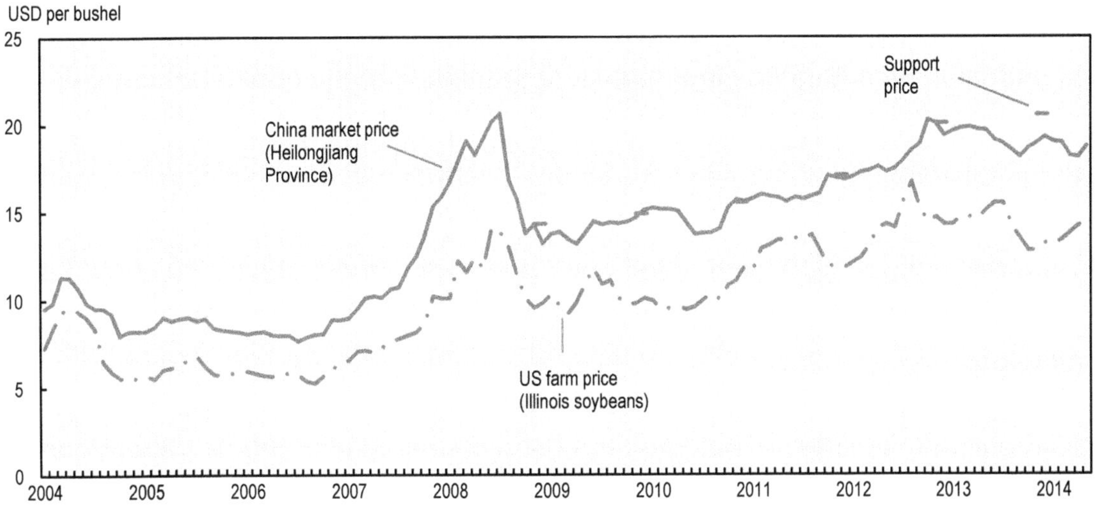

Source: USDA, Economic Research Service analysis of data from China National Grain and Oils Information Center, China National Development and Reform Commission, and USDA, National Agricultural Statistics Service.

The government's expectations were crushed when India lifted its export ban on rice shortly after the programme was implemented and as a result, world price did not increase as much as Thailand had expected. The programme eventually led to huge stockpiles of rice as the government kept speculating for higher prices. The programme ultimately was abolished in February 2014. Most rice farmers, who were intended to profit from the programme, were left worse off since no funds were available to pay them.

Public rice stocks in **Malaysia** are managed by PadiBeras National Berhad (BERNAS), a private company traded on the Kuala Lumpur Stock Exchange. BERNAS purchases paddy from farmers at a guaranteed minimum price, manages farm input subsidies, runs milling operations, maintains the nation's rice stockpile, and acts as the sole importer of rice. This privileged position was extended in 2011 for another 10 years. So far, no studies were found that examine the effectiveness of the buffer stock in achieving price stability.

4.4 Other impacts of recent public stockholding policies

The country examples show that buffer stocks and social safety net stocks have varying degrees of success in achieving their objectives. However, besides their performance, it is also important to examine whether these stockholding policies have other impacts on society. In certain cases, these negative impacts can even offset any benefit that was created by the stockholding programme. The most significant impacts of stockholding policies relate to their effects on distributional outcomes, the government's budget, the displacement of the private sector and spillovers to neighbouring countries.

Distributional impacts

The distributional impacts of buffer stocks and social safety net stocks validate the importance of effective targeting and setting simple objectives. Several country case studies (e.g., Kenya, Zambia, Indonesia and Ethiopia) that reported on the success of buffer stocks at raising producer prices pointed out that these higher prices were mostly captured by the wealthier and large scale farmers. In the case of social safety net stocks, targeting is also crucial to ensure that those who are most food insecure are the beneficiaries of the food distribution programmes. However, targeting still remains one of the main weaknesses of these programmes. There are not only exclusion errors, where people who should be targeted do not receive the benefits, but also inclusion errors, where people who are not in need of assistance enjoy undue benefits. Nearly 70% of the beneficiaries of Indonesia's Raskin, for example, are not poor. As a result, there is less subsidised rice available for the people who need it the most (World Bank, 2012a).

In cases where producer price support objectives are paired with the objective of providing lower prices to the consumers, poor and food-insecure consumers risk being hurt multiple times. First, consumers are paying indirectly for the higher prices for producers through taxes that fund the programme. Second, higher producer prices often translate to higher consumer prices, which are difficult to counterbalance by food distribution programmes. In the Philippines, for example, the share of rice that was bought at subsided prices by the poorest households in 2007/08 was only around 10%. The remaining rice was sold at prices above world market level (World Bank, 2007). Finally, due to inefficient targeting, poor consumers risk not being reached by food distribution programmes.

Fiscal impacts

The fiscal impact of stockholding programmes is often cited as one of its main downsides. The direct costs for public stocks include storage costs, transport costs, management costs, acquisition costs and the costs associated with distribution. These costs escalate as the programme increases the size of its stock and/or tries to achieve multiple objectives. The volume of India's public wheat and rice stocks, for example, more than tripled between 2005 and 2013. This led to an increase of almost 200% in nominal terms of the food grain carrying costs[7] for FCI over that period (Saini and Kozicka, 2014). Public spending on stocks can amount to as much as 2% of GDP and is often larger than public spending on agriculture and research (World Bank, 2012b).

The spending on public stocks also creates opportunity costs, as less funding is available for other public programmes which might be more efficient at reducing price risk. In many eastern and southern African countries, volatility is a result of poor infrastructure and low resilience against shocks. These problems would be best addressed by investing in infrastructure and agricultural research and development. The scale of costs of buffer stocks thus leads to major opportunity costs because not enough investments are made in those programmes that are best suited to tackle volatility. World Bank (2012b) notes that as a result, buffer stocks in Kenya, Malawi and Zambia are even thought to increase price volatility because they were not able to address the causes of volatility and took away resources from programmes that could.

Crowding out of the private sector

Public stock programmes can disincentivise the private sector to participate in stockholding and trading activities. In particular, when the purchase and release of grain for public stocks is unpredictable, it becomes riskier and costlier for the private sector to invest in trade and storage (Jayne and Tschirley, 2009). Faced with greater insecurity, the private sector will withdraw from storage and trade, and with less actors in the market to stabilise prices, this will eventually exacerbate the instability of food prices.

The private sector can also be discouraged to partake in domestic market activities when the size of the public stockholding programme is large. In India, for example, 75% of marketable surplus is procured by the government, which leaves very little grain available for the open market (Saini and Kozicka, 2014). When the private sector is crowded out, the government will face an even bigger role in stabilising prices, which adds additional pressures on the budget.

International spillovers

Stockholding policies are designed as domestic policies, but their impacts can transcend national borders. When big players on the world market acquire or release large amounts of stock, this can create international spillover effects. The acquisition, whether from domestic production or through imports, can lead to a decrease in supply in the world market and hence a potential increase in the world market price. On the other hand, releasing large amounts of stocks may depress world market prices. These effects are not limited to large countries, as the same effect can be caused by a group of relatively smaller countries acting in the same way. However, when large countries implement large stockholding programmes, this inevitably generates nervousness on the international markets as it is often uncertain how much stock will be acquired or released, when and at which price.

Buffer stocks can also impact neighbouring countries through the trade barriers that are often created to defend the price band. In particular, countries need to have control over their imports and exports to effectively implement a floor price and ceiling price. Import tariffs or tariff quotas help countries maintain their floor price, while export restrictions are used to apply their ceiling price. The implementation of these trade barriers can have significant impacts on prices in other countries and hence on their food security and poverty situation.

4.5 Conclusions

This chapter reviews the recent literature on the performance of buffer stocks and social safety net stocks. The effectiveness of buffer stock programmes is evaluated by analysing whether the programmes were able to achieve their objective(s) of reducing overall volatility, increasing producer prices and/or stabilising consumer prices. The performance of social safety nets is analysed by examining food security indicators such as consumer prices and domestic price volatility. The review focuses on country case experiences in the last 15 years.

As stockholding policies are almost always associated with other policy instruments such as administered prices, trade policy instruments, import and export monopolies, it is not possible to disentangle the effects from these other instruments. This explains why none of the case studies controlled for any other factors that might have influenced the performance or impact of stockholding policies.

In terms of volatility, some country case studies showed that these stockholding programmes were associated with lower overall price volatility. Interestingly, the countries that reported a reduction in overall price volatility had implemented a drastic change in their trade policies or had linked their stockholding programmes to trade policies. This observation raises two important issues. First, in those countries where the change in trade policy was rather radical (e.g. an export ban), trade most probably had a more significant impact on volatility than stocks. The reports do not explicitly provide proof for this statement as none of the studies control for any of the confounding factors that might have influenced price volatility. What is clear though is that countries that isolate their domestic markets from the international markets using trade measures such as bans are able to shield themselves from international price volatility. However, when international prices are stable, countries with strong trade barriers are potentially exposing themselves to more instability because domestic market shocks are typically more severe and frequent that international ones. Second, buffer stocks can only work efficiently in countries that can control their trade flows. In particular, a country implementing a buffer stock scheme needs to be able to insulate its own economy from the world market; otherwise the stabilisation effects of the buffer stock dissipate into the international market.

Even though buffer stocks necessarily lead to the creation of trade barriers, openness to international trade would, usually, offer more price stability because it pools production risk and because international markets exhibit lower price volatility than domestic markets. While a buffer stock might succeed at lowering price volatility for some period of time, the risk remains that this programme collapses. Once a stabilisation programme breaks down, the resulting surge in price volatility will offset any price stabilising effects of the original programme.

Buffer stocks that explicitly aimed to raise producer prices seemed to have been relatively successful at reaching their objective. However, there are some caveats. First of all, these policies do not always reach their targeted audience. Instead of reaching poor farmers, the benefits of the schemes can be accrued by well-off farmers, traders or marketers. Additionally, these programmes are often a huge drain on the budget. Even though the strategy is to buy low and sell high, this is a tactic that often does not work and as a result the country can be left with massive stockpiles and/or a fiscal deficit. Finally, buffer stocks that guarantee producers an artificially high price can cause several indirect economic costs. They can lead to higher consumer prices, tend to lower wage competitiveness, and can reduce agricultural diversification (World Bank, 2012b). The fact that consumer prices often rise as a result of buffer stock schemes is in direct conflict with any food security objectives of the programme.

There is little evidence of buffer stocks stabilising consumer prices. This is mainly due to the fact that buffer stocks are more adept by nature at preventing price drops than curbing price hikes and are more often used to raise prices. Also, stocks that were bought with the purpose of stabilising prices are not necessarily released with the same purpose and could end up in regular distribution programmes. The fact that it is hard to trace these stocks complicates the analysis.

The literature provides a very detailed explanation on why buffer stocks have typically failed. The most common causes are the unsustainable fiscal costs, conflicting objectives of the programmes, crowding out of the private sector and other agricultural investments, poor management and non-transparent working of the programmes. The reasons why buffer stocks failed in the past are in general also the reasons why they appear to be currently failing. The overwhelmingly negative experiences with buffer stocks clearly suggest that countries would be better off without these policies. However, they are politically attractive and it is important to keep track of them as they will undoubtedly influence domestic prices and have very large fiscal impacts while in some cases they will also have international spillovers that influence the food security of other countries.

The success of social safety net stocks depends largely on having well-defined objectives and effective targeting. In cases where targeting is poorly executed the distributional impacts can be very significant. Social safety net stocks are usually less controversial than buffer stocks, mostly because they do not influence prices directly and have a food security objective. However, when large players on the world market decide to build stocks, the objective for the creation of these stocks is not relevant to its trading partners. Whether the stock is created for the purpose of price stabilisation or to improve food security, the fact remains that when the stock is built, a large amount of cereals might not reach the world market. Moreover, there is also the risk that these large stockpiles might get dumped on the world market at any time. It is therefore necessary to also monitor social safety net stocks.

Notes

1. Agricultural Policy Analyst, Agro-food Trade and Markets Division, Trade and Agriculture Directorate, OECD. The views expressed in this chapter are those of the author and do not necessarily reflect those of the OECD or OECD member governments.
2. Countries that released stock at subsidised prices include: Algeria, Bangladesh, Benin, Bolivia, Brazil, Cambodia, Cameroon, People's Republic of China, Costa Rica, Dominican Republic, Egypt, Eritrea, Ethiopia, Guatemala, Guyana, Honduras, India, Iraq, Jordan, Kenya, Lebanon, Malawi, Malaysia, Mauritania, Nepal, Nigeria, Pakistan, Philippines, Korea, Senegal, Sierra Leone, Thailand, Togo, Viet Nam, Yemen (Wiggins and Keats, 2009).
3. The study focuses on national public stocks which are composed of physical commodities (grains or food). This study does not consider stocks that are held by private actors, that are held at regional or international level, or that are virtual in nature.
4. This classification is based on the classifications used in World Bank (2012b).
5. See also AFD (2014) for an overview of the different definitions that are used in the literature to classify stocks.
6. Price volatility in World Bank (2012b) is defined as the standard deviation of the logarithm of the first price differences.
7. Carrying costs are the costs incurred to maintain stocks and include the costs of warehousing, stock maintenance, etc.

References

Abbott, P. (2012), "Stabilisation Policies in Developing Countries after the 2007-08 Food Crisis", in Agricultural Policies for Poverty Reduction, OECD Publishing, Paris. DOI: http://dx.doi.org/10.1787/9789264112902-8-en.

AFD (2014), "Food Reserves and Regulating Market Volatility in Africa". *A Savoir* No. 23, http://www.afd.fr/webdav/site/afd/shared/PUBLICATIONS/RECHERCHE/Scientifiques/A-savoir/23-VA-A-Savoir.pdf.

Carter, C.A., F. Zhong, and J. Zhu (2012), "Advances in Chinese Agriculture and its Global Implications", *Applied Economic Perspectives and Policy*, Vol. 34(1), 1-36. DOI: http://dx.doi.org/10.1093/aepp/ppr047.

Dorosh, P. (2009), Price stabilisation, international trade and national cereal stocks: World price shocks and policy response in South Asia, *Food Security*, Vol. 1:137-149.

Dorosh, P. and H. Ahmed, (2009). Foreign Exchange Rationing, Wheat Markets and Food Security in Ethiopia. Ethiopia Strategy Support Program 2 (ESSP2) Discussion Paper No. ESSP2 004. International Food Policy Research Institute, Washington, DC.

FAO (1997). "Strategic grain reserves - Guidelines for their establishment, management and operation", *FAO Agricultural Services Bulletin*, Rome. http://www.fao.org/docrep/w4979e/w4979e00.htm#Contents.

FAO, FIDA, IFPRI, FMI, OCDE, CNUCED, WFP, WORLD BANK AND WTO (2011). "Price Volatility in Food and Agricultural Market: Policy Responses", Background Policy Report for the G20 Summit in Paris in November 2011, Rome.

FAO (2014). *The state of food insecurity in the world, 2014*, Food and Agriculture Organisation, Rome.

FAO-GIEWS (2014), Food Price Data and Analysis Tool. http://www.fao.org/giews/pricetool/ Accessed November 2014.

FCI (2014), http://fciweb.nic.in/ Accessed November 2014.

Gale, F. (2013), *Growth and Evolution in China's Agricultural Support Policies*, ERR-153, US Department of Agriculture, Economic Research Service, Washington, DC.

Gouel, C. (2013). Food price volatility and domestic stabilisation policies in developing countries. In: Chavas J.-P., D. Hummels and B. Wright (ed.), *The Economics of Food Price Volatility*, University of Chicago Press, Chicago.

Intal, P.S., L.F. Cu and J.A. Illescas (2012), "Rice Prices and the National Food Authority", Discussion paper series No. 2012-27, Philippine Institute for Development Studies, Makati City, Philippines.

Jayne, T.S. (2012), "Managing food price instability in East and Southern Africa", *Global Food Security*, Vol. 1(2): 143–149. DOI: http://dx.doi.org/10.1016/j.gfs.2012.10.002.

Jayne, T., R. Myers and J. Nyoro (2008), "The Effects of NCPB Marketing Policies on Maize Market Prices in Kenya", *Agricultural Economics*, Vol. 38: 313-25.

Jayne, T.S. and D. Tschirley (2009), "Food price spikes and strategic interactions between the public and private sectors: markets failures or governance failures?", in *FAO Commodity Market Review 2009-2010*.

Mason, N.M., and R.J. Myers (2013), "The effects of the Food Reserve Agency on maize market prices in Zambia", *Agricultural Economics*, Vol. 44(2): 203–216. DOI: http://dx.doi.org/10.1111/agec.12004.

McCreary, I. (2012), "Food Reserves in India. Canadian Foodgrains Bank", *Occasional Paper*, Canadian Foodgrains Bank, Winnipeg, MB.

McCulloch, N. and C.P. Timmer (2008), "Rice Policy In Indonesia: A Special Issue", *Bulletin of Indonesian Economic Studies*, Vol. 44(1): 33-44.

Minot, N. (2010), "Food price stabilisation: Lessons from eastern and southern Africa", Paper prepared for the Fourth African Agricultural Markets Program (AAMP) policy symposium, Agricultural Risks Management in Africa: Taking Stock of What Has and Hasn't Worked, organised by the Alliance for Commodity Trade in Eastern and Southern Africa (ACTESA) and the Common Market for Eastern and Southern Africa (COMESA). Lilongwe, Malawi, 6-10 September 2010.

Minot, N. and S. Rashid (2013), "Technical inputs to proposed Minimum Support Price (MSP) for wheat in Ethiopia", *Policy Note*, International Food Policy Research Institute, Washington DC.

OECD (2009), *Agricultural Policies in Emerging Economies 2009: Monitoring and Evaluation*, OECD Publishing, Paris. DOI: http://dx.doi.org/10.1787/agr_emerging-2009-en.

OECD (2012), *OECD Review of Agricultural Policies: Indonesia 2012*, OECD Publishing, Paris. DOI: http://dx.doi.org/10.1787/9789264179011-en.

Poulton, C. et al. (2006), "State intervention for food price stabilisation in Africa: Can it work?" *Food Policy*, Vol. 31.

Rashid, S. and A. Negassa (2011), "Policies and Performance of Ethiopian Cereal Markets. Ethiopia Strategy Support Program 2 (ESSP 2)", *Working Paper* No. 21. International Food Policy Research Institute, Washington, DC.

Saini, S. and M. Kozicka (2014), "Evolution and Critique of Buffer Stocking Policy of India", *ICRIER Working Paper* No. 283, Indian Council for Research on International Economic Relations, New Delhi, India.

Tangermann, S. (2011). "Policy Solutions to Agricultural Market Volatility: A Synthesis; ICTSD Programme on Agricultural Trade and Sustainable Development" *Issue Paper* No. 33; ICTSD International Centre for Trade and Sustainable Development, Geneva, www.ictsd.org.

Tobias, A et al. (2012), *Handbook on rice policy in Asia*, International Rice Research Institute (IRRI), Philippines.

Wiggins, S. and S. Keats (2009), *Volatile World Food Prices and Their Implications: Grain Stocks and Price Spikes*, Overseas Development Institute, London.

World Bank (2012a), "Targeting Poor and Vulnerable Households in Indonesia", *Working Paper* 67218, World Bank, Washington DC.

World Bank (2012b), "Using Public Food Grain Stocks to Enhance Food Security", Report Number 71280-GLB, World Bank, Washington DC.

World Bank (2007), "Philippines: Agriculture Public Expenditure Review", Technical working paper, Manila and Washington, DC.

Wright, B. D. (2012), "International Grain Reserves And Other Instruments to Address Volatility in Grain Markets", *The World Bank Research Observer*, 27(2): 222-260. DOI: http://dx.doi.org/10.1093/wbro/lkr016.

Xu, Z., Y. Xi, and S. Zhang (2010), "Analysis on the Implementation, Mechanisms and Effects of 2008/2009 National Corn Provisional Purchase Policy", *Issues in Agricultural Economy*, Vol. 3: 16-23.

ORGANISATION FOR ECONOMIC CO-OPERATION AND DEVELOPMENT

The OECD is a unique forum where governments work together to address the economic, social and environmental challenges of globalisation. The OECD is also at the forefront of efforts to understand and to help governments respond to new developments and concerns, such as corporate governance, the information economy and the challenges of an ageing population. The Organisation provides a setting where governments can compare policy experiences, seek answers to common problems, identify good practice and work to co-ordinate domestic and international policies.

The OECD member countries are: Australia, Austria, Belgium, Canada, Chile, the Czech Republic, Denmark, Estonia, Finland, France, Germany, Greece, Hungary, Iceland, Ireland, Israel, Italy, Japan, Korea, Luxembourg, Mexico, the Netherlands, New Zealand, Norway, Poland, Portugal, the Slovak Republic, Slovenia, Spain, Sweden, Switzerland, Turkey, the United Kingdom and the United States. The European Commission takes part in the work of the OECD.

OECD Publishing disseminates widely the results of the Organisation's statistics gathering and research on economic, social and environmental issues, as well as the conventions, guidelines and standards agreed by its members.

OECD PUBLISHING, 2, rue André-Pascal, 75775 PARIS CEDEX 16
(51 2015 06 1 P) ISBN 978-92-64-23388-1 – 2015

www.ingramcontent.com/pod-product-compliance
Ingram Content Group UK Ltd.
Pitfield, Milton Keynes, MK11 3LW, UK
UKHW051504290926
15471UKWH00008B/1401

9 789264 233881